THE SPANISH LEGAL SYSTEM

AUSTRALIA
LBC Information Services
Sydney

CANADA and USA
Carswell
Toronto

NEW ZEALAND
Brooker's
Auckland

SINGAPORE and MALAYSIA
Thomson Information (S.E. Asia)
Singapore

THE SPANISH LEGAL SYSTEM

By

ELENA MERINO-BLANCO, Lda. en Derecho
Lecturer in Law, University of the West of England, Bristol

LONDON • SWEET & MAXWELL • 1996

Published in 1996 by
Sweet and Maxwell Limited of
100 Avenue Road, Swiss Cottage
London NW3 3PF

Typeset by Selwood Systems, Midsomer Norton
Printed and bound in Great Britain by
Butler and Tanner Ltd, Frome and London

No natural forests were destroyed to make this product:
only farmed timber was used and re-planted.

ISBN 0 421 54930 0

A CIP catalogue record for this book is available
from the British Library

All rights reserved. UK statutory material in this publication is
acknowledged as Crown copyright.

*No part of this publication may be reproduced or transmitted in any
form, or by any means, or stored in any retrieval system of any nature
without prior written permission, except for permitted fair dealing
under the Copyright, Designs and Patents Act 1988, or in accordance
with the terms of a licence issued by the Licensing Agency in respect of
photocopying and/or reprographic reproduction.
Application for permission for other use of copyright material
including permission to reproduce extracts in other published works
shall be made to the publishers. Full acknowledgement of author,
publisher and source must be given.*

© Elena Merino-Blanco
1996

A mi familia

Preface

This book seeks to provide an introduction to the Spanish legal system for English readers, by explaining the history, sources, institutions of the State, court structure and main principles of procedure. It is hoped that it will be of interest to students, practitioners, academics or simply those who are interested in the Spanish Legal system because of cultural or commercial reasons.

The idea of writing a book about the Spanish Legal system came as a response to the almost absolute lack of materials on Spanish law in English addressed to the English reader. Readers of this book need not be Spanish linguists nor have access to original source material.

While not seeking to provide specific advice on Spanish substantive law, nor to be a guide to the practitioner, this book intends to provide a sufficient introduction for the reader to be able to undertake further study on specialised areas.

Emphasis is placed on the distinctive characteristics of the Spanish legal system such as the co-existence of "foral" or regional laws with national civil law, the territorial and political division of the State into Autonomous Communities and the relationship between central State legislation and autonomous legislation. The reader is also made aware of some of the major distinctions between Civil and Common law systems, for example, the division between public and private law, the importance of codification, the system of sources and the significance of the Constitutional Court and its proceedings.

Where possible Spanish terminology has been retained because of the difficulties of accurate translation; when this has been done the legal concept behind the term has been explained by way of a footnote. In particular, the Spanish method of citing sources of law has been retained.

Any mistakes are entirely the author's own. The law as stated is that up to June 1, 1995. As a consequence recent legal changes, such as the introduction of the jury in criminal proceedings, have been mentioned but are not discussed extensively.

Elena Merino-Blanco
June 1, 1995

Acknowledgments

This book would have not been possible without the generous help of my colleague at the University of the West of England, Sue Farran, who has patiently read endless drafts and made useful comments, discussed legal terminology and in general has provided encouragement and support from the start of this project. It is only fair to say that I would not have been able to conclude this book without her help.

I am also grateful to my good friend José Ignacio Martínez of bufete Lupicinio Rodriguez, Madrid, for his valuable assistance providing up-to-date Spanish material. Useful Spanish material was also provided by Beatriz Martin Rueda and Carles Prat.

Thanks are also due to Fiona Geddes (University of the West of England), the personnel at the Colegio de Abogados de Madrid, and Jordi Ojeda for their various contributions.

Last but not least, I would like to express my gratitude to Mike for patiently coping with me being either busy or tired for more months than I care to remember.

Contents

Preface	iv
Table of Cases	xv
Table of Legislation	xvii
Table of European, International and Foreign Legislation	xxvii
Table of Abbreviations	xxix

1. Introduction to the Spanish legal system   1

1. Legal History	1
Historical introduction	1
2. Constitutional history	16
3. Codification	20
4. Spain today: a social and democratic constitutional state	24
5. The Spanish conception of law	27
6. The division between public and private law	28

2. Sources of law   29

1. Introduction	29
2. Primary sources of law	30
La ley (legislation)	30
Types of *ley*	31
La costumbre (customary laws)	41
Los principios generales del derecho (general principles of law)	43
3. Complementary sources	44
La jurisprudencia (case law)	44
The decisions of the constitutional court	46
4. Explanatory sources	47
La doctrina (legal writings)	47
5. Autonomy and the system of sources: the relationship between state law and the law of the Autonomous Communities	47
6. Interpretation, application and efficacy of the laws	51
Interpretation of the law	51
The role of equity	53
Efficacy of the laws: territorial application and time-span	53

3. Constitutional Organs of the State — 57

1. The Crown — 57
   Functions of the King — 58
2. *Las Cortes Generales* (Parliament) — 59
   Composition — 59
   Status of Members of Parliament — 62
   The law-making process — 63
3. The Government and the Public Administration — 67
   The Government — 67
   The Public Administration — 71
4. The judicial power: courts and court structure — 76
   Organisation and government of the Judiciary — 78
   Classification of the courts — 80
5. *El Ministerio Fiscal* (the Public Prosecution Service) — 94
6. *El Tribunal Constitutional* (the Constitutional Court) — 95
   Composition and functions — 95
   The different proceedings of the Constitutional Court — 98

4. The legal professions — 105

1. Introduction: legal education in Spain — 105
2. *Abogados* — 107
   European Community lawyers — 111
3. *Procuradores* — 112
4. Representation and defence of the State: *Abogados del Estado* — 113
5. *Jueces y Magistrados* — 113
6. *Secretarios judiciales* — 116
7. *Fiscales* — 116
8. Auxillary personnel in the administration of justice — 118
   Oficiales, auxilares y agentes — 118
   Policía judicial — 118
   Other technical auxiliaries of the administration of justice — 118
9. Civil servants — 119
10. *Notarios* — 119

5. Civil procedure — 123

1. General characteristics — 123
   Inquisitorial and adversarial proceedings — 123
   Orality and written proceedings — 124
2. Sources of civil procedure — 125

3. International jurisdiction of the Spanish courts	125
4. Courts of first instance in civil proceedings	129
5. Main civil proceedings	132
Proceedings for provisional remedies	132
Declarative proceedings	134
6. *Recursos* (appeals)	147
Recurso de reposición	147
Recurso de súplica	147
Recurso de queja	147
Recurso de apelación	147
Recurso de casación	148
Recurso de revisión	148
7. Enforcement of judgments	149
General	149
Enforcement of domestic judgments	150
Enforcement of foreign judgments	151
8. Judicial costs	155
9. Legal aid	155

6. Criminal procedure   157

1. Criminal law and criminal procedure	157
2. Principles of criminal procedure	157
3. Sources of criminal procedure	159
4. Parties	160
5. The court	164
6. Main criminal proceedings	166
Preliminary stage	167
La instrucción	174
The public hearing	179
7. *Recursos*	186
8. Costs and legal aid	189
9. Enforcement	190
Glossary	193
Index	207

Table of Cases

I. European Cases

Case 6/64, *Costa v. ENEL*:[1964] E.C.R. 585; [1964] C.M.L.R. 425 36
Case 29/76, *LTV v. Eurocontrol*: [1976] E.C.R. 1541 127

II. Sentencias de Tribunal Constitucional

STC 2/81, *Caso Ley de Bases de Régimen Local*, of February 2, 1981 99
STC 51/81, *Caso LOACE* of February 13, 1981 32
STC 6/81, of March 16, 1981 32
STC April 18, 1981 184
STC 29/82 of March 17, 1982 40
STC 51/82 *Caso Art. 137 L.P.L.* of July 19, 1982 40
STC 11/83 *Caso RUMASA decreto-ley* of February 23, 1983 38
STC 35/83 *Caso Hermanos Bengoechea v. T.V.E.* of May 11, 1983 102
STC 38/83 *Caso Ley de Elecciones Locales* of May 16, 1983 ....32, 33
STC 70/83, *Caso LOAPA* of August 5, 1983 32
STC 47/84 *Caso Jefe de Servicio de Renfe* of April 4, 1984 40
STC 51/85 *Caso Castells* of April 10, 1985 63
STC 77/1985 *Caso L.O.D.E.* of June 27, 1985 73
STC 30/86 *Caso de Juntas de Guernica* of February 20, 1986 63
STC 60/86 *Caso R.D. Ley de Medidas Urgentes de reforma
   administrativa* of May 20, 1986 68
STC 108/1986 *Caso Ley Orgánica del Poder Judicial, II*, of July 29, 1986 79
STC 520/86, *Casotutela judicial efectiva* of October 10, 1986 184
STC of June 3, 1987 137
STC of November 3, 1987 137
STC 118/88 *Caso Materias Clasificadas* of June 20, 1988 62
STC of July 12, 1988 .... 92, 164
STC 45/89 *Caso I.R.P.F.* of February 20, 1989 100
STC of December 29, 1989 184
STC 3/90 of January 15, 1990 178
STC *Caso Ley Organica del Poder Judicial III* of March 29, 1990 99
STC 119/90 *Caso Idigoras – Aizpurúa – Alcalde* of June 21, 1990 62
STC 150/90 *Caso Recargo del tres por ciento* of October 4, 1990 99
STC 28/91 *Elecciones al Parlamento Europeo* of February 14, 1991 37
STC 64/91 *Caso Apesco* of March 22, 1991 ....34, 99
STC 84/95 of July 8, 1995 188

III. Autos del Tribunal Constitucional

ATC 69/83 of January 17, 1983 40

ATC 579/1990 Caso Ley asturiana de caza of November 28, 1990 99

IV. Dictamen del Tribunal Constitucional

DTC Caso Tratado de la Unión Europea of July 1, 1992 101

V. Sentencias del Tribunal Supremo

STS of February 10, 1866 45
STS of June 30, 1866 45
STS of December 10, 1894 47
STS of July 1, 1897 129
STS of March 26, 1906 47
STS of June 10, 1916 47
STS of June 27, 1941 52
STS of February 22, 1960 129
STS of May 30, 1961 129
STS of February 8, 1964 149
STS of April 28, 1975 149
STS of June 30, 1977 143
STS of November 14, 1981 186
STS of April 15, 1986 154
STS of November 4, 1986 184
STS of April 28, 1987 ....30, 34
STS of September 30, 1988 184
STS of December 21, 1988 36
STS of January 11, 1989 178
STS of April 17, 1989 34
STS of June 16, 1989 184
STS of June 17, 1989 184
STS of February 25, 1991 184

Table of Legislation

I. Constitution Española

1978 Constitución Española
    art. 1 .... 43, 57, 72
        (2) 64
        (3) 24
    art. 2 60
    art. 9(1) 26
        (2) 78
        (3) 38, 55, 72
    art. 10(1) 25
    art. 11(2) 191
    art. 13(2) 35
    art. 14 .... 26, 43, 102
    art. 15 .... 177, 190
    arts. 15–19 102
    arts. 15–29 .... 26, 32
    arts. 15–30 98
    art. 16 25
    art. 17 .... 162, 171, 172
        (1) 171
        (2) 172
        (3) 163
        (4) 172
    art. 18 177
    art. 23(1) 181
    art. 24 .... 125, 159, 162
        (1) 137, 139
        (2) 159
    art. 25 23
        (3) 172
    art. 26 78
    art. 27 25
    art. 29 26
    art. 30(2) 102
    arts. 30–38 26
    art. 36 73
    art. 46(1)(b) 102
    art. 53 26
        (1) 26, 32, 37
        (2) 26, 102
        (3) 26

1978 Constitución Española
    —cont.
    art. 54 .... 26, 33, 74
    art. 56(1) 58
        (3) 78
    art. 62(1) 58, 71
        (2) 58
        (3) 58
        (9) 69
    art. 63 62
    art. 64(2) 58
    art. 66 59
    art. 71 166
        (3) 63
    art. 72(1) 62
    art. 73 62
    art. 75(1) 60, 62
        (3) 61
    art. 76 62
    art. 78 62
    art. 79 62
    art. 80 62
    art. 81 .... 26, 31, 32, 33
        (1) 32, 37
    art. 82(1) 39
    arts. 82–85 71
    art. 84 65
    art. 86 .... 38, 60
        (1) 37, 38
        (2) 38
        (3) 38
    art. 87 .... 39, 64
        (2) 65
        (3) 33, 65
    art. 88 68
    arts. 88–91 39
    art. 92(2) 69
    art. 93 .... 33, 34, 36
    art. 94(1)(a)(b)(c)(d)(e) 34
        (2) 34

1978 Constitución Española
—cont.
art. 95 .... 35, 98, 101
(1) 35
art. 96 34
(1) 33, 35
art. 97 .... 41, 71
art. 98 .... 67, 69, 70
(1) 67
art. 99 .... 60, 68
(2) 71
art. 100 68
art. 102 70
art. 103 .... 73, 78, 95
(1) 73
arts. 103–107 73
art. 105(a) 74
(b) 74
art. 106 73
art. 112 .... 68, 69
art. 115 68
(1) 69
art. 116(2) 68
(3) 68
art. 117 .. 77, 114, 157, 190
(1) 77
(3) 78
(5) 78
(6) 78
art. 119 .... 155, 156
art. 120 .... 124, 159
(1) 159
(2) 159
art. 121 188
(2) 79
art. 123 81
(1) 78
art. 124 .... 95, 117
(1) 95
art. 125 .. 95, 179, 180, 181
art. 126 .... 118, 167
art. 131 65
art. 134 65
art. 137 .... 41, 72
art. 143 48
art. 144 .... 48, 49
art. 146 48

1978 Constitución Española
—cont.
art. 147(1) 48
art. 148 48
art. 149 48
(1) 50
(6) 160
art. 149(2) 51
(3) 50
(5) 50
art. 151 48
art. 152(1) 81
art. 159 98
(4) 98
art. 161(1)(a) 98
(b) 98
(c) 98, 103
(d) 104
(1) 99
(2) 49, 74, 103
art. 163 98
art. 164 100
art. 165 33

II. Leyes Orgánicas

L.O. 1/1979, of September 26, General Penitenciaria 190
L.O. 2/1979, of October 12 del Tribunal Constitucional 41, 46, 49, 95
art. 1 .... 46, 97
art. 2(2) 41
art. 8 104
art. 10(b) 103, 104
art. 27(2) 35, 62, 98
art. 28(2) 32
art. 32(2) 99
art. 27 59
art. 35(1) 100
art. 37 59
art. 38 100
art. 40 100
(2) 160
art. 43(1) 102

L.O. 2/1979, of October 12 del Tribunal Constitucinal—cont.
   art. 44(1) 102
   art. 50 102
   art. 59(3) 98, 104
   art. 62 103
   art. 63 103
   art. 64(3) 103
   art. 78 35
      (1) 101
   art. 340 49

L.O. 3/1980, of April 22 del Consejo de Estado . 40

L.O. 3/1981, of April 6 del Defensor del Pueblo 33, 74, 75
   art. 25 75

L.O. 2/1982, of May 12 del Tribunal de Cuentas 75

L.O. 8/1983, of June 25 de Reforma urgente y parcial del Código Penal   23

L.O. 10/1983, of August 16 166

L.O. 11/1983, of August 25 de Reforma universitaria 106

L.O. 3/1984, of January 26 Reguladora de la Iniciatiava Popular 33, 65

L.O. 6/1984, of May 24 de Habeas Corpus ... 92, 172

L.O. 6/1985, of July 1 del Poder Judicial 41, 46, 79, 88, 93, 125, 185
   art. 3(1) 78
   art. 4 .... 78, 144
   art. 5(1) 46
   art. 9(2) 80
      (6) 129
   art. 11 183
   art. 19(1) 170
   art. 21(2) 126
   art. 21–5 126
   art. 22 ....129, 138

L.O. 6/1985, of July 1 del Poder Judicial—cont.
   art. 22(1) 128
      (2) 128, 129
      (3) 128
   art. 30 80
   art. 42 129
   arts. 42–48 130
   art. 43 129
   art. 52 80
   art. 53 81
   art. 56(2) 130
   art. 62 80
   art. 71 81
   art. 73 89
      (2)(a) 130
        (b) 89
   art. 80 81
   art. 82 91
   art. 84 81
   art. 87 92
   art. 89 81
   art. 90 81
   art. 92 81
   art. 97 81
   art. 99 94
      (1) 81
   art. 107(4) 80
   art. 110 41
   art. 200 115
   art. 219 115
   art. 229(1) 124
   art. 232 159
   art. 237 159
   art. 240(2) 124
   art. 248(3) 144
   art. 266 186
   art. 292–297 188
   art. 299 113
   art. 348–77 80
   art. 436 108
   art. 436–442 163
   art. 439(2) 108
   art. 440(2) 189
   art. 443–445 118
   art. 447(1) 113
   art. 472–483 116

L.O. 6/1985, of July 1 del
Poder Judicial—cont.
art. 505 119
L.O. 10/1985, of August
2 de autorización para la
ratificación del Tratado
de Accesión a las Comunidades Europeas 34
L.O. 2/1986, of May 13 168
L.O. 4/1987 of July 15 86, 167
L.O. 3/1988, of May 25 166
L.O. 4/1988, of May 25 166
L.O. 7/1988, of December 28 .... 91, 92, 93
117, 164, 166
L.O. 2/1989, of April 13 167
L.O. 3/1989, of June 21 23, 131, 150
L.O. 5/95, of May 22 del
Tribunal Jurado ... 166, 180, 181, 182

III. Estatutos de Autonomía

L.O. 4/1978, of December 18 de Estatuto de Autonomía de Cataluña 89
L.O. 7/1979, of December 18 de Estatuto de Autonomía del País Vasco 89
L.O. 1/1981, of April, de Estatuto de Autonomía de Galicia 89
L.O. 4/1982, of June 8 de Estatuto de Autonomía de la Región de Murcia 89
L.O. 5/1982, of July 1 de Estatuto de Autonomía de Valencia 89
L.O. 6/1982, of August 10 de Estatuto de Autonomía de Aragón 89

L.O. 13/1982 of August 10 de Estatuto de Autonomía de Navarra 89
L.O. 1/1983 de Estatuto de Autonomía de Extremadura 89
L.O. 2/1983 de Estatuto de Autonomía de Islas Baleares 89

IV. Leyes

Ley del Notariado, of May 28, 1862 .... 120, 121
art. 1 121
Ley of July 19, 1944 .. 137
Ley de Sociedades Anónimas of July 17, 1951 . 24
Ley de Régimen Jurídico de la Administratión del Estado of July 26, 1957 . 69
Ley de Procedimento Administrativo of July 17, 1958 40
art. 129–37 40
Ley 62/1978, de protección jurisdiccional de los derechos fundamentales de la persona of December 26 ....26, 161, 166, 170
Ley 40/1979, of December 10 166
Ley of July 20, 1980 .. 131
Ley 30/81 por la que se regula el Estatuto Orgánico del Ministerio Fiscal of December 30 95
Ley 10/1983, de organización de la administración central del Estado of August 16 ..68, 69
Ley 25/1983, de incompatibilidades des altos cargos of 26 December 70

TABLE OF LEGISLATION xxi

Ley 26/84 General para la Defensa de los Consumidores y Usarios of July 19	24
Ley 10/1984, of ?	124
Ley 30/1984, de medidas para la reforma de la función publica of August 2	113
Ley 34/1984 Novela de modificación de la L.E.C., of August 6	45, 135, 146
Ley 4/1985 por la que se regula el procedimiento de extradicción of March 21	166
Ley 9/85 Cambiara y del Cheque of July 16, 1985	
Ley 25/1986, of December 24	155, 189
Ley 30/1986 de abolición de las tasas judiciales of December 24	156
Ley General de Cooperativas of April 2, 1987	24
Ley de Mercado de Valores of 1988	24
Ley 23/1988, Letrados de Estado of June 28	113
Ley 36/1988, of December 5	138
Ley 38/1988 de demarcación y planta judicial of December 28	80, 125
Ley 18/1989, of July 25	177
Ley 19/1989, of July 25	24
Ley 3/92 of ?	80
Ley 4/92 Reguladora de la Competencia y el procedimento de los juzgados de menores of June 5	167
Ley 10/1992, de Medidas Urgentes de Reforma Procesal of April 30	125, 166
Ley de Procedimiento Laboral of April 27	85

V. Reales Decretos y Decretos Legislativos

Decreto of November 21, 1952	38, 39, 137
art. 45	140
art. 46	139
R.D. – Ley of January 4, 1977	93
R.D. – Ley of January 4, 1977	93
R.D. 2046/1982 of June 30	112
R.D. 2090/1982, of July 24	107, 108, 163
R.D. 545/83	95
art. 2–6	160
art. 3	170
art. 4	170
art. 5	170
art. 22	95
art. 25	95
art. 27	95
R.D. 1209/1984, of June 8	120
R.D. 849/1985 of June 5	113
R.D. 1030/1985 of June 5	112
R.D. 1030/1985 of June 19	155
R.D. 2169/1985 of November 27	113
R.D. 118/1986 of January 24	163
R.D. 607/1986 of March 21	111
R.D. 769/1987 of June 19	168

R.D. 1497/1987 of November 27 105
R.D. 429/88 of April 29 116
R.D. 1062/1988 of September 16 111
R.D. 122/1989 of February 3 125
R.D.-Ley, 1564/1989 of December 22 24
R.D.-Ley 339/1990 of March 2 177
R.D. 1424/1990 of October 26 105
R.D. 147/1991 of February 15 108
R.D. 1665/1991 of October 25 111
R.D. 1728/1991 of November 29 120
R.D. 13/1992 of January 17 177

VI. Otras Disposiciones

Reglamento del Congreso de los Diputados of February 10, 1982
  arts. 10–14 166
  art. 20(3) 62
  arts. 23–8 61
  art. 30.2 60
Reglamento de la Ley General Penitenciania of May 8, 1981
  art. 44 197
  art. 45 197
  art. 46 197
  art. 58 197
  art. 98 197
  art. 242(2) 197
Reglamento del Senado of May 25, 1982
  art. 21 166
  art. 22 166
  art. 5.1 60

Reglamento del Senado of May 25, 1982—cont.
  art. 11 62
  art. 12 62
  art. 23(1) 63
  arts. 28–34 61
Reglamento Notarial of June 2, 1994 .... 121, 120
  art. 2 121

VII. Códigos

1881 Ley de Enjuiciamiento Civil
  art. 3 112
  art. 10 110
  art. 12 110
  art. 40 131
  art. 13 156
  art. 14 156
  art. 15 156
  art. 20 156
  art. 30 156
  art. 45 131
  art. 47 131
  art. 52 131
  art. 54 131
  art. 55 .... 131, 150
  art. 63 131
  art. 74 124
  art. 79 138
  art. 125(2) 131
  art. 140 133
  arts. 260–71 137
  arts. 326–33 175
  art. 340 144
  art. 359 144
  arts. 373–379 147
  arts. 381–389 147
  art. 398(1) 147
  arts. 401–403 147
  art. 423 155
  art. 483 130
  arts. 484–86 130
  art. 486 146
  art. 489 .... 131, 148

TABLE OF LEGISLATION xxiii

1881 Ley de Enjuiciamiento
Civil—cont.
art. 523 155
art. 525 137
art. 526 137
art. 530 137
art. 532 145
art. 533 131
    (1) 129, 138
    (2)(3)(4)(5)(6)
    (7) 129, 138
art. 534 138
art. 535(1) 138
art. 536(2) 138
art. 537 139
art. 538(3) 139
art. 540 139
art. 542(1) 138
    (3) 139
art. 546 140
art. 547(3) 140
art. 549(2) 140
art. 578 ....140, 141
art. 583 140
art. 644 155
art. 645 155
art. 667 143
art. 670 143
art. 671 143
arts. 681–82 137
art. 689 139
art. 694 124
art. 701 143
art. 720 146
art. 733 131
art. 773 137
art. 919 .... 131, 149, 150
arts. 921–7 150
art. 924 150
arts. 928–31 150
arts. 951–956 130
arts. 951–958 151
art. 952 154
art. 954 154
art. 958(11) 130
arts. 1397–1418 133

1881 Ley de Enjuiciamiento
Civil—cont.
art. 1400 155
arts. 1419–27 134
art. 1428 134
art. 1429 150
arts. 1429–1531 150
art. 1621 133
arts. 1631–85 133
arts. 1633–50 133
arts. 1633–75 133
arts. 1651–62 133
arts. 1676–85 133
art. 1687 141
art. 1692 45
    (5) 45
art. 1697 147
art. 1796 ....148, 149
arts. 1796–1810 148
art. 1798 149
art. 1800 149
art. 1801 149
art. 1802 149
1885 Ley de Enjuiciamiento
Criminal 70
art. 2 160
art. 10(15) 175
art. 14 92
    (1) 164
art. 61(2) 175
    (6) 175
art. 100 163
art. 101 161
art. 104 ....161, 170
art. 105 ...... 160, 161, 170
art. 108 161
art. 110 162
art. 118 ....169, 170
arts. 123–5 189
art. 126 189
art. 127 189
art. 141 185
art. 142 186
art. 159 186
art. 215 159
art. 240 189
art. 241(2)(3)(4) 189

1885 Ley de Enjuiciamiento
 Criminal—cont.
art. 242	189
art. 259	168
art. 260	169
art. 261	169
art. 262	168, 75
art. 263	169
art. 264	168
art. 270	170
(II)	161
art. 271	170
art. 280	162
art. 283	168
art. 297	168
art. 299	158
art. 306	178
art. 311	170
art. 312	170
art. 336	175
art. 343	175
art. 384	178
(1)	178
art. 400	176
art. 410	182
arts. 410–450	176
art. 420	182
art. 433	182
arts. 451–455	176
art. 483	158
arts. 486–488	171
art. 487	171
art. 489	171
art. 490	171, 172, 173
arts. 501–525	173
art. 504	173
art. 505	173
art. 508	173
art. 520	163, 172
(1)	172
(2)(a)	163
art. 523	173
arts. 529–542	173
art. 530	173
arts. 589–614	174
art. 622	178
art. 623	178

1885 Ley de Enjuiciamiento
 Criminal—cont.
art. 631	179
art. 632	179
art. 680	179
arts. 688–689	180
arts. 688–740	179
art. 701	180
(vi)	158
arts. 701–722	182
art. 702	182
art. 708	158, 182
art. 712	182
arts. 729–32	158
art. 733	184, 186
art. 739	185
art. 740	185
art. 741–2	185
art. 742	185
arts. 750–756	166
arts. 770–797	166
art. 779	166
art. 781	160
art. 785	178
art. 789(2)	191
(3)	178
art. 790	178
arts. 790–792	166
art. 795	186
arts. 804–823	166
art. 795(2)(3)(8)	187
art. 796	187
art. 847	187
art. 849(1)(2)	187
art. 850	187
art. 851	187
art. 901(a)	188
art. 902	188
art. 954	188
art. 955	188
art. 957	188
art. 960	189
art. 961	189
art. 962	178

1889 Código Civil
art. 1	30
art. 6	29

1973 Código Penal
    art. 1 157
    art. 8 163
        (2) 162
    art. 15 162
    art. 19 163
    art. 22 163
    art. 34 191
    art. 35 191
    art. 36 191
    art. 89 191
    art. 91 191
    art. 92 190
    art. 101 163
    art. 109 189
    art. 160 70
    art. 161 70
    art. 163 70
    art. 238 162
    art. 325 169
    art. 325(II)(III) 170
    arts. 326–8 182
    art. 338 169
    art. 340(a)(1) 177
    art. 385 164
    art. 431 161
    art. 443 161
    art. 463 161
    art. 467 .... 161, 170
        (v)(vi) 170
    art. 487 161

1973 Código Penal—cont.
    art. 499 162
    art. 505 175
    art. 515 175
    art. 529 174
    art. 563 161
    art. 590 164
    art. 594 164
    art. 596 164
    art. 586 161
Código Civil
    art. 1 ....29, 30, 41, 42, 140
        (1) 46
        (6) 46
    art. 2 41
        (1) 54
        (3) 55
    art. 3 .... 42, 51, 53
        (1) 52
        (2) 53
    art. 4 54
    art. 12 140
    arts. 13–17 54
    art. 90 150
    art. 91 150
    art. 93 150
    art. 434 142
    art. 1154 53
    art. 1215 140
    art. 1216 121
    art. 1280 121

Table of European, International and Foreign Legislation

1791	French Constitution		
	art. 5	58	
	art. 16	16	
	art. 14	126	
1807	Napoleonic Code		
	art. 14	21	
1811	Austrian Civil Code		
	art. 7	43	
1896	Convenio of November 19 (between Spain and Switzerland)	152	
1908	Convenio of May 30 (between Spain and Columbia)	127	
1908	Convenio of May 30 (between Spain and Columbia)	127	
1908	Convenio of December 26 (between Spain and Columbia)	152	
1927	Convenio of November 21 (between Spain and Czechoslovakia .	152	
1929	Warsaw Convention for the Unification of certain rules relating to Air transport	127	
1945	Statute of the International Court of Justice		
	art. 38	43	
1949	German Constitution ..	97	
1950	European Convention for the protection of fundamental rights and fundamental freedoms (Rome)	176	
1952	Convention relating to the Arrest of Sea-Going ships	127	
1954	Hague Convention relating to some rules on Civil Procedure ...	138	
1956	Geneva Convention on certain rules relating to the carriage of goods by Road	127	
1957	EEC Treaty (Treaty of Rome)		
	arts. 59–60	111	
	art. 60	111	
1961	Vienna Convention on diplomatic relations .	127	
1963	Vienna Convention on Consular relations ...	127	
1968	Convention on Jurisdiction and enforcement of judgements in civil and commercial matters (Brussels Convention) 126, 127, 151, 152		
	art. 1 ....127, 152		
	art. 5–15	128	
	art. 16	127	
	art. 17	127	
	art. 19	128	
	art. 27 ....153, 154		
	(4)	153	
	art. 28 ....153, 154		

1968	Convention on Jurisdiction and enforcement of judgements in civil and commercial matters (Brussels Convention)—*cont.*	1987	Convenio of May 4 (between Spain and Czechoslovakia) 127
	art. 32 152	1987	European Convention on the Prevention of Torture 176
	art. 59 153	1988	Convention on Jurisdiction and the enforcement of judgements in Civil and Commercial matters between EEC and EFTA Member States (Lugano Convention) 127, 152
1969	Convenio of May 28 (between Spain and France) 127, 152		
1969	Convention on Liability for Oil pollution damage 127		
1969	Convention on special missions 127		art. 19 128
1973	Convenio of May 22 (between Spain and Italy) 127, 152		art. 27 153
			art. 28 153
		1989	Convenio of May 30 (between Spain and Israel 127
1983	Convenio of November 14 (between Spain and Germany 127, 152		
		1991	Convenio of April 17 (between Spain and Mexico 127
1984	Convenio of February 17 (between Spain and Austria) 127, 152		
		1992	Treaty of Maastricht 36
1986	Single European Act ...35, 36		

Table of Abbreviations

A.D.	Anno Domini
Ap.	Apartado
Art.	Articulo
ATC	Auto del Tribunal Constitucional
BC	Brussels Convention (1968)
BOE	Boletín Oficial del Estado
Cap.	Capítulo
CC	Código Civil
CCo	Código de Comercio
CE	Constitución Espanola
CGPJ	Consejo General del Poder Judicial
CP	Código Penal
DA	Disposición Adicional
DTC	Dictamen del Tribunal Constitucional
EA	Estatuto de Autonomía
EA	Estatuto de la Abogacía
ECR	European Court Reports
EOMF	Estatuto Orgánico del Ministerio Fiscal
INSALUD	Instituto Nacional de la Salud
INSS	Instituto Nacional de la Seguridad Social
J.	Juzgado
L.	Ley
LAU	Ley de arrendamientos urbanos
LC	Lugano Convention (1988)
LDPJ	Ley de Demarcación y Planta Judicial
LEC	Ley de Enjuiciamiento Civil
LECrim	Ley de Enjuiciamiento Criminal
LO	Ley Orgánica
LOACE	Ley Orgánica de la Administración Central del Estado
LODE	Ley Orgánica del Derecho a la Educación
LODP	Ley Orgánica del Defensor del Pueblo
LOPJ	Ley Orgánica del Poder Judicial
LOREG	Ley Orgánica del Regimen Electoral General
LORIP	Ley Orgánica Reguladora de la Iniciativa Popular
LOTC	Ley Orgánica del Tribunal Constitucional
LPL	Ley de Procedimiento Laboral

LRJAE	*Ley de Regimen Jurídico de la Administración del Estado*
LSC	*Ley de Seguridad Ciudadana*
RD	*Real Decreto*
RDL	*Real Decreto-ley*
RLGP	*Reglamento de la Ley General Penitenciania*
RS	*Reglamento del Senado*
Secc.	*Sección*
STC	*Sentencia del Tribunal Constitucional*
STJCE	*Sentencia del Tribunal de Justicia de la Comunidad Europea*
STS	*Sentencia del Tribunal Supremo*
TC	*Tribunal Constitucional*
TCEE	*Tratado de la Comunidad Económica Europea*
Tit.	*Título*
TS	*Tribunal Supremo*
TSJ	*Tribunal Superior de Justicia*
TVE	*Television Espanola*
UCM	*Universidad Complutense de Madrid*
Vol	*Volumen*

Chapter One
Introduction to the Spanish legal system

1. LEGAL HISTORY

HISTORICAL INTRODUCTION

Early influences

Very little is known about the peoples who inhabited the Iberian peninsula before the first Roman invasion. The first inhabitants are thought to have been Celts and Iberians and there is little evidence of their customary laws.[1] Among the Iberian tribes, the most socially and culturally developed were the inhabitants of the South-East due to their commercial contacts with Greeks and Phoenicians. These Iberians had some written laws.[2] A common feature of all primitive customary laws is that they are personal laws, meaning, only applicable to the family or local group. When contact with other groups became necessary the tribes established different agreements called *pactos de hospitalidad o clientela* (hospitality agreements) which regulated the relationships between people belonging to different groups.[3]

Iberia was incorporated with Rome after two centuries of fighting[4]

---

[1] The problem with the sources of this period is the general absence of written sources; only some stones—*teseras*—hand-written in what is thought to be "Iberian" have been found. However, these cannot be translated because this language is still unknown. Francisco Tomás y Valiente, *Manual de Historia del Derecho Español* (1992) p. 75. For an overview of "primitive laws" in Spain see, E. Gacto Fernández y otros, *El Derecho Histórico de los Pueblos de España* (7th ed., 1992), pp. 46–55.

[2] According to the Roman historian *Estrabon* (III, 1, 6), the inhabitants of Tartessos—today's Seville—had laws in verse. See Pérez-Prendes, "*El mito de Tartessos*" (1974) 134 *Revista de Occidente* 183–204.

[3] These agreements were evidenced in bronze tablets; some of these have been found by archaeologists, for example, the Bronze of Astorga. See F. Tomás y Valiente, *op. cit.*, pp. 78–9.

[4] From the battle of Cissa against Carthago 218 B.C. to 19 B.C., "*Hispania pacata*" under Emperor Augustus.

and for the first time all the inhabitants of the peninsula became subject to the same political power. However, the presence of Rome and its influence was unequal in the different territories of what became Hispania. Some tribes demonstrated great resistance and offered little chance of long-term influence to their colonisers, retaining their traditions and ways of living; while other groups—mainly the Mediterranean population and the tribes of the valley of the river Guadalquivir—soon adopted the Roman culture and way of life.[5]

The main change introduced by the Romans was the urbanisation of society. Roman administrative and political life was organised around the *urbs*. However, and as a consequence of the principle of personality of the laws common to the ancient world, Roman law only applied to Roman citizens. All the other citizens of the Empire were subject to their personal laws.

The first romanisation of Hispania started with the administrative regulations dictated by Rome for the organisation and the government of the conquered territories. Hispania was organised into provinces according to a *lex provinciae* which gave legal status to the different urban and municipal entities, respecting the local laws in all matters not regulated by the *lex*. Only those who acquired Roman citizenship were subject to Roman law—the *ius civile*. The other inhabitants of the Empire were the *peregrini*, free men within the borders of the Empire whose relationships were governed by the *ius pereginum*; the *latini*, who were an intermediate category enjoying some of the benefits of Roman citizens[6] and, therefore, were subject to Roman law in some aspects of their life[7]; and the slaves, who lacked any legal capacity. The relationships between people belonging to these different groups were articulated according to the *ius gentium*, a special system of law originating from the *ius civile* and the general rules of the other systems.

In A.D. 212 Emperor Caracalla gave Roman citizenship to all inhabitants of the Empire except slaves. This measure did not, however, totally eliminate local pre-Roman laws, which were still applied in some areas and which undoubtedly influenced the way of understanding and applying the rules of Roman law.[8] It is not possible, therefore, to say that the same Roman law was applied throughout the territories of Hispania since local customs adapted the law to the circumstances and needs of each

---

[5] This was, quite possibly, due to the fact that these peoples were accustomed to contacts with foreigners by trading with Phoenicia and Carthage.

[6] They enjoyed the *ius commercii* but not the *ius connubii*, *ius honorum* or the *ius sufragii*. See, F. Tomás y Valiente, *op. cit.*, p. 86.

[7] The term used to designate the mixture of their own law and the *ius civile* applicable to the *latinii* was *ius latii*.

[8] F. Tomás y Valiente, *op. cit.*, p. 87.

area.[9] Also, classical Roman law was never applied in Spain since this was conceived around the procedure of the *cognitio per formulas*, which was only applied in Italy, while provinces applied the *cognitio extra ordinem*. Some Roman legislation of this period was given to Hispania exclusively, such as the *lex ursonesis, lex salpesana lex malacvitana* or the "Bronzes of *Vispasa*".[10]

It was the Roman law of the postclassical period and what has been called "vulgar" Roman law,[11] which had more influence in the provinces of the Empire. The Roman Emperors tried to address the crises of the Empire in the third century by becoming more and more absolutist. The laws of the Emperor become progressively the only source of law and the great works of classical jurist-consults—Paulus, Gaius, Ulpianus and Papinianus—started to become a source of reference, since the quality of the works of the post-classical jurists was in clear decline.

While the Western Empire collapsed due to social and economic changes towards ruralisation and the feudal society of the Middle Ages, the eastern part of the Empire achieved its full splendour. Contact with the Hellenic culture, highly developed in disciplines such as logic and ethics, created a law of higher quality and sophistication than the law of the Western Empire. This culminated with the *Corpus Iuris Civilis* of Justinian A.D. 528–533. The *Corpus Iuris Civilis* had four parts and twelve books: the *Digest* or *Pandectas*, which was a collection of the works of the great jurisprudence of the classical period; the *Institutiones*, based on the *Instituta* of Gaius written for the teaching of the law; the *Codex*, which was a code of imperial legislation from Adrian to Justinian; and the *Novella*, which contained different enactments made after the publication of the *Codex*. The importance and influence of this work was enormous since it survived the Dark Ages and was rescued by medieval Italian scholars, influencing the whole of occidental legal culture.

At the time of the fall of the Roman Empire in A.D. 746, Hispania had already suffered the invasion of different barbarian tribes, mainly the Suevoi, Vandals and Alans. In order to fight these invasions the Roman Emperors asked for the help of another barbarian tribe, the Visigoths, who had already settled in other parts of the Empire[12] and were highly influenced by Roman culture. Their presence was not very numerous until A.D. 507 when Alarico II was defeated in Gaul by the Francs and this began a large scale immigration towards the South.

---

[9] See E. Gacto Fernández, *op. cit.*, pp. 68–71.
[10] For more detail see, *ibid.*, pp. 73–97.
[11] There is no consensus among writers about the term "vulgar Roman law". See F. Tomás y Valiente, *op. cit.*, p. 94.
[12] Mainly in Gaul (France).

4 INTRODUCTION TO THE SPANISH LEGAL SYSTEM

However, the number of Visigoths in Spain was never more than five per cent of the population.[13] The Visigoths were mainly peasants, with a few aristocratic families. It is doubtful whether they mixed with the Hispanic population[14] although they probably mixed with the Roman aristocracy. Their presence in Spain was very dispersed and they mainly occupied the north of the central plateau, establishing their capital in Toledo. They encountered great resistance in the North where some tribes, like the Basques, were never properly romanised or subjected to the Visigothic power.

The *leges* and *iura* of the Roman post-classical period remained in force in Gaul and Hispania long after the fall of the Empire. Most of the barbarian tribes only had customary laws, of which there is no surviving evidence. Whilst the Visigoth kings produced legislation, this co-existed with Roman law since it was primarily concerned with the distribution of land between Romans and Visigoths. The main legal works of the Visigoths were the *Código de Eurico*[15] and the *Breviario de Alarico* or *Lex Romana Visigothorum*[16]. The *Lex Romana Visigothorum* was not a compilation of Visigoth law but of Roman law. It was composed of *leges*, *iura*[17] and an *interpretatio* or interpretation of each text. Its influence was enormous and it was applied—in Hispania, and particularly in Gaul—for centuries. However, it was Recesvinto, who in A.D. 654, produced the main work of Visigoth law, the *Liber Iudiciourum*. The *Liber* was divided into 12 books and included all the laws passed by the different Visigoth kings. It was revised on two occasions and new legislation was added to it. It was widely applied and its influence persisted well after the Moslem invasion of Spain. These three main "codes" were applied in the whole territory dominated by the Visigoths[18], although local customs were respected in those matters not covered by the Visigoth codes.

In A.D. 711 the defeat in Guadalete meant the fall of the Visigoth monarchy and the beginning of the Moslem presence in Spain which was to remain for eight centuries. Although this factor differentiates

---

[13] F. Tomás y Valiente *op. cit.*, p. 98.

[14] Due partly to the cannon laws at the time which forbade mixed marriages. This rule was later incorporated in the *Breviario*. See below.

[15] Probably passed in A.D. 476 after the fall of the Empire. It has been described as a monument of "vulgar Roman law" although it incorporates some germanic customs, F. Tomás y Valiente, *op. cit.*, p. 102.

[16] A.D. 506.

[17] Mainly imperial constitutions and different versions of the *Instituta of Gaius*, the *Sententiae of Paulus* and the *Responsa* of Papinianus.

[18] There are important discrepancies about the personality of territoriality of Visigoth legislation. See F. Tomás y Valiente *op. cit.*, pp. 107–8 for a brief explanation of the main positions and a detailed bibliography.

Spanish history from other European countries[19] the changes were not as drastic as some historians have suggested. In fact, Visigoth society was in a clear and irreparable crisis before the Moslems arrived in Spain. On the other hand, most of the Visigoth aristocracy stayed and entered into different agreements with the invaders by which the Visigoths kept most of their land and power. Also, most of the Hispano-Roman population received the "invaders" with little resistance[20] and regarded them as a possibly better alternative than the Visigoth monarchy, which anyway was really as foreign as the Moslems.

The Hispano-Roman population which stayed in the peninsula—the vast majority—was allowed to keep its religion, customs, law and property by recognising the Moslem authority and paying a tax; however, some of this population converted to *Islam* and became subject to Muslim law. The *Liber Iudiciourum* was still applied, although with unavoidable modifications due to the absence of an unitary power to enforce it. Also some of the parts of the *Liber*—those about political organisation like criminal law and procedure—were not tolerated by the government of Al-Andalus. The co-existence of different religions meant that different systems of law were applied to each group—Jews, Moslems and Christians—under the Moslem tolerance.[21]

The beginning of the Visigoth and Christian resistance against the Moslems—*la reconquista*[22]—meant in legal terms, the beginning of the fragmentation and diversification of the law. Different Christian kings needed the help of feudal lords who imposed their own rules within their territory and established a difference between the law applied in cities and the law of rural areas.

From the eighth until the thirteenth century the law became increasingly local, and after the eleventh century was expressed by the different *fueros municipales*. The Christian kings of the period were weak and did not create much legislation; instead, they adopted and preserved the old law—the *Liber*. The kings did not start to create law until the sixth or seventh century, and when this happened it was in order to resolve all those situations for which the old *Liber* did not have an answer. In the new Christian kingdoms municipal law was mainly concerned with

---

[19] Spain was never a part of the Holy Roman Empire and the Moslem invasion and subsequent *reconquista* meant it had a different history from that of other European countries.

[20] Which explains the fact that within eight years the Moslems were in control of practically the whole of the territory, while it took two centuries for the Romans to conquer Spain.

[21] A good account of the law of the period is provided by E. Gacto Fernández, *op. cit.*, pp. 144–8.

[22] For an account of this period in English, see O. Robinson, *European Legal History* (2nd ed., 1994) pp. 117–19.

criminal, administrative or procedural law. In those areas in which the Visigoths never had effective control, *i.e.* the north of Spain, primitive laws were still applicable and when these people moved south, towards Castile,[23] they took their law with them—a law which was never romanised—refusing to acknowledge the *Liber* and resolving their disputes by nominating local judges.

The wars against Moslem domination lasted eight centuries, during which the different Christian kingdoms moved south as they recaptured new territories. One of the main problems of the time was the lack of population in some areas, especially on the borders of Moslem territories. In order to encourage Christian settlements in these areas the Christian kings granted a special law for each of these settlements with different privileges. These laws were known as *cartas pueblas* or *fueros*. They contained a few rules about administrative organisation and the rights over the use of the land.

In the tenth century, the King of León and the independent Count of Catalonia started to legislate, that is, to produce laws of general applicability for the whole of the territory under their control. The most important of these Christian laws were the *Usatges de Barcelona*, which, without derogating the *Liber*, replaced it in those areas in which it had become obsolete; the *Fuero de Aragón* and, at a later date, the *Fuero de Castilla*. In Castile a royal policy of unification of local laws was implemented by Fernando III and Alfonso X. Fernando III translated the *Liber* into Castilian calling it *Fuero Juzgo*. He chose this text as the law to be applied to all the re-conquered territories. The increasing power of the monarchy was also evident in the law of the time; Alfonso X imposed a *Fuero Real* in different areas of Castile, where it encountered severe opposition because it increased the powers of the crown and eliminated customary laws and rights.

The formation of the "ius commune".

The most important work in the history of Roman law was the *Corpus Iuris Civilis* of Justinian. However, published in A.D. 533 after the fall of the Western Roman Empire, it was not generally known or applied in Western Europe, with the exception of the territories kept under the control of Byzantium. Although Roman legal tradition was constant in Spain through the application—albeit irregular—of the *Liber*, this was not accompanied by the study of Roman law.

In Northern Italy the tradition of studying the sources of Roman law survived during the Dark Ages and experienced a renaissance in the

---

[23] At the time dependent on the Christian kingdom of León.

seventh century. One of the factors influencing the re-birth of the study of Roman law was the fact that European society at the time gravitated around two concepts: the Empire and Christianity. Charlemagne rebuilt an empire in place of the fallen Roman Empire, the "Holy Roman Empire", where all Christian people lived under the powers of the Emperor and the Pope. This Empire needed an unitary law which applied to all people; in contrast to the diversification of customs of the Germanic tribes and Roman law, the law of the last great Empire seemed to provide the logical answer.

In the sixth century new manuscripts of the *Corpus* were found in Italy, and in Bologna, Innerius, a teacher of the School of Arts gave autonomy to the study of law by creating a new method: the *Gloss*.[24] The studious of Bologna worked with the original texts of the *Corpus Iuris Civilis* introducing comments and annotating the original texts at the margin with the aim of discovering and explaining the true sense of the different books of the *Codex*. The Glossators did not, however limit their work to an analysis and exegesis of Justinian's work but also cultivated other methods like the *Summa* or the *Quaestiones disputae*. The *Summa* was a systematic study of one of the books of the *Corpus*, or of a law or title of the *Digest*. The *Quaestiones disputae* consisted of the discussion of a legal problem taking into account all the different approaches from several writers, analysing these and reaching a solution which was better adjusted to justice. The important names of this school are Azzo and Accusio. The later drafted the *Glossa Ordinaria*, a collection of all previous glosses, which acquired a wide circulation being itself studied by the Post-Glossators.

Parallel to the study of the *ius civile* was the study of canon law. The increasing power of the Church meant the Popes of the seventh and eighth centuries produced an enormous amount of *Decretals* which were the object of a study similar to the study of the *ius civile*.[25]

In the eighth century, the centre for the study of law moved from Italy to France where a new method, the Commentary, started to be practised in the University of Orleans. This school tried to adapt the law to the problems of real life, abandoning to a certain extent the study of the original texts of the *Corpus* and concentrating on creating an integrated system of municipal law and Roman law. The main difference between Commentators and Glossators was that while the Glossators' main purpose was to find the literal sense of the different texts of the *Corpus*, the Commentators went further afield in their study, trying to discover

---

[24] See O. Robinson, *op. cit.*, pp. 42–58.
[25] The main collections are the *Decretals Gregorii IX* complied by Raimundo de Peñafort in 1234, and the *Clementinas* elaborated in 1298.

the sense or "ratio" behind each disposition. In doing this they established the relationship of each text with the others, interpreting the rules of the *Corpus* in order to solve the practical legal problems of the time. The Commentators also produced *Consilia*, which was advice to the judges[26] and the parties in practical problems and which constituted a useful instrument for the introduction of Roman law into legal life.

The *ius commune* was a law made by lawyers—the scholars—integrated not only by Roman and canon law but also by the works of the scholars, known as "doctrinal writings".

Reception of the "ius commune" in the Spanish territories and integration of the different systems of law.

Whilst it is possible to talk in general terms about the reception of the *ius commune* in countries like France by establishing a difference between the *pays de droit écrit* and the *pays de droit coutumier*[27] it is not possible to make general remarks about the situation in Spain. Although in those territories such as Catalonia, where the *Liber* had a general application, the reception of the *ius commune* was easier and more complete, each of the different kingdoms and territories adopted a different approach to the integration of the *ius commune* with the laws of the king and with their traditional laws. These differences need to be understood because they are the basis of the different civil legal systems that today still exist in Spain—*los derechos forales*.[28]

Catalonia was the Spanish territory in which the *ius commune* penetrated to the greatest extent, due to the extensive Roman and Visigoth influence, its geographical proximity to the South of France, and the continuous commercial relations with the Italian republics. After Catalonia, the new kingdoms of Valencia and Mallorca, which did not have an autonomous, developed system of customary law, were also eager to implement the *ius commune*. The small kingdom of Navarra was the territory where the *ius commune* had a later and lesser influence, followed by the Basque provinces. These were hardly romanised at all, having local and differentiated customs which were firmly entrenched in the population.

In Castile and Aragón the penetration of the *ius commune* was quite complex. The local population strictly adhered to their local laws and opposed the imposition of royal legislation of Roman law. The kings

---

[26] Who at the time were not legal experts.
[27] F. Tomás y Valiente, *op. cit.*, p. 201; C. Dadomo & S. Farran, *The French Legal System* (1993) p. 5.
[28] "Foral laws" or regional customary laws.

oscillated in their positions as to the implementation of the *ius commune*. On one hand, the *ius commune* supported the idea of a king with power to legislate and as such was favoured by medieval kings; on the other, the *ius commune* was a highly developed system of great technical quality, which made the legislation of the king superfluous since, in theory, every problem could be resolved according to the *ius commune*. The solution to this dilemma consisted in declaring the primacy of royal legislation, recognising some traditional customary laws and the supplementary application of the *ius commune* in those areas where the above proved insufficient. However, the prestige of Roman and canon law, and the fact that the study of law at universities consisted of the study of the *ius commune*, meant that lawyers applied Roman law to resolve the cases. It was necessary for the kings to make several decisions forbidding this practice and specifying that only in the absence of royal or local rules could the parties or the judge resort to the application of Roman law. The integration of the laws in each of the different kingdoms will be considered since, as already explained, these differences in political organisation and legal institutions are the basis of the Spanish system today.

During the *Reconquista*, Spain was composed of different Christian kingdoms, to which the newly recaptured territories were incorporated with different degrees of autonomy. Some of these kingdoms were ruled by the same "Crown". This procedure culminated in 1492 when, after the conquest of Granada by Isabel and Fernando, Spain was unified under two Crowns: Castile and Aragon.[29] The "King of Spain" was officially king of all and every kingdom, "Prince of Catalonia" and "Lord of Vizcaya", but his power was unequal in the different territories because each of these kept its political personality and legal institutions and allowed the king different degrees of intervention.[30]

(1) **Navarra**

The small kingdom of Navarra had a uniform system of traditional local laws integrated mainly by unwritten customs and *fueros municipales*. This uniformity of local laws culminated in a general law for the whole kingdom called the *Fuero General de Navarra*. This law was respected by the different kings, who agreed to maintain the traditional law and subsequently passed little legislation. The penetration of the *ius commune* was late and minimal since there were no universities in the territory and it was only in the late fifteenth century that judges and lawyers

---

[29] Which in turn are integrated by different kingdoms.
[30] See F. Tomás y Valiente, *op. cit.*, pp. 282–97.

started to look at the *ius commune* for answers which could not be provided by the traditional law.

(2) Aragón

In Aragón traditional laws were of a high technical quality. The original Parliament—*las Cortes*—passed laws of general application known as *Fueros*, of which the most important was the *Fuero de Aragón* of 1274. However the *Fuero* was only applicable in the absence of a special local law, which always had preference. The *ius commune* was hardly applied although the *Fuero de Aragón* of 1274 had a provision of hierarchy of sources by which, in the absence of local law and of a provision in the general *Fuero*, it was possible to judge according to canon and Roman law.

(3) Catalonia

The main characteristics of the legal system of Catalonia in the Middle Ages were the great quality of their late local laws, the powerful penetration of the *ius commune*, and the development of early legislation.[31]

The main cities of Catalonia made written compilations of their local laws—*Costums*. These *Costums* were integrated by three different elements: local customs, some of them immemorial; privileges given by the king to the locality; and decisions of the local courts.[32] Separately from the different local laws, Catalonia started developing an independent law of the Principate, the main example of which was the *Usatges*, a compilation of feudal laws. Economic changes towards a mercantile society in the eighth and fourteenth centuries increased the powers of cities and demands for a new legislation. This legislation was given by the king and the *Cort General*.[33] The power of the king was always limited by the *Corts*.[34]

The reception of the *ius commune* was general and extensive in Catalonia. The *Costums* established a system of hierarchy of sources by which if there were neither local customs, nor other provision by the *Usatges*, the *Dret Comú* (*ius commune*) should be applied. Lawyers however, constantly applied the *ius commune* in the resolution of disputes to such an extent that in 1251, King Jaime I, considering that the application of Roman law was overtaking the application of specific

---

[31] F. Tomás y Valiente, *op. cit.*, p. 214.
[32] Among these *Costums* the most famous were: the *Costums de Tortosa* (1181) the *Consuetudines de Horta* (1296), the *Consuetudines ilerdenses* (1228), the *Recognoverunt proceres* (1284) and the *Consuetuts de la Ciudat de Barcelona* (date unknown).
[33] A parliament consisting of nobles, churchmen and the representatives of the cities.
[34] See F. Tomás y Valiente *op. cit.*, pp. 216–20.

Catalan laws, passed a restrictive order by which the pleading of Roman laws in judicial proceedings was forbidden except in cases in which there was not a local law applicable to the resolution of the dispute.

(4) Mallorca

Mallorca was a new kingdom incorporated under the Crown of Aragon but populated mainly by Catalans who imported their legal culture into the island. Mallorca did not seem to have a body of local laws and its specific law was constituted by royal legislation. The *ius commune*, either as directly applicable supplementary law or introduced by Catalan law, was widely applied. However, in 1439, in order to emphasise the autonomy of Mallorca in respect of Catalonia, a royal disposition forbade the application of the *Usatges* and declared that the supplementary law in Mallorca was the *ius commune*.

(5) Valencia

The new kingdom of Valencia, which was also incorporated under the Crown of Aragon but had autonomous political personality, was also greatly influenced by the *ius commune*. When King Jaime I decided to give a new law to Valencia this law was the *ius commune*. For four centuries, from 1229 to their expulsion in 1609, a large part of the population was integrated by the Moors who were allowed to keep some of their customs by royal decree. The local law was mainly absorbed by the *Furs* of 1240, by which different prerogatives were granted to the city of Valencia and later extended to different territories of the kingdom. Most of the rules of the *Furs* are directly taken from the *Codex* and the *Digests* of Justinian but were also influenced by canon and Catalan law.

(6) Castile

The largest and most powerful Crown of Castile, consisting of Castile and León, followed a different policy from Aragón in the respect of the autonomy of the different kingdoms. In effect Castile soon imposed its law and its political institutions on most of its territories and its kings legislated extensively. After Alfonso XI promulgated the *Ordenamiento de Alcalá* in 1348, only one law was applicable in Castile, Galicia, Asturias, León, Andalucia, Extremadura and Murcia and later to the newly acquired territories of Canarias and Granada. Only the Basque provinces kept their own law and legal institutions.

In Castile it is possible to talk about a royal legislative policy. The three early main works are the *Fuero Real*, the *Especulo* and most importantly, the main legal work of Spanish history *Las Siete Partidas*. The *Fuero Real* of 1255 was originally passed by Alfonso X for Aguilar de Campoo and Sahagun. The aim of the *Fuero Real* was to supply uniform rules for the resolution of legal disputes. The *Fuero* was progressively extended to different territories, often with little or no resistance from the population, since some of these territories already had their customary laws and more importantly, regarded the *Fuero Real* as an interference with local autonomy mainly because of the provision that judges were to be designated by the king instead of chosen by the local people. This *Fuero Real* was legally influenced by the *Liber* and canon law. However, the major legal work of the time was the *Código de las Siete Partidas*. Divided into seven books it covered questions of canon law, political power, procedure, matrimonial law, contracts, succession and criminal law. It was translated into Portuguese and in the nineteenth and twentieth centuries into English, and applied in the territories under Spanish domination in America. At the beginning it was a doctrinal text but its increasing prestige made it generally applied law until the nineteenth century. The influence of Roman-canon law in the *Partidas* is clear and decisive in the Spanish legal tradition.

(7) Basque country

The most distinctive feature of the territories and the peoples inhabiting what today is known as the Basque country is their language: the "*Euskera*".[35] *Euskera* is one of the rare examples of "island languages" which survived both the Indo-European and Roman influences. The Basques also avoided, to a large extent, the influences of the different cultures which invaded the Spanish peninsula through history. Confined to the remote and mountainous areas around the Pyrenees and the North of Spain, brave, and reluctant to encounter any external influence, they had little contact with the Romans, the Visigoths or the Moslems. When they descended to Castile at the time of the "reconquest" their customary laws did not seem to be homogeneous or very developed. As with their language, which had many dialects, so their customs seemed confined to small groups and communities.

F. Tomás y Valiente[36] points out some common characteristics of the laws of the three territories[37] during the medieval period. There is a coexistence of non-written customary law in rural areas with privileges and laws given by the King of Castile to the inhabitants of the cities (*villas*). Also, in the fourteenth century, in order to eliminate the violence which was an obstacle to any trade and even movement in the different territories, the inhabitants of the cities created associations called *Hermandades* or *Juntas* with capacity to dictate rules (*Ordenanzas*)

---

[35] F. Tomás y Valiente, *op. cit.*, p. 250.
[36] See *ibid.*, p. 252.
[37] Vizcaya, Alava and Guipozcoa.

for the judgment and punishment of crime. Although the Basque provinces were incorporated under the Crown of Castile the *Cortes* of Castile did not have power to legislate for Alava, Vizcaya and Guipúzcoa. In order to resist the attempt to extend to them the Castilian sources (*Fuero Real* and *Partidas*) in the fourteenth and fifteenth centuries, customary Basque laws were compiled in writing. These compilations of customs[38] and the general rules emanated from the different *Juntas*, constituted the main body of law in the provinces of Vizcaya, Alava and Guipúzcoa.

Absolutism

The powers of the King gradually increased during the sixteenth and seventeenth centuries and so did the volume of legislation. This created two main problems. The first problem was of a practical nature and this was the confusion among judges and lawyers as to which rules were still applicable and which not, since most of the new legislation did not repeal the former. The solution to this problem came by way of "compiling", that was, organising the different existing laws according to a chronological or systematic criteria in order to make it easier for the user to find the applicable provision. Most of the compilations of the time were started at instances of the king, although there were some important private collections. In general the compiler only transcribed the existing laws, organising these according to the chosen criteria but without altering the letter or substance of the provisions. However, in Castile, where the amount of legislation surpassed that in other territories, some authors attempted the difficult technique of "recasting the texts" by which all the different provisions refering to the same point were reformulated in a new one—which did not always respect the original aim and spirit of the rule. Among the most important collections of the time were the *Ordenamiento de Montalvo* of 1484 and the *Nueva Recopilación* of 1567.

The second problem was of very different nature and related to the relationship between this increasing legislation and the different systems of law existing in Spain at the time. After the unification of Spain in 1492 following the defeat of Boabdil in Granada by Isabel I of Castile and Fernando V, Spain was ruled by a unitary Crown with different kingdoms, each of which had its own political and legal constitution which was threatened by the laws imposed by the King of Castile. The King progressively became more absolute, legislating by ways of *pragmáticas* (laws given by the King without consultation with the *Cortes*

---

[38] *Fuero de Ayala* (1373) in Vizcaya, *Fuero Viejo de las Encarnaciones* (1394) and *Fuero Viejo de Vizcaya* (1452).

or Parliamentary assemblies) and legislating with effect in all the different territories. Felipe IV started an expansionist policy consisting of extending the political institutions of Castile to all other territories. These institutions were less democratic than those found in other territories because they granted greater powers to the King to the detriment of the local authorities. Some of the laws made by the King during this period were contrary to the laws generally approved by the different *Cortes* and assemblies and contrary to the traditional laws recognised in those territories. The solution to this conflict was found in the different legal formulas expressed by the local political organisations—*Cortes*— which, while acknowledging the power of the King to legislate, implemented the formula *obedézcase pero no se cumpla* which consisted in delaying the application of the royal legislation until the King, once he had been informed of the conflict with the local laws, resolved this in one way or another.

This formula was established by the *Cortes de Burgos* in 1379 but resistance to royal legislation and the defence of local laws was important in other kingdoms. In Navarra, where the legal system was clearly less romanised and "royalist" than in any other kingdom, a system of prior control by the *Consejo Real de Navarra* was established, by which all dispositions of the king needed to be approved by the *Consejo* before they could be applied in Navarra. This was known as the *pase foral* and was also generally practised in Guipúzcoa, Vizcaya and Alava until the nineteenth century. Catalonia and Aragón also protected their respective systems of law by similar formulas. In Catalonia a *constitución* passed by Fernando V in 1487, through the formula *poc valdria*, allowed the non-application of any laws contrary to the laws of the Principate. In Aragón control was effected by the *Justicia Mayor*.[39]

However, it was the Spanish War of Succession after the death of Carlos II and the triumph of Felipe V, which provided the excuse to abolish most of the local laws and effectively unify civil law in Spain. Catalonia, Aragón, Valencia and Mallorca supported the cause of Arch-Duke Carlos against the grandson of Louis XIV[40] and, when the Bourbon King won the throne, were severely punished, having their autonomy and laws curtailed.[41]

---

[39] The *Justicia Mayor* is a typical institution of Aragón; he was a judge between the King and the kingdom. See, for an explanation of his role, F. Tomás y Valiente, *op. cit.*, p. 296.

[40] Catalonia and Aragón, followed by Mallorca and Valencia, distrusted the centralism of the Bourbons which they believed to be incompatible with the autonomy enjoyed by those regions and supported the cause of the Austro-German candidate after Felipe V was already proclaimed King of Spain.

[41] Particularly Aragón. The main consequence was that most public institutions were abolished in those territories and consequently their particular public law. Only the

The Age of Enlightenment

The factor which was to be of greater influence on legal thought in the eighteenth century and which would constitute the theoretical basis for the new order of the next centuries, was the philosophical movement, which originated in the sixteenth and seventeenth centuries, based on the enlightenment of reason for the discovery of laws governing the physical world of nature. If reason could explain the functioning of nature and the laws to which this was subject, reason should also be able to explain the laws governing human nature and so draw the principles according to which men should be governed.

The School of Natural law, of which the main representatives were Grotius, Hobbes, Puffendorf and Wolff, proclaimed that philosophy would provide the general principles of Natural Law and that the legislator should create a systematic body of law based on these principles and according to which the different nations would be ruled. These principles, together with the theory of individual natural rights of Locke, Montesquieu's political theories expounded in *De L'Esprit des Lois*, and the Rousseaunian ideas of the "social contract", provided the ideological background of the Age of Enlightenment which quickly spread throughout Europe.

The legal principles of absolute monarchies by which the king could legislate according to his wishes—creating laws to which he was not subject himself—the division of society into different groups enjoying diverse privileges and the arbitrary system of justice administered by those chosen by the King, were duly criticised by Montesquieu, Kant, Mirabeau and Rousseau as contrary to reason and the natural order. Three new principles emerged from this new conception of the world: the principle of legality,[42] according to which both the universe and human nature are subject to laws; the principle of rationality, by which those laws governing humanity are derived from the natural laws by the use of reason; and the principle of nationality, which recognises the differences existing between different nations and according to which positive law, following the principles of natural law, must be adapted to the circumstances of each nation. The philosophical and political ideas of the period were reflected by two major trends in legal history: the creation of a state of law governed by a supreme rule—the Constitution—and codification of law.

---

institutions of Navarra and the Basque provinces survived together with the Castilian ones, now extended to most territories.

[42] Recognised by the 1791 French Constitution, Tit. III, Chapt. II, s. I, art. 3, first sentence: "There is no authority superior to the law".

Bourgeois revolution and liberal state

The society of the *Ancien Régime* was characterised by the differences between men who did not enjoy equal rights. Power rested upon ownership of the land which was controlled by the nobles and the Church. The King was the only person who could create law, a law which protected the interests of the dominant classes. Economic changes towards capitalism needed a new legal framework and the elimination of the old law. The new society born of the *Ancien Régime* proclaimed the equality of all men—although this was more a formal declaration used by the bourgeoisie for its own benefit rather than a real achievement—the free circulation of wealth and the liberalisation of the ownership of land. In legal terms the main difference was that the absolute monarchy was replaced by a liberal state governed by a supreme law—the Constitution.

2. CONSTITUTIONAL HISTORY

The Constitution, according to the principles and ideas of the Revolutionaries and the philosophers of the Age of Enlightment, was the supreme law by which free men could decide how they wanted to organise themselves as a State.[43] The Constitutional text, therefore, defined the political structure of the State and established the individual rights and freedoms of the citizens. In this respect the written constitutions of Europe of the eighteenth and nineteenth centuries served the dual purpose of being a bill of rights and a statement of the political principles of organisation of the State.

In Spain the principles of the bourgeois revolution penetrated quite late compared to other European countries, particularly France, since the sociological conditions were quite different.[44] Also, the fact that France was at the time Spain's enemy, created a situation of resistance to some of the ideas exported from the neighbouring country. According to F. Tomás y Valiente[45] the revolutionary period in Spain can be divided into three phases.

The first phase extended from 1808 to 1833. Napoleon, according to his imperial plans, invaded Spain in 1808 and proclaimed José Bon-

---
[43] According to the ideas of Kant "the State is a society of free men over which nobody has power". F. Tomás y Valiente, *op. cit.*, p. 422.
[44] Spain did not have such a powerful urban bourgeosie nor were the peasants so determined to break with the old regime.
[45] See F. Tomás y Valiente, *op. cit.*, p. 404.

aparte, his brother, King of Spain. On May 2, 1808 the War of Independence started, first as a movement to fight the invader, but later it developed into a war against the very foundations of the old regime. In a situation where there was a power vacuum—Fernando VII was absent and José Bonaparte was not recognised as the legitimate king by most of the population—the Spanish revolutionaries formed themselves into *Juntas*. All the provinces not occupied by the enemy elected their representatives in 1810 and the first *Cortes* (Parliament) met in Cádiz in order to draft a Constitution. The first Spanish Constitution was approved in Cádiz in 1812. It was strongly influenced by revolutionary ideas on the recognition of individual rights and the division of powers, establishing a Constitutional Monarchy. The Constitution of Cádiz of 1812 was a radical text which transformed society and recognised the principle of national sovereignty (article 3, Constitution of 1812), the division of powers—with a uni-cameral Parliament which "with the King" makes the laws which are executed by the King and the courts of justice. Other important principles of this first constitutional text were the principles of unity of codes and unity of jurisdiction. However, King Fernando VII, after coming back from exile, abolished the Constitution in 1820 and the country returned to being subject to an absolute monarchy. In 1820 a liberal *coup d'état*, the *Pronunciamiento de Riego*, re-established the 1812 Constitution, which was again abolished by the King in 1823. The re-establishment of the absolutism from 1823 to 1833 meant the frustration of the revolutionary achievements.

The second period of the process took place from 1836 to 1856. During this time a Constitutional State was definitively established, the regime of land ownership modified[46] and the Church deprived of much of its power. The nobility remained a socially powerful group but was now closer to the ideas of the bourgeoisie. The Constitutions of the period (1837 and 1845) were moderate. The Constitution of 1837 combined some of the ideas of the 1812 Constitution but made important concessions to the moderate sector, especially in the organisation of the powers of the State. The Parliament was now bi-cameral, with a Senate elected partly directly and partly by the King, and a Congress which was wholly elected. The powers of the Crown were, in general, reinforced. However, this flexible Constitution was modified in 1845 in order to change the principle of national sovereignty (sovereignty became shared between the nation and the King) and to reinforce, even more, the powers of the Crown.

The third and last stage of the revolutionary period was the most democratic. It started with the revolution of 1868 and ended with the

---

[46] On the transformation of the ownership of land or *desamortización* see, *ibid.*, pp. 406–14.

return of a Bourbon King, Alfonso XII, in 1874. In 1868 Generals Prim, Serrano and Topete, led a revolution which ended with the expulsion of Queen Isabel II and the establishment of a new monarchy under Amadeo I of Saboya.[47] The European political climate, the loss of the colonies in America and the dissatisfaction of the working classes, together with the errors of the monarchy, created the foundations for the later republican revolution. Some consensus was reached between the bourgeoisie and the popular classes and, for the first time, universal suffrage was recognised, culminating in the 1869 Constitution which clearly recognised a wide variety of individual rights, including freedom of association, freedom of expression and religion and basic human rights. The 1869 Constitution recognised national sovereignty and included the division of powers with a clear pre-eminence of Parliament over the Executive. Important laws were passed in this period: the Criminal Code of 1870; the Organic Law of the Judiciary of 1870; and the Code of Criminal Procedure of 1872. Subsequently, the bourgeoisie became a conservative class, once it had achieved most of its demands and a new order favourable to its interests had been established.

However, the renunciation of the throne by Amadeo of Saboya, because of the impossibility of ruling a country while there were continuous political struggles between opposing parties, opened the door to the establishment of the First Spanish Republic in 1873. The 1869 Constitution remained applicable, despite the fact that it endorsed the monarchy as the form of government, while the republicans waited for a new constitution to be drafted. In 1873 a project for a republican-federal constitution was presented by a commission presided over by Emilio Castelar. The project retained the rights and freedoms of the 1869 Constitution and introduced Krausist ideas on a multiple conception of sovereignty recognised at different levels: individual, local, regional and federal. Indeed, the main novelty lay in the conception of Spain as a federal state, according to which several states, reflecting the historic territories, could each have their own constitution together with the generic constitution for the central State. The President of the Republic acquired some of the traditional powers of the King, becoming an arbitrator between the different territories. However, the general climate of political instability and anarchy made the implementation of the Constitution impossible and in 1874 the *coup* of General Pavía ended the republican government and the son of Isabel II, Alfonso XII, returned as King of Spain.

---

[47] It was thought that a King belonging to a different royal family would be more suitable for the new conception of the State as a constitutional monarchy. At the time a large sector of the population, especially the regions which opposed Felipe V during the

The monarchic return of 1874 and the moderate Constitution of 1876 meant returning to the option of a constitutional monarchy which had been unsuccessfully tried during the previous century. Even if the 1876 Constitution kept some of the rights recognised in the 1869 text, the Government enjoyed wide powers to suppress these. The State became Catholic again and the King shared sovereignty with the nation and, therefore, the power to legislate with parliament. This Constitution remained applicable for more than twenty years and important legislation of the period included the Criminal Procedure Code of 1882 and the Civil Code of 1889.

In 1917 General Primo de Rivera seized power and a dictatorship was imposed until 1931. The last government of the dictatorship in 1931 decided to call for municipal elections in order to test the political climate of the country[48] and on April 12, 1931 the socialist and republican parties obtained an overwhelming majority. King Alfonso XIII understood that the country clearly opted for a Republic and he left the country on April 14, 1931.[49] On the same day the Second Republic was peacefully proclaimed. The provisional government of the Second Republic called elections for constituent *Cortes*, after modifying the electoral laws in order to have the first truly democratic elections. Women were allowed to vote for the first time and the old electoral register was modified in order to prevent the manipulation of the electorate. This democratically elected Parliament approved the 1931 Constitution, the application of which was interrupted by the victory of General Franco in the Civil War, but had a considerable influence on the current 1978 Constitution. The Constitution of 1931 had an advanced social content. Although it recognised private ownership this was limited on the grounds of the "national interest" and contained provisions according to which ownership could be nationalised, especially in respect of those services which affected the common interest. Article 1 declared Spain to be "a Republic of workers organised in a system of freedom and justice. All the powers come from the citizens". As to the territorial organisation of the State, article 1 declared that "the Republic is an 'integral' State, recognising the autonomy of municipalities and regions". This republican constitution did not establish a federal state but lay the foundations of today's State of Autonomies because it recognised the right of the different territories to form themselves into autonomous regions and approve an *Estatuto de autonomía*.[50]

Spanish War of Succession, were against the Bourbon royal family which was identified with the absolutism of the *Ancien Régime*.
[48] Note that the Monarchy agreed with the dictatorship.
[49] Although he did not renounce his rights to the throne.
[50] See below, Chap. 2, p. 47 *et seq.*

Catalonia approved its *Estatuto* by a law of September 15, 1932, the Basque country by a law of October 6, 1936 and Galicia on June 28, 1936, although this last was never ratified in *Cortes*. Valencia, Aragón and Andalucia did not see their projects of *Estatuto* approved due to the outbreak of the Civil War in 1936 and the later dictatorship of General Franco following his victory.

From 1939 to 1975 Spain was under the right-wing dictatorship of General Franco who imposed an autocratic system around his person and abolished the republican Constitution and with it most of the rights and freedoms acquired during the revolutionary period. Catholic, unitary (no rights of autonomy were recognised in any of the historical regions) and highly centralised, Spain was ostracised by the international community until 1975 when, after Franco's death, the Monarchy in the person of King Juan Carlos I, was re-established.[51]

3. CODIFICATION

Codification of civil law

Although the idea of the having all the laws in a single body was not a novelty[52] the ideas of the philosophers of the Natural Law School, that the law was an organised system of rules derived from nature, was articulated by the creation of codes. A code would consist of a body of legislation which contained all the general principles on which subsequent legislation would be based. The existence of a single source whereby the rights recognised by the Constitution—especially ownership and individual freedom—could be established in an universal way provided the bourgeoisie with legal certainty. A code could also be presented as the instrument with which to achieve a break with the past and consolidate the new order recognised in the constitutional text.

Prussia, Austria[53] and France were the first European countries to have codes. However, it was the French *Code Civile* of 1804 which was the greatest of them all because of its technical perfection and the fact that it was elaborated in a country which already had a bourgeoise revolution. The influence of the French Civil Code has been enormous. It was

---

[51] About this period and the political transition to democracy, see, among others: Paul Preston, *The Triumph of Democracy in Spain* (1986).
[52] Indeed the best example is the *Corpus Iuris Civilis* (A.D. 527–60) and before it the *Codex Gregorianus* (A.D. 291), *Codex Hermogenianus* (A.D. 295) and the *Codex Theodosianus* (A.D. 439).
[53] On the Prussian and Austrian codification see O. Robinson, *op. cit.*, p. 250; F. Tomás y Valiente, *op. cit.*, p. 477.

implemented and copied in several countries and inspired the codification of civil law in others, among them, Spain.

The first Spanish Civil Code was not approved until 1889, nearly a century after the French Civil Code. Although greatly influenced by the *Code Civile* in its principles, structure and systematisation, the codification of civil law in Spain presented peculiar characteristics due to the resistance of customary local laws to abolition and unification. The late publication of the Civil Code meant that during most of nineteenth century Spanish civil law was founded on the surviving customary local laws of the different communities[54] and the law of sources as old as the Code of the *Siete Partidas* and the *Ordenamiento de Alcalá*. In fact, it was the existence of different systems of civil law which slowed down the process of codification, together with a reaction against the centralisation of power in the nineteenth century. Although the Constitution of 1812 introduced the idea of drafting a civil code, several unsuccessful projects[55] were proposed until in 1885, Francisco Silvela, then Minister of Justice, presented a draft Civil Code containing important concessions for the application of *foral* and local law which would remain applicable, and establishing that the civil law contained in the Code would be supplementary in those territories which had their own customary *foral* law. According to the project of 1885 the different *foral* laws would be compiled in appendices and added to the Civil Code. The project presented by Francisco Silvela was in fact a *Ley de Bases*[56] which was to be developed by the *Comisión de Codificación*.

In 1889 the Civil Code was approved and came into force on May 1, 1889. The Civil Code has a Preliminary Title on the sources, application, interpretation and efficacy of the Law. It is divided into four books: persons, property, acquisition and transfer of property and obligations. It is influenced by Castilian traditional law, particularly the Code of *Siete Partidas*, in subjects such as marriage and matrimonial property, and Roman law—as found in the *Ordenamiento de Alcalá*—in the area of contract. Principles of *foral* law are reflected in succession rules, although here the different *foral* regimes are respected. Foreign influences come mainly from the Code Napoleon and from different Ibero-American Codes, which themselves incorporated principles and ideas of the French Code. Politically the Code is a product of the liberal conception of the nineteenth century which is reflected in the protection of individual freedom, especially in contract law, and the protection of private ownership which is understood as an absolute right.

---

[54] The ones which were not abolished by Felipe V. See above.

[55] For an explanation of these different projects and the problems they encountered see F. Tomás y Valiente, *op. cit.*, pp. 546–50.

[56] A law establishing guidelines which were subsequently developed by a commission and later approved in Parliament.

As far as the appendices of *foral* law originally planned are concerned, only Aragón presented its appendix in 1925. This was of poor quality and was severely critised and quickly subject to a project of reform. In 1946 a national meeting in Zaragoza rejected the idea of these appendices and agreed that different compilations should be drafted in order to elaborate a General Code of Civil law containing Common Civil law and the different aspects of *foral* law. Compilations with *foral* law were approved between 1959 and 1973, these included the laws of Catalonia, Aragon, Navarra, Baleares, Galicia, Alava and Vizcaya[57].

Codification of criminal law

The Codification of other areas of law, envisaged since the 1812 Constitution, followed an easier path. Criminal Law, influenced by Roman law and canon law was one of the areas of law most severely criticised by the philosophers of the Age of Enlightment.[58]

Although the 1812 Constitution declared the principle of unity of Codes for the whole of the national territory, due to the political circumstances of the time[59] it was necessary to wait until the liberal triennial (1820–23) for the publication of the first Criminal Code in Spain, the *Código Penal* of 1822. This was only applied from January 1, 1823 to April 1823 when it was derogated by Fernando VII. The second Criminal Code was approved in 1848; shorter, and with a more modern approach, this was modified in 1850 by the absolutist government. The third Code was a product of the 1868 Revolution and was approved in 1870. Although originally intended only to be temporary—it was known as the "Summer Code"—paradoxically it had the longest application period. Derogated during the dictatorship of Primo de Rivera by the Criminal Code of 1928, it was re-established in 1932 during the Second Republic and modified again in 1932. The "New State" of General Franco introduced several modifications to the Criminal Code of 1870 which was formally still applicable. These culminated in 1944 with a Criminal Code in line with the principles and ideas of the *Régimen*. This Code, despite the political circumstances under which it was drafted, remained applicable, with some important modifications, after the 1978 Constitution.

Since the change of political orientation under a new democratic

---

[57] See Castán Tobeñas, *Derecho Civil Español, Común y Foral* (1982) pp. 294–352 for an exposition of the different systems of *foral* law.
[58] Montesquieu, in his famous book *De L'esprit des lois* (1748) advocated a new and rational criminal law and criminal procedure since criminal law during the *Ancien Régime* took a line of extreme cruelty, especially on punishments.
[59] See above.

system, the most important reforms to the 1870 Code[60] have been effected by the LO 8/83, of June 25, "Partial and Urgent Reform of the Criminal Code", and the LO 3/89 of June 21 updating the Criminal Code, by which some of the principles contained in the Constitution were introduced into the Criminal legislation. However, the situation of Criminal law in Spain has been severely criticised from a number of different perspectives and several projects for a new Criminal Code have been unsuccessfully presented. Among these it is worth mentioning the project for Criminal Code of 1980 and the draft outline of 1983. A new Criminal Code has been recently approved in Parliament.[61] This introduces, as main reforms, a substantial modification of the system of punishment (according to article 25 CE[62]), new types of crimes in order to reflect the changes observed in society, namely in the areas of socio-economic[63] and environmental crimes, the protection of fundamental rights such as the right to honour, with the introduction of a new and rather vague category described as "crimes against moral integrity".[64] It also proposes the modification of crimes against sexual freedom in order to depart from the traditional protection of women and to extend this protection to all citizens who are victims of sexual attacks without differentiating on the ground of gender.[65]

Codification of commercial law

Commercial law was first codified in 1829. Since the late eighteenth century there had been demand for a general Code of maritime law and a general Code for commercial proceedings in order to overcome the diversification of laws produced by the different *Consulados*.[66] The *Código de Comercio* of 1829 had an excellent technical quality although it left some areas, such as the stock market, to be regulated by special legislation. However, the expansion of capitalism and the radical economic liberalism of the late nineteenth century soon meant that the provisions

---

[60] As subsequently modified.
[61] The new Criminal Code was approved by Congress on November 8, 1995 with the abstention vote of the Conservative group.
[62] art. 25 CE: "*Las penas privativas de libertad y las medidas de seguridad estaran orientadas hacia la reeducacion y reinsercion social y no podran consistir en trabajos forzados . . . en todo caso tendra derecho a unn trabajo remunerado . . . acceso a la cultura y al desarrollo integral de su personalidad*".
[63] Crimes relating to trade marks, intellectual property, and consumers.
[64] See art. 169 of the Project.
[65] It is not possible to give a detailed description of all the reforms introduced, and to some extent it is necessary to await the publication of the definitive text.
[66] See F. Tomás y Valiente, *op. cit.*, "Mercantile law from the XII to the XVIII Centuries" pp. 346–68 and "Codification of Commercial Law" pp. 507–19.

of the 1825 Commercial Code were inadequate and a new Code was drafted and approved in 1885. Very similar in its structure to the 1825 Code, the 1885 text is still applicable although a variety of laws have been passed in order to reflect changes in the commercial world. Among these the most important have been the *Ley de Sociedades Anónimas* in 1954 modified in 1989,[67] *Ley Cambiaria y del Cheque* (1985), *Ley del Mercado de Valores* (1988), *Ley General de Cooperativas* (1987), *Ley General para la Defensa de los Consumidores y Usuarios* (1984).

4. SPAIN TODAY: A SOCIAL AND DEMOCRATIC CONSTITUTIONAL STATE

On December 6, 1978 a Constitution was approved by national referendum and sanctioned by the King on December 27. It was drafted by a constitutional commission composed of representatives of the main political forces winning the 1977 elections.[68] The main aspects to be determined by the Constitution were: the definition of the form of government, the relationship between Church and State, the territorial structure of the State, and the powers of the Head of State and the Executive in respect of Parliament.[69] Together with these, the definition of the fundamental rights and freedoms and the establishment of a system of guarantees for the protection of these, was also in the minds of the draftsmen of the Constitution and the political forces at the time. As to the form of government—monarchy or republic—the dilemma was solved in favour of the monarchy since all political forces agreed that the price to pay for a peaceful transition to democracy was the acceptance of the monarchy as a form of government.[70] The Constitution in article 1(3) declares that the form of government is a parliamentary monarchy.[71] Sovereignty rests upon the nation which elects its representatives to a bi-cameral Parliament.[72]

As to the relationship between Church and State, there was a considerable debate between the parties of the left who supported a declaration of total separation of Church and State, such as the one contained

---

[67] By the *RDL*, 1564/1989 of December 22; see also *Ley* 19/1989 of July 25, adapting Spanish legislation on companies to EEC law.
[68] The constitutional commission was integrated by three deputies from UCD, one from PSOE, one from PCE-PSUC, one from AP and one from the Catalan minority.
[69] According to M.A. Aparicio, in *Introducción al Sistema Político y Constitucional Español* (1991) p. 42.
[70] See J. Solé Tura, *Los Comunistas y la Constitución* (1978) pp. 69–70.
[71] See below, Chap. 3, for an explanation of the role of the Crown in the Spanish System.
[72] For the role of Parliament see below, Chap. 3, p. 25

in the 1931 Constitution, and the more conservative UCD (centre) and AP (right) who fought in order to preserve at least some of the powers of the Church. Article 16 represents a compromise between these two positions by declaring that "No religion is the religion of the state ... The public powers will co-operate with the Catholic Church and other faiths".[73] Perhaps the major problems of the relationship between State and Church arose in connection with an area traditionally dominated by the Church—education.[74] The Catholic Church was reluctant to lose its ideological and economic monopoly on private education and the "representative political parties", the UCD and the AP ensured by the drafting of article 27 CE, the preservation of this power.[75]

The territorial organisation of the State was one of the most difficult problems to solve, partly because even within the different political groups the position as to whether to opt for a federal or unitary state was not clearly defined. The Constitution chose, in Title VIII, an unitary but decentralised State by which the different historical territories were recognised as having to achieve different degrees of autonomy according to the procedure set forth in Title VIII. Today, similarly to the Italian regional State, Spain is composed of seventeen autonomous communities each of which has an autonomous Parliament and Executive[76] with powers shared with the central or national Parliament and the Executive.

As far as the definition and protection of fundamental rights and freedoms are concerned the 1978 Constitution is a progressive text along the lines of the Italian Constitution. Although it is not possible here to include a detailed study of the fundamental rights and freedoms recognised by the Constitution and the systems for their protection, a few of the most important aspects will be indicated.

The first consideration refers to the role that the fundamental rights and freedoms play in the whole legal system. To this effect article 10.1 CE states that the laws should be interpreted according to the system of fundamental rights recognised by the Constitution. These rights and freedoms are thereby placed in a position of principles informing the interpretation and application of the rules of the whole legal system.

---

[73] art. 16 CE "Ninguna confesión tendrá caracter estatal. Los poderes públicos tendrán en cuenta las creencias religiosas de la sociedad española y mantendrán las consiguientes relaciones de cooperación con la Iglesia católica y demás confesiones."

[74] M.A. Aparicio, *op. cit.*, p. 44.

[75] art. 27 recognises the right of creation of educational centres to individuals and groups and thereby to the Catholic Church. However the development of art. 27 has been controversial.

[76] References are made throughout the text to the powers of the autonomous communities. See, especially, Chap. 2, pp. 47–51.

The second consideration relates to the guarantees established for the effective implementation and protection of fundamental rights. These guarantees are not limited to jurisdictional procedures, as indicated below, but encompass a wider system which integrates the principle of subjection of all citizens and public powers to the Law (article 9(1) CE), with the declaration of the principle of legality of article 53.1, according to which the regulation of the exercise of fundamental rights and freedoms is reserved to formal *leyes*, and, for some of these, to *leyes orgánicas* (article 81)[77]; the introduction of specific institutions such as the *defensor del pueblo* (article 54)[78]; the regulation of the right of petition (article 29 CE) and the description of the functions of Parliament in this area.

The third point to consider is that the "Fundamental rights and duties" of Title I of the Constitution are divided into three types of rights depending on the protection available to them. The first group of rights and freedoms is integrated by article 14—principle of equality—and articles 15–29 CE—which include the fundamental rights and freedoms of section 1, Chapter 2, Title I. The second group is integrated by articles 30–38; and the third by the rights recognised in Chapter 3, Title I, "Principles informing the social and economic policy". The difference between these "types" or categories of rights, established in article 53 CE, is the form of protection against any violation of these "rights".[79] Article 53(2) makes provision for a special summary procedure for the protection of the rights recognised in articles 14 and section 1, Chapter 2, Title I, articles 15–29.[80] Also, these rights can be pleaded in the Constitutional Court by the procedure of *recurso de amparo*.[81] The rights recognised in Chapter 1, should be pleaded according to ordinary proceedings and are excluded from the possibility of being protected directly by the Constitutional Court according to the procedure of *recurso de amparo*. As for the protection of the principles informing social and economic policy, article 53(3) establishes that although these shall inform legislation and judicial practice they can only be pleaded in court according to the laws by which they have been developed.[82]

---

[77] See Chap. 2, pp. 31–33.
[78] See Chap. 3, p. 74.
[79] Note that there are different classifications of fundamental rights. For example Luis López Guerra in *Introducción al Derecho Constitucional* (1994) pp. 104–11, makes the distinction between "rights of freedom", "rights of participation" or political rights, "social rights" or second generation rights and, "solidarity rights" or third generation rights.
[80] *Procedimiento preferente y sumario* as developed by the *Ley 62/1978 de protección jurisdiccional de los derechos fundamentales de la persona* of December 26.
[81] See below, Chap. 3, pp. 101–103.
[82] For a greater detail on the exposition of the system of fundamental rights and freedoms, see M.A. Aparicio, *op. cit.*, pp. 100–109 and the bibliography therein cited.

5. THE SPANISH CONCEPTION OF LAW

The word *derecho* is associated with the idea of justice and rectitude, as opposed to what is unjust, illegal or irrational.[83] When used in common language *derecho* has different meanings. First, *Derecho* (capital) means all the rules according to which society is organised. In this sense, *Derecho* is equivalent to the English word "Law". Secondly, the word *derecho* (non-capital) is used as an equivalent to the English word "right". Thirdly and last, *Derecho* is also used to designate legal science, that is, the study of the rules of law.

The first meaning of the word *Derecho*, is an objective sense and designates the rules according to which society organises itself; but only certain type of rules can be included in the concept of legal rules. There are other rules which clearly influence and govern human behaviour but cannot be included in the term *Derecho*; these are moral, religious or social rules. The difference between a rule of law and other rules is that rules of law have two distinct characters: they are bi-lateral and imperative. Law is always concerned with the conduct or behaviour of a person in relationship with others; in this sense, the rule of law is bi-lateral because it creates at the same time a duty for one party and a power or right for the other.[84] Law is also imperative in the sense that every rule of law contains a mandate imposing certain behaviour on all those subject to the rule and encompasses a sanction in case of disobedience.[85]

The second meaning of the word *derecho* (right) or *derecho* in a subjective sense makes reference to the power that the legal system confers on individuals to act in a specific way and at the same time to expect a certain behaviour from others. In this sense the owner has the right of enjoyment of his property and the power to exclude others from that enjoyment, or the creditor has the right to be paid and the power to demand payment from the debtor.

The word *derecho*, comes from the latin word *directum* which is the past form of the verb *dirigere* which, according to Castán Tobeñas,[86] means "that which is according to rule" or "that which leads to an end". *Derecho* is thus, associated with the idea of "rectitude and direction".[87]

---

[83] Castán Tobeñas, *op. cit.*, pp. 58–60.
[84] Moral or social rules only impose duties and do not create rights or powers.
[85] This sanction can be more or less perfect depending on the case. For example in Public International law, it is difficult sometimes to impose sanctions on sovereign states.
[86] *op. cit.*, p. 58.
[87] In other languages this idea is also found in the terms used for *derecho*: *dret* in Catalan, *droit* in French, *diritto* in Italian, *recht* in German and "right" in English. See the very interesting etymological study by Castán Tobeñas, *op. cit.*, p. 58.

It is interesting to note, however, that the Romans used the word *ius* to designate what today is known in Spanish as *Derecho* (Law). The displacement of the word *ius* for *directum* has different explanations[88] but several words connected with the Law derive from this Latin word: *justicia, justo, juez, jurídico, jurista*, etc.

6. THE DIVISION BETWEEN PUBLIC AND PRIVATE LAW

The classical division between public and private law comes from the great Roman jurists. Ulpianus, in a definition included in the *Institutiones*, defined public law—*ius publicum*—as the law which regulates the political aspects of the State while private law—the *ius privatum*—comprises the rules which regulate the relationships of citizens among themselves. Many criteria have been discussed by scholars concerning the classification of public and private law: the type of interest—general or private, protected and/or the character, imperative or dispositive—however, all of these have been criticised and today the predominant criteria establishes the differences between private and public law on the basis of the subjects involved in the legal relationship. In this sense, public law is the part of the law which regulates relationships in which the State is involved whenever they act as such, or as the Roman jurists used to put it, whenever they exercise *"imperium"*; and private law includes all those rules which organise the relationship of private citizens between themselves.

This distinction between private and public law, which does not exist in Common Law countries, has been basic to Civil Law countries. However, the development of new branches of law and the increasing intervention of the State in many areas traditionally governed by private law has given rise to a growing scepticism as to the utility of such differentiation or even its existence today. Some authors write about three areas of law; public, private and mixed, which of course, diminishes the importance of the original division.

The traditional branches of public law are: criminal law (*derecho penal*), administrative law (*derecho adminsitrativo*), procedural law (*derecho procesal*), tax law and public international law.

Private Law in turn includes civil law (*derecho civil*), commercial law, private international law and originally labour law, although the latter is heavily regulated by the State and can be included in the third or mixed category.

---

[88] See, again, Castán Tobeñas, *op. cit.*, p. 59 and the bibliography therein provided.

Chapter Two
Sources of law

1. Introduction

The expression "sources of law" can be interpreted in different ways. It can be understood as the origin of the rules of law. In this sense Parliament would be a "source of law", because the *leyes* are enacted by the Chambers of Parliament; in the same sense the Executive would be another "source of law" because it produces regulations. However, this is not the meaning that the expression "sources of law" commonly has in legal theory. When we speak about the sources of law of a given legal system what we are referring to are all those rules which constitute "the Law". From a functional perspective the sources of law are everything which provides rules for the judge when having to decide a case.[1]

Traditionally, the regulation of the sources of law was to be found in the Spanish Civil Code. The old article 6 contained a mandate to the judge, in the absence of any rule of written law—*ley*[2]—to apply the local custom and the general principles of the law. By a law of March 17, 1973 a Preliminary Title was introduced in the 1889 Civil Code and in article 1 the sources of the Spanish legal system were established as being: *la ley, la costumbre y los principios generales del derecho*.[3] In this preliminary title there are also rules concerning the application of the law, the interpretation of legal rules, the role of "equity"[4] and the personal, territorial and life-time effect of the laws. This group of rules has been referred to as "material constitutional law"[5] because they provide and establish the basic framework of the operation of the system. The sources of the law as defined in the Civil Code have been described as "traditional sources of law" in contrast to the sources described in the 1978 Constitution. The Civil Code itself is a subsidiary source for all the other

---

[1] Ignacio del Otto, *Derecho Constitucional, Sistema de Fuentes* (1991), p. 72.
[2] *Ley* is a formal Act of Parliament but can also be translated as "Law" or "legislation". When referred to as a source of law, *ley* means any rule of law emanating from the State.
[3] *Ley*, in the sense explained above, custom and the general principles of the law.
[4] "Equity" or *equidad* is understood as the equivalent of justice. See below.
[5] Ignacio del Otto, *op. cit.*, p. 85; against, Díez Picazo, *Sistema de Derecho Civil* (1992), Vol I.

areas of the law as *derecho común ó general*, but it needs to be remembered that, for each branch of the law, the sources can be re-defined and to some extent varied. A good example of this is criminal law, where, by virtue of the "principle of legality" only written law promulgated by the State is a recognised source of law. Other examples are administrative law, tax law and labour law where the traditional sources of article 1 of the Civil Code are limited or extended.

The sources of law in Spain can be divided into three categories: primary sources of law, which provide judges with the law directly applicable to the case; complementary sources, the power and scope of which derives from a primary source; and explanatory sources, which give guidance to the person applying the law as regards the meaning of the primary sources. What is considered to be a source of law in any given legal system is closely connected with and dependent on the legal history of the system.[6]

2. PRIMARY SOURCES OF LAW

LA LEY (LEGISLATION)

The word *ley*, when used as synonym for legislation, has a broad meaning encompassing all written law emanating from the State: the Constitution, ordinary legislation, rules of law emanating from the government by virtue of legislative delegation or special powers derived from the Constitution[7]—*decretos-leyes, decretos legislativos*, and decisions of the Constitutional Court. In this respect *ley* is any rule of written law which has a certain position in the hierarchy of sources—*fuerza de ley*— and not only the rules emanating from Parliament's[8] broad category of *ley*, but rules from very different sources can be found and even the Constitution itself would be included.

However, when the Civil Code mentions *la ley* in article 1, it is not only referring to the rules created by the State's legislative power according to different procedures and in respect of different matters, but also to the rules created by the Government[9] and the Public Administration in the exercise of their executive power. *Ley*, thus, is any written

---

[6] See Chap. 1 for a brief summary of the history of the Spanish legal system.
[7] See below.
[8] There is a distinction between *ley* in a formal sense, *i.e.* Acts of Parliament and *ley* in a material sense, *i.e.* general measures by another authority with the same value and position in the hierarchy of sources. For a comparison with the French legal system, see Dadomo & Farran, *op. cit.*, p. 60 *et seq.*
[9] *Reglamentos, decretos, ordenes*. See below.

rule of law created by the state. All these different types of rules and the relationship between them will be examined in this chapter.

TYPES OF *LEY*

Leyes orgánicas[10]

When the 1978 Constitution was approved, it was difficult to achieve agreement on some fundamental matters. The political consensus, reached by the different political forces during the period of "political transition"[11] as regards the organisation of the State and the minimum levels of civil rights and liberties, could not cover all the basic aspects which make up a State. Some matters therefore had to be left to the legislator but at the same time these aspects were so fundamental that it was thought to be inappropriate to leave them to the arbitrary will of the majority political party in power. This explains why the use of *leyes orgánicas* became a necessary device.

Leyes orgánicas are a special type of statute required by the Constitution for the regulation of certain matters, subject to special requirements for the procedure of elaboration, approval, modification and derogation. Article 81 of the Constitution states that *"leyes orgánicas* regulate fundamental rights and civil liberties, approve of the *Estatutos de Autonomía*[12] the general electoral regime and any other matter provided for by the Constitution".

Leyes orgánicas are different from ordinary legislation in two ways: first, as to the subject matter of the regulation, they relate to specific matters (article 81 CE); and secondly, because there are different formal requirements for their approval due to the fundamental character of the areas to which they relate.[13]

As to their position in the hierarchy of sources of law, *leyes orgánicas* are subject to the Constitution, otherwise they would be declared unconstitutional by the Constitutional Court.[14] As regards other types of *ley*, in particular ordinary legislation, *leyes orgánicas* are at the same level because they are only a different type of *ley*. Whether a matter should or should not be regulated by a *ley orgánica* depends on whether that matter

---

[10] *Leyes orgánicas* could be translated by "organic laws", but this is not widely accepted terminology and therefore the original Spanish word will be used.
[11] See Chap. 1, p. 24.
[12] See below.
[13] *Leyes orgánicas* need to be approved by an absolute majority of the Congress (art. 81 CE), while ordinary legislation only requires a simple majority for its approval.
[14] See below, Chap. 3, pp. 95 *et seq*.

is specified in article 81 CE or another constitutional provision. If it is, then the ordinary legislator cannot regulate that matter and any ordinary *ley* purporting to do so would be unconstitutional because it would contravene article 81 CE. If the matter is not specifically designated as requiring a *ley orgánica*, the ordinary legislator can regulate it, and the *ley ordinaria* is then subject only to the Constitution. The relationship between *leyes orgánicas* and ordinary *leyes* is, therefore, a question of subject-matter, not hierarchy. The problem arises when a *ley orgánica*, while regulating matters specified in the Constitution as requiring such legislation, goes beyond these and regulates other matters not specifically so reserved. In this case the question is, can an ordinary *ley* modify or abrogate this legislation? Article 28(2) of the LOTC[15] clearly states that the Constitutional Court can declare any *ley*, which modifies or derogates a *ley orgánica*, unconstitutional. At first, this seems to indicate that ordinary legislation cannot modify or abrogate any regulations contained in a *ley orgánica*. However, the Constitutional Court, in a decision of 1981,[16] had declared that if a *ley orgánica* regulates any other matter beyond the areas delimited in the Constitution it would only have the value of an ordinary *ley*, and as such it could be modified or abrogated, as regards these matters, by later ordinary legislation.

The matters reserved for a *ley orgánica* are listed in article 81(1) CE. Some clarifications are necessary at this point. First, as to the "development of fundamental rights and civil liberties", the stipulation that a *ley orgánica* must be used in this area must be interpreted[17] as referring only to Chapter II, section 1, of Title I, articles 15–29 CE, because this section is the only one which is entitled "Of fundamental rights and public freedoms". Any other interpretation of article 81 CE would create the situation in which ordinary legislation would become almost redundant because Title I of the Constitution includes the principles of economic and social policy which are present in almost every regulation. Also, "development" means "development of the recognition of the right in the Constitution",[18] not every regulation on the exercise of the right, because that is a matter for an ordinary *ley* under article 53(1) CE.[19]

Secondly, as to the regulation of the "general electoral regime" by a *ley orgánica*, the Constitutional Court understands[20] this to cover not

---

[15] *Ley Orgánica del Tribunal Constitucional* LO 2/1979 of October 3.
[16] STC 51/81 of February 13.
[17] STC 70/1983 of August 5.
[18] STC 6/1981 of March 16.
[19] "*Los derechos y libertades reconocidos en el Capítulo segundo del presente Título vinculan a todos los poderes públicos. Solo por ley, que en todo caso deberá respetar su contenido esencial, podrá regular el contenido de tales derechos y libertades...*"
[20] STC 38/1983 of May 16.

only general elections but also local elections. This regulation by a *ley orgánica* extends to all "basic and primary aspects of the electoral regime and not only the right to vote".[21]

The approval of the *Estatutos de Autonomía* by a *ley orgánica*, will be discussed later in the context of Autonomic Laws.[22] The last matter specifically requiring a *ley orgánica* under article 81 CE is an open category "any other matter as determined by the Constitution". The matters determined by the Constitution include; the regulation of the institutions of the State; *Defensor del Pueblo*[23] (article 54 CE), *Consejo de Estado* (article 107 CE), *Tribunal Constitucional*[24] (article 165 CE), and other important matters such as the popular legislative initiative[25] (article 87(3) CE).

International treaties

(a) Incorporation into the legal system: Types of treaties

International treaties are automatically incorporated into the Spanish legal system once they have been duly signed and ratified.[26] Spain adopts a monist system of incorporation of international rules into domestic law. This means that no further action by the legislative or any other body of the State is necessary to confer binding force on an international agreement.[27] The Constitution draws a distinction between different types of treaties; in all of them, the conditions for their validity are *ex ante* as to whether they have been properly entered into; if they have, they are automatically incorporated into the legal system and bind all citizens and public powers.

Three types of international treaties are identified in the Spanish Constitution:

(1) Article 93 treaties, which confer some of the powers of the State on an international organisation. For these treaties a *ley orgánica*[28] authorising the signing of the treaty is necessary. Probably the most famous and typical example of this type of treaty is the Treaty of the Accession of Spain to the European Com-

---

[21] STS 38/1983 of May 16.
[22] See below.
[23] LO 3/1981 of April 6, *del Defensor del Pueblo*. See below, Chap. 3, p. 74.
[24] The Constitutional Court, *LOTC* 2/1979 of October 12.
[25] LO 3/1984 of January 26, *reguladora de la iniciativa popular*; see below, Chap. 3, p. 65.
[26] "Any international treaty signed and ratified according to the rules of international law and this Constitution will be part of the legal system" (art. 96(1) CE).
[27] Dualist systems such as in England require an Act of Parliament to enact a treaty.
[28] This is one of the matters specifically provided for in the Constitution requiring a *ley orgánica*.

munities, the ratification of which was authorised by a *ley orgánica*.[29]

Once the approval to ratify the treaty is given by a *ley orgánica*, the treaty will automatically be incorporated into domestic law on its publication[30] in the official journal.[31] As the international treaty has given authority to the international organisation, the legislation produced by the organisation—derivative or secondary law of the European Communities—will be automatically obligatory in Spain with no need for any further action by the internal powers. The Supreme Court has confirmed the "direct efficacy and supremacy of European Community Law due to the partial assignment of sovereignty to the Community Institutions".[32] Along the same lines, the Spanish Constitutional Court has expressed that "the binding force of Community Law comes from the Accession Treaty according to article 93 of the Spanish Constitution" (*STC* 61/1991, *caso APESCO*, F.J.4).[33]

(2) The second type of treaty is that requiring prior authorization by Parliament through an agreement of both Chambers at the request of the Executive. These treaties, *rationae materiae*, are of a political or military character and affect the territorial integrity of the State, the rights and freedoms guaranteed in Title I of the Constitution, or create financial obligations on the State. For example, the participation of Spain in NATO required previous authorization by Parliament. According to article 94 (1)(a),(b),(c),(d),(e) CE, the authorisation of Parliament is necessary prior to the ratification of any treaty if this involves a modification or abrogation of any law or the need for any legislative measure for its implementation.

(3) Any other treaty not included in (1) or (2). The Executive can sign and ratify these treaties and there is a requirement only to inform Parliament following such ratification (article 94(2) CE).

---

[29] LO 10/1985 of August 2, authorising the ratification of the Treaty of Accession to the European Communities, Lisbon and Madrid, June 12, 1985.
[30] art. 96 of the Spanish Constitution.
[31] *Boletín Oficial del Estado* (BOE).
[32] STS of April 28, 1987, *Depositos Francos* (*Sala* 3, 1987); in the same sense STS of April 17, 1989, *ITE Canario* (*Sala* 3, 1989) Cdo. 2.
[33] For the most recent analysis of the relationship and applicability of European Community Law in Spain, see Pablo Perez Tremps, *Constitucion Española y Comunidad Europea* (1994) pp. 133, 134.

(b) The position of treaties in the hierarchy of sources of law

The position of international treaties is clear in respect of their subordination to the Constitution.[34] There is a procedure whereby enquiries may be made to the Constitutional Court as to whether a treaty conflicts with the Constitution. The Government and/or Parliament can require the Constitutional Court to make a ruling as to whether the treaty is or is not against the Constitution.[35] If the treaty is contrary to the Constitution the latter will need to be modified before the signing of the treaty (article 95(1) CE).[36] There is also a *post facto* control by the Constitutional Court according to article 27(2) LOTC.[37] Since the treaty has a hierarchical position equivalent to the *ley*, the Constitutional Court can declare that all or some of the provisions of the treaty are "unconstitutional" and so inapplicable.[38]

A problem arises in respect of the relationship between treaties and ordinary laws. Treaties (without distinction) are treated in the same way as ordinary legislation as regards their constitutional control. However, other differences arise between treaties and ordinary legislation. The active force of the legislation, its capacity to abrogate or modify other rules of law, including other legislation, is not applicable to international treaties. Only when a treaty has been signed with the previous approval of the legislative power can a treaty abrogate or modify other legislation because the previous approval of Parliament means an extension or delegation of legislative power. On the other hand, the force of ordinary legislation is restricted when applied to a treaty (article 96.1) because the provisions of a treaty can only be modified, abrogated, or suspended in accordance with the procedure established in the treaty itself. If a provision of a treaty and a rule of domestic law are in conflict, the provision of the treaty prevails.

This particular situation regarding treaties has led to doctrinal controversy concerning the superior position of international legislation over domestic legislation. However, rather than looking at this question in terms of hierarchy, the special status of the treaty can be explained by the principle of *pacta sunt servanda* and thus the impossibility of unilateral modification of the terms or obligations assumed under a treaty.

---

[34] art. 95 of the Spanish Constitution *a sensu contrario*.
[35] arts. 95(2) CE and 78 LOTC. See below, Chap. 3, p. 101.
[36] For instance art. 13(2) of the Constitution was modified on August 27, 1992 in order to allow the signing of the Single European Act.
[37] See below, Chap. 3, p. 98.
[38] In this case the Executive will have to take measures in order to modify its international obligations.

(c) European Community law

The accession of Spain in 1986 to the European Community and the subsequent ratification of the Single European Act and the Treaty of the European Union meant a cession of State powers in favour of an international organisation. The application and position of the original treaties in the Spanish legal system did not create major problems. The treaties are rules of International law and if properly signed they are directly applicable as a part of the national system once they have been published in the Official Journal.[39] A different problem is the applicability of the "derivative law" of the European Communities. By derivative law is meant the rules produced by the Institutions of the Community. Here, again, the Spanish legal system adopts a monist approach. In the same way as the treaties are rules of International Law directly applicable in domestic situations without the need for any further action by the internal legislative power, so is derivative law, since it is a consequence of the obligations imposed by the treaty. There is no provision other than article 93 CE in Spanish law on which to base the application of the derivative law of the Communities. The Supreme Court has expressed and reinforced this view: "European Community Law has direct effect and supremacy over national law by virtue of the partial cession of sovereignty brought about by the accession to the European Community".[40] The question of the direct effect of Community legislation has never been controversial in Spanish law, due perhaps to Spain's late joining of the Community and the numerous decisions of the European Court of Justice concerning the direct effect and supremacy of Community law. The Spanish Supreme Court has totally accepted the position of the European Court of Justice on the direct effect of regulations[41] and directives.[42]

Another area concerning the relationship between Community legislation and internal rules is the question of the resolution of conflicts between rules of both systems. After the famous decision of the European Court of Justice *Costa/ENEL* (1964),[43] the principle of precedence of Community law over national law is one of the pillars on which the system rests. The Spanish Constitutional Court has held that any conflict between Community legislation and domestic legislation has to be

---

[39] The problem of applicability is more difficult for States with a dualist position such as England.
[40] STS of April 28, 1987, *Depositos Francos*; also, STS of April 17, 1987, *ITE Canario*. For a general discussion on the topic, see Pablo Pérez Tremps, *op. cit.*, pp. 127–49.
[41] STS of April 17, 1987, *ITE Canario*.
[42] STS of December 21, 1988, *Contrabando de Tabacos* (*Sala* 2, 1988). For more references, see Pablo Perez Tremps, *op. cit.*, p. 137.
[43] STJCE *Costa/ENEL*, of July 15, 1964.

Leyes ordinarias

Since the French Revolution the word *ley* has been used to designate all the rules dictated by the organ of popular representation according to a certain procedure. *Ley* is the rule of law approved by Parliament according to the procedure established in Title III, Chapter 2 of the 1978 Constitution[45] and the rules of law approved by the legislative organs of the Autonomous Communities.

Almost any matter can be regulated by ordinary legislation,[46] and some of these matters are specifically reserved for the *ley*.[47] However, due to the lengthy procedure for approval of ordinary legislation in Parliament and to the complexity of some of the matters that need to be regulated in modern societies, the number of formal *leyes* is relatively small compared with other types of legislation, namely *decretos-leyes* and *decretos legislativos*[48] which hierarchically are in the same position as ordinary legislation but are made by the Executive.

Decretos leyes

In cases of urgency and extreme need, the Executive has the power to introduce rules which have the force of *ley*. This power of the Executive is recognised by the Constitution (article 86.1) and it is commonplace in comparative constitutional law.[49] The limits imposed by the Constitution on this power—which indeed modifies the original division between the legislative, executive and judicial powers[50]—are both formal and substantive. The substantive limitation is that the *decreto-ley* may not affect the organisation of the basic institutions of the State, the

---

[44] STC 28/1991 of February 14, *Elecciones al Parlamento Europeo*. For a further discussion on the subject see. A. Sánchez Legido, *Las relaciones entre el Derecho Comunitario y el Derecho interno en la Jurisprudencia del Tribunal Constitucional* pp. 184–5. Pablo Pérez Tremps, *op. cit.*, pp. 146–8.

[45] See below, Chap. 3, pp. 63–65.

[46] With the exception of the matters reserved to *leyes organicas* by art. 81(1) CE. See above.

[47] *Reserva de ley formal* for example the regulation of the rights and freedoms of Chap. 2 of the Constitution can only be done by a *ley* according to art. 53(1) CE.

[48] See below.

[49] art. 16 of the French Constitution, art. 81 of the German Constitution, and art. 77 Italian Constitution recognise the same power of their respective Executives. In all three the power of the government is restricted to cases of extreme urgency and/or need.

[50] As established during the French Revolution.

civil rights and liberties contained in Title I of the Constitution, the organisation and powers of the Autonomous Communities or the general electoral regime. The formal limit is the need to submit the *decreto-ley* to Congress for approval and ratification within a period of thirty days. The validity of this type of legislation is therefore conditional on the ratification or rejection by Congress (article 86(2) CE). If it is approved, Congress can "convert" the *decreto-ley* to an ordinary *ley* by an expedited procedure (article 86(3) CE).

The existence of this power of the Government to legislate gives rise to important and difficult questions about the controls to which this type of rule is subject. The main question is the relationship between a *decreto-ley* and the subsequent *ley* of Parliament when the *decreto-ley* has been converted,[51] and whether the new *ley* and the original *decreto-ley* are two different rules which can be subjected to the control of the Constitutional Court separately, or whether the new *ley* has retroactive effects and the *decreto-ley* is a "project of *ley* with anticipated effects".[52] The Constitutional Court, in a rather unclear decision in 1983,[53] held that it is possible to question the validity of an original *decreto-ley* as to whether the requirements of "urgent and extraordinary need" were present, but when the content of the *decreto-ley* has been incorporated into a formal *ley*, what should be examined is the constitutionality of the new *ley* which thereby has "some retrospective effects". This solution seems to give the new *ley* retrospective effect which is contrary to article 9(3) CE and also, according to some writers deprives the restrictions set out in article 86(1) of any meaning.[54]

Decretos legislativos

While the Executive, in the case of *decretos-leyes*, using the power given by the Constitution in article 86, decides that the regulation of some matters requires swift action, there are other cases in which Parliament decides that some legislation would be better drafted by the Executive because of the nature of the matter. In these cases Parliament

---

[51] See Ignacio del Otto, *op. cit.*, pp. 206–209 for a detailed consideration and analysis of the topic.
[52] In the words of Ignacio del Otto, *op. cit.*, p. 208.
[53] STC 11/1983, *caso RUMASA*. By *decreto-ley* of February 23, 1983 the Executive expropriated the *Grupo RUMASA* which belonged to J.M. Ruiz-Mateos. This *decreto-ley* was confirmed shortly afterwards by Congress according to art. 86.2 CE. On June 29, 1983 a *ley* substituted the original *decreto-ley* because it was argued that an expropriation affected fundamental rights and could not be made by this type of legislation according to art. 86.1 CE.
[54] However, the solution of the Constitutional Court is followed by the majority of writers, and warmly supported by Ignacio del Otto, *op. cit.*, p. 208–209.

delegates its legislative power to the Executive. The legislation passed by the Executive following delegation by Parliament is called *decreto legislativo*.

Legislative delegation is a practice common in all European States. Article 82(1) of the Spanish Constitution establishes the power of Parliament to delegate to the Government the right to pass rules which have the force of *ley*. These rules are different from those mentioned previously—*decreto-ley*—for whereas with *decretos-leyes* the Government is exercising one of its own powers, here Parliament has conferred this power on the Executive which must observe the limits set out by Parliament.

Any delegation of power must be exercised within strict limitations. It can only be made for a specific matter, it must be expressly allowed by a *ley*[55] of Parliament, and for a finite period of time. It cannot apply to matters reserved for a *ley orgánica*[56] or the general budget of the State. The delegation can be articulated in two ways. In the first instance—*textos articulados*—Parliament dictates a *ley de bases*[57] fixing the principles, criteria, object, limits and scope of the delegation and the text which will be created. The second instance is the authorization for consolidating legislation which already exists but is scattered. Here the limits are easier to establish as the Executive has to reorganise pre-existing legislation but cannot introduce or create new rules.

Control of this method of legislating can be exercised by the courts in the ordinary way once the text has come into existence. Also the enabling or delegating *ley* can establish additional controls. In the case of *decretos-legislativos* there is no control by Parliament after the promulgation of the text as is the case with *decretos-leyes*.[58] Problems arise when the Government acts *ultra vires*, that is, when it goes further than authorised by the enabling law. The doctrine has different opinions as to what happens with rules passed outside the scope of the power given by the delegation. As it is a rule having the force of law, a judge who has to apply it has two options: not to apply that part of it which is tainted by *ultra vires*,[59] or to require the Con-

---

[55] A formal *ley*, approved according to the procedure of arts. 87–91 CE. See above, and for more detail Chap. 3, pp. 63–65.
[56] See above: matters reserved for a *ley orgánica*.
[57] Basic legislation.
[58] See above.
[59] Because, according to E. García de Enterría, *Curso de Derecho Adminsitrativo* (1993) p. 250 *et seq*, the rules contained in the *decreto legislativo* tainted by *ultra vires* do not have the nature or the value of *ley*; they have the same value as any of the dispositions dictated by the Executive in the exercise of its regulatory power; and these regulations of the Executive need not be applied by the ordinary judge when they are contrary to a *ley* or to the Constitution. Compare, however, the view of Ignacio del Otto, *op. cit.*, pp 190–4.

stitutional Court to give a ruling on the constitutionality of the whole text.[60]

Reglamentos, decretos, and other administrative dispositions

The term *reglamento*[61] refers to any general legal rule dictated by the Public Administration or, more generally, by the Executive. The formalities required by these rules and the different organs from which they emanate give rise to different types of *reglamentos* which are hierarchically organised. At the top of the scale of *reglamentos* are the *decretos* of the Council of Ministers; below these, the *ordenes* of the Ministers or of the Delegated Commissions; underneath, *instrucciones* and *circulares* from inferior authorities and members of the administration. The procedure and requirements for drafting these dispositions are established by the Administrative Procedure Act 1954, articles 129–37. *Reglamentos* are rules of law due to their generality and are different from other administrative acts which are only individual acts. These rules dictated by the Administration are always subject to the *ley* and the judge has no power to apply any reglamentary disposition which is contrary to a *ley*. A *reglamento* can also be challenged in the Administrative Court and declared null and void.

Traditionally *reglamentos* have been classified in two groups. Independent *reglamentos* or *praeter legem*, which regulate matters without legislative coverage; and executory *reglamentos*, or *reglamentos secundum legem*, which develop an existing *ley*.[62] In this case it is necessary to request the opinion of the *Consejo de Estado*.[63] A different classification is that which distinguishes between *reglamentos jurídicos* and *reglamentos administrativos*. *Reglamentos jurídicos* are those which create or modify the rights and duties of citizens, for example the Road Traffic Code; these *reglamentos* affect citizens independently of any special relationship with the Public Administration. *Reglamentos administrativos* are those dictated by the administration for the organisation of its activities and only affect the citizen who is in a special relationship with the administration, for example, because he is a inmate in prison, or using a public hospital.[64]

---

[60] The Constitutional Court has affirmed its competence in this matter SSTC 29/82; 51/82; 47/84 and *Auto* 69/83 of January 17.

[61] Which can be translated by "regulation", and should not be confused with the *reglamentos* of the Chambers of Parliament which are the rules that the Chambers pass in order to organise their own functioning and which have the same value as a *ley*.

[62] A good example of this second type are the *Reglamento del Registro Civil* or the *Reglamento Hipotecario* which develop the *Ley del Registro Civil* and the *Ley Hipotecaria* respectively.

[63] art. 22.3 LO 3/1980 of April 22, *del Consejo de Estado*.

[64] Ignacio del Otto, *op. cit.*, p. 218 and E. García de Enterría, *op. cit.*, p. 257 *et seq*.

PRIMARY SOURCES OF LAW 41

The power to pass *reglamentos* is vested in the Executive by article 97 of the Constitution,[65] but other constitutional organs of the State also enjoy "regulatory" power; these are the *Consejo General del Poder Judical*[66] and the Constitutional Court which can regulate their own organisation, personnel and services.[67] The territorial entities which have recognised autonomy by the Constitution—municipalities, provinces and Autonomous Communities[68]—also enjoy regulatory power.

LA COSTUMBRE (CUSTOMARY LAWS)

According to article 1 of the Preliminary Title of the Civil Code, *la costumbre* (Custom) is a primary source of law, the second source after the *ley*. However, this is subject to some qualifications. Custom will only be applied by a judge if there is no applicable *ley*, it cannot be contrary to morals or public order and needs to be proved.

Historically the first definition of customary laws was given in *Las Partidas*:[69] "Custom is non-written law, applied by men for a long time". This definition provides a starting point for the examination of customary laws. The first characteristic is that customs are "non-written law"; while legislation is normally written[70] customs are usually not. However, there is nothing to prevent customary laws from being compiled or reduced to writing;[71] probably the best example is provided by international trade rules such as the rules governing documentary credits transactions which have been reduced to writing[72] but which do not have a value other than that of mercantile usage. The fact of whether a rule is written or not, is not enough to characterise customary laws as being different from legislation. The second characteristic of customs is the origin of these rules. Customary laws, it is said, do not originate from the State but from society. This second characteristic, however, necessitates the continuous practice of the custom by the social group which has created these rules.

In order to be rules of law, customs must satisfy some requirements. The first is the existence of a practice—a "usage". This practice does

---

[65] "*El Gobierno . . . ejerce la función ejecutiva y la potestad reglamentaria de acuerdo con la Constitución y las leyes*".
[66] See below, Chap. 3, pp. 78–80.
[67] arts. 2.2 LOTC and 110 *LOPJ*.
[68] art. 137 CE.
[69] See Chap. 1, p. 12.
[70] It has to be written: art. 2 Civil Code.
[71] For example "foral laws" of customary origin had been compiled as was the *droit coutumier* in France during the sixteenth and seventeenth centuries.
[72] *Uniform Customs and Practice for Documentary Credits, Publication 500*. International Chamber of Commerce, Paris 1993.

not need to be for any special length of time but a single use clearly does not create a custom. The second traditional requirement for customs to be considered as sources of law is the existence of an *opinio iuris*. This means the existence of a general conviction about the obligatory character of the customary rule. Together with the requirements of "continuous and regular practice" and *opinio iuris*, the Civil Code establishes that customs cannot be contrary to morals or to public order, although if the custom is a source of law it is difficult to think how it can be immoral unless the legislator when drafting the Civil Code was thinking of uses or practices which were not customs properly so called. In order to accord with public order, since customs only apply in the absence of legislation, the public order must be established by the general principles of the law.[73]

As a source of law custom has some special features. It is an independent source since it is created and developed totally independently from any other source;[74] it is a subsidiary source because it will only apply if there is no written provision of State origin (a relevant *ley*); and it is a secondary source in the sense that it needs to be pleaded and proved to the satisfaction of the court.[75]

Depending on the relationship between customary laws and written legislation there are different types of customs: customs which are contrary to legislation—*contra legem*; customs which interpret a legal or customary rule according to the law—*consuetudo secundum legem*; and customs which regulate situations for which there is no written legislation—*extra legem* or *praeter legem*. Customs *contra legem* are excluded by article 1 of the Civil Code because customs are only operative in the absence of legislation, never against it. As to the second type or customs *secundum legem*, their value lies in the interpretation of the application of the rules of law, but judges are not bound by this interpretation.[76] The third type of customs—*praeter legem*—are generally recognised by article 1 of the Civil Code and are, thus, a source of law.

---

[73] Note that after the 1978 Constitution the majority of the Doctrine indicate that the references to "public order" are references made to the Constitutional public order.

[74] It is due to this characteristic that custom is included among the primary sources.

[75] Since the principle *iura novit curia* does not extend to customary laws.

[76] art. 3, when setting the rules for the application and interpretation of the rules of law does not mention "usual or customary" interpretation as one of the criteria to be taken into account.

LOS PRINCIPIOS GENERALES DEL DERECHO (GENERAL PRINCIPLES OF LAW)

Much controversy surrounds the third source of law in the Spanish Civil Code—the general principles of the law. The existence of some form of "superior" principles was recognised in ancient Greece[77] and inherited by Rome where the idea of a *ratio iuris*[78] underlying the rules of law was commonly accepted. When Codification started in France the issue was much discussed. However, the French Civil Code did not contain any mention of these "natural laws" probably due to the idea that the Code was a product of reason. It was the Austrian Civil Code of 1811, the first of the modern Codes, which first contained a reference to these principles.[79] The concept of "natural legal principles" or "general principles of the law" gained popularity in modern legal theory[80] and today general principles of the law are recognised as a source of international law.[81] General principles of the law are the basic rules reflecting the convictions of a community in respect of its organisation. These general principles permeate the whole legal system. Modern constitutions make formal declarations of the values considered fundamental by the community; article 1 of the 1978 Constitution says that the values underlying the Spanish legal system are freedom, justice, equality and political diversity. In Spanish law these general principles have a twofold function: first, they are a source of law, though a subsidiary source; secondly, they inform the other sources. A good example is provided by the principle of "equality", which is one of the fundamental values recognised by article 1 CE and further developed in article 14, which prohibits any form of discrimination. This principle informs all areas of the law, for instance civil or criminal procedure have to respect it by granting to all parties to the proceedings equal opportunities;[82] other examples of legislation incorporating this principle are the rules organising access to the civil service or employment law.

---

[77] Where references were made to *agrafos nomos*, or non-written law derived from nature, or moral and religious convictions.

[78] *Ratio iuris* or *natura rerum* was the law constituted or derived from the nature of things.

[79] art. 7 of the Austrian Civil Code of 1811 stated: "If it is not possible to decide a question according to written law ... it will be decided according to natural legal principles".

[80] Especially among the followers of the School of Natural Law. See above, Chap. 1, p. 15.

[81] art. 38 of the Statute of the International Court of Justice, recognised as the most authoritative statement on the sources of international law, provides that: the Court ... shall apply, ... (c) "the general principles of law recognised by civilised nations".

[82] See below, Chap. 5.

44   Sources of Law

3. Complementary Sources

LA JURISPRUDENCIA[83] (CASE LAW)

Strict separation between the creation and the application of rules of law originated in the French Revolution and rests on the idea that the application of a rule of law is only an operation consisting of giving practical effect to an abstract concept which has already foreseen and provided for the consequences of any concrete case.[84]

This concept has been strongly criticised since the nineteenth century because in every case in which the law is applied there is a choice. The text of the rule of law is not always clear, and even if it is, the generality of its terms necessarily encompasses a certain degree of choice, with the result that the application of the law by any judge always requires the exercise of some freedom and reflects the creative aspect of the law.

In the Spanish conception of the "State of Law" or "Democratic State"[85] the principles of legal certainty, equality and unity of the law require restrictions to be imposed on the freedom of the judge. In Anglo-Saxon countries the restriction of the freedom of the judge in the exercise of this jurisdictional function is achieved by giving binding force to the criteria with which the court has decided previous cases in the past. This rule, known as *stare decisis*, originated not as an answer to the problems of applying existing rules of written law but as a substitute for it. Anglo-Saxon law is to a large extent a system of case law. Even if there is a statute (written law of Parliament) this is applied within a safe-guard provided by the previous applications of the same provision by the courts. The principle of *stare decisis* operates horizontally and vertically in order to ensure uniformity of justice organized from the top of the Court structure; at the same time the possibility of abandoning the precedent, with greater or lesser freedom depending on the court, ensures the evolution of the law.

In Continental Europe limitation of the judge's freedom in the application of the law was achieved by creating a special organ, *ad hoc*, a *Tribunal de Casación*, the function of which is to elaborate a doctrine about how the rule of law must be interpreted. The origin of the system is the *référé législatif* introduced in France in 1790, by which, if the judge has doubts about the interpretation of a rule of law he must ask

---

[83] Although the term *jurisprudencia* in Spanish law can be used to describe "the science of law" as in the English term "jurisprudence", it also means case law, or more exactly, the case law of the Supreme Court. The term is used here with this second meaning.

[84] According to the famous quote from Montesquieu in *De L'Esprit des Lois*: "The judge is the mouth pronouncing the words of the law".

[85] *Estado de Derecho* or *Estado Democrático de Derecho* (art. 1 CE).

Parliament to give an interpretation. Later, a *Tribunal de Casación*,—a political organ dependent on Parliament—was created for this. The *référé legislatif* was later eliminated and the *Tribunal de Casación* became a "real" court, independent of the legislative power and with jurisdiction to rule on all mistakes on the application of the law by the judges.[86] The system has some similarities with the Anglo-Saxon system, the main difference being that only the decisions of the Supreme Court have binding force.[87]

In Spain, the 1812 Constitution, created a Supreme Court—*Tribunal Supremo*—which in principle only had jurisdiction to rule on decisions of the inferior courts which were allegedly against the law. This was done through a *recurso de nulidad*, a special type of appeal in which the Supreme Court had to determine whether the decision was null because it was found to contravene the law. In 1855 the *Ley de Enjuiciamiento Civil*[88] expanded the functions of the Supreme Court and the new appeal—*casación*—allowed the Supreme Court to decide not only if decisions were against the law, but also, whether judicial decisions of the lower courts were against the established legal doctrine[89] of the Supreme Court.[90] Today article 1692(5) of the Civil Procedure Act[91] acknowledges the possibility of an appeal in *casación* in cases in which there is an infringement of the *jurisprudencia*.[92]

The introduction of "infringement of the *jurisprudencia*" as a new ground of *casación*, has added a new dimension to the traditional debate about the nature of the decisions of the Supreme Court. It seems that if a citizen can appeal because the *jurisprudencia* has not been respected, it is because it is a source of law, and as such, it must be applied by the judge in the resolution of a case. Some authors[93] maintain that "the

---

[86] In Ignacio del Otto, *op. cit.*, p. 293.
[87] In Spanish law the *jurisprudencia* includes only the decisions of the Supreme Court, not the decisions of other courts, STS of June 30, 1866 and STS of February 10, 1886 among others. Castán Tobeñas, *op. cit.*, p. 515.
[88] Civil Procedure Act.
[89] The term "legal doctrine" or *doctrina legal* is synonymous with *jurisprudencia*. What the Supreme Court controlled, therefore, was the respect of its own *jurisprudencia*, which brings the Spanish model closer to the Anglo-Saxon.
[90] According to Federico de Castro, *Derecho Civil de España, Parte general* T.1 (1st ed., 1942), p. 418, the introduction of the ground "infringement of legal doctrine" was necessary in order to adapt the *recurso de casación*, which was imported from France to the Spanish legal tradition which acknowledged a *recurso de injusticia notoria* which was possible not only when the judge gave judgment against a written *ley* but also when the judgment was against the "straight application and interpretation of the law".
[91] Introduced by the *Ley* 34/1984 of August 6 which modified the old art 1692 of LEC.
[92] See below, Chap. 6, p. 148.
[93] Especially Puig Brutau, *La Jurisprudencia como fuente del Derecho (Interpretación creadora y arbitrio judicial)* (1951) p. 7.

46   Sources of Law

theoretical difference between continental legal systems and the Anglo-Saxon system is not so important in practical terms, because the *ley* and other officially accepted sources of law have a limited scope which is insufficient to resolve all the individual cases", Puig Brutau affirms that "Spanish Civil law is, to a certain extent, a system of law created by the judges, because judicial decisions have a highly persuasive value, independently of their formal recognition as a source of law".[94] However, the wording of the Civil Code is clear[95] on what the sources of law are: *la ley, la costumbre y los principios generales del derecho*. The *jurisprudencia* "will complement" the legal system and is the tool by which the uniform application of the above sources of law is guaranteed".[96] The *jurisprudencia*, therefore, is a complementary source and the duty of the judiciary, therefore, is to ensure that the Supreme Court creates *jurisprudencia* and the lower courts respect it.[97]

THE DECISIONS OF THE CONSTITUTIONAL COURT

The Constitutional Court is an organ of the State. The function of this Court is to interpret the Constitution and assess the conformity of the sources of law with the Constitution.[98] The decisions of the Constitutional Court are referred to as *jurisprudencia constitucional*, but their value is very different from the *jurisprudencia* of the Supreme Court because what the Constitutional Court controls is the compliance of legislation with the Constitution. When the Constitutional Court declares a statute to be unconstitutional and so null and void, this interpretation is superior to the interpretation of the legislator. This rule places the Constitutional Court's decisions on the same level as the Constitution itself in the hierarchy of sources. The decisions of the Constitutional Court have to be applied by the ordinary courts according to article 5(1) *LOPJ*.[99]

---

[94] Compare the view of F. de Castro, *op. cit.*, (2nd ed. 1949), p. 508.
[95] art. 1(1) CC, "The sources of law are *la ley, la costumbre y los principios generales del derecho*".
[96] art. 1(6) CC "*La jurisprudencia complementará el ordenamiento jurídico con la doctrina que, de modo reiterado, establezca el Tribunal Supremo, al interpretar y aplicar la ley, la costumbre y los principios generales del derecho*".
[97] This is the majority view supported by Castán Tobeñas, *op. cit.*, pp. 520–3; F. de Castro, *op. cit.*, p. 508, Alabadalejo, *Instituciones de Derecho Civil* (1985), pp. 127–47; Lacruz Berdejo, *Elementos de Derecho Civil*, I (1980), pp. 61 *et seq*.
[98] art. 1 *LOTC*: "The Constitutional Court is the supreme interpreter of the Constitution".
[99] art. 5(1) *LOPJ*: "The courts shall interpret and apply the law according to constitutional principles and the interpretation of these principles by the Constitutional Court in any type of process".

4. EXPLANATORY SOURCES

LA DOCTRINA (LEGAL WRITINGS)

The third category of sources of law are those from which no directly applicable rule of law can be derived, but whose value lies in the clarification and interpretation they provide for the application of the primary sources. Among these are doctrinal and legal writings.

Legal writings were of great influence in Roman law,[1] and in historic Spanish law.[2] However, the Civil Code does not mention legal writings among the sources of law, not even with a complementary character and the Supreme Court has denied this character.[3] The value of legal writings in the system of sources is that they provide a clarification of the other primary sources of law.

5. AUTONOMY AND THE SYSTEM OF SOURCES: THE RELATIONSHIP BETWEEN STATE LAW AND THE LAW OF THE AUTONOMOUS COMMUNITIES

Autonomy is the power of individuals or groups to give themselves regulations within the framework of another, wider and superior, legal system. Spain, according to the territorial model set up by the 1978 Constitution, is a State of Autonomies; that is, a unitary State in which territorial entities—the Autonomous Communities—exercise the powers attributed to them by the Constitution. Amongst these powers is the power to legislate on certain matters. This produces the effect that in the Spanish legal system there are two levels or types of legislation: the rules of law of the State, which have effect in the whole country, and the rules created by the Autonomous Communities—in matters within their competence—which have effect only in the territory of the Community.

Without going into political theory and explaining the differences between a federal state and a state of autonomies a general remark seems appropriate at this stage. In a federal state the member states of the federation give themselves a Constitution within the framework of the Federal Constitution. However the main institutional rule of the Auton-

---

[1] See Alvaro D'Ors, *De la prudentia iuris a la jurisprudencia del Tribunal Supremo"* in *"Información Jurídica"* (1947).
[2] In Catalonia, legal writings were a source of law accepted by the Supreme Court if uniform and widely accepted. Castán Tobeñas, *op. cit.*, pp. 528–9.
[3] STS of December 10, 1894, STS of March 26, 1906, STS of June 10, 1916, among others.

omous Communities—the *Estatuto de Autonomía*—is produced by the Central State. This has consequences for the status and character of the laws produced by the Autonomous Communities, because if several independent states get together in a federation their different legal systems, which were complete and provided regulation for every matter, will have to renounce those rules concerning matters which are now within the competence of the federation. In the Spanish situation, however, the departure point is a State's legal system which is complete in the sense that there are no limitations on the matters which can be regulated, and within this legal system the Autonomous Communities's sub-legal systems consist of those matters under authority of each of the autonomies. The result is that the rules of the State system on matters which are within the jurisdiction of the Autonomous Communities are not abrogated, but remain applicable, although of a supplementary character. One could say that the Spanish legal system is made of a sub-system which is complete and general, and several partial and territorial sub-systems which have a priority of application on the matters within their scope.

The *Estatuto de Autonomía* is the "basic institutional rule" of each Autonomous Community[4]; it is the *Estatuto* which creates the Autonomous Community, defines its territory, and gives powers to the community. The Constitution only establishes the framework which makes possible autonomy, but it is up to the *Estatuto* to give a meaning and substance to the constitutional possibility. The *Estatutos de Autonomía* are approved by the procedure of the *leyes orgánicas*.[5] They are, therefore, laws of Parliament which, like any other, are sanctioned by the King. However, there are important differences between an *Estatuto de Autonomía* and other laws of Parliament. Before the *Estatuto* can be approved by Parliament there is a whole procedure, called *proceso de iniciativa autonómica*, by which the different provinces express their will to become an Autonomous Community that needs to be followed. The Constitution establishes two procedures of access to autonomy: the so called "quick way" or *vía rápida* (article 151 CE), and the "normal way" or *vía normal* (article 143, 144 and 146 CE). The *vía rápida* allows a greater initial autonomy.[6] In order to be able to obtain autonomy, the municipalities of the territories involved must vote and choose to become autonomous and integrated into a Community. Parliament can only intervene to grant autonomy to a single province without historic

---
[4] art. 147(1) CE "*Los Estatutos de Autonomía serán la norma institucional básica de cada Comunidad Autónoma . . .*".
[5] Although with some important differences which justify a separate study.
[6] arts. 148 and 149 CE.

tradition (article 144 CE),[7] or when it is necessary in order not to leave a single province which has not integrated into an Autonomous Community.[8] The drafting of the *Estatuto* is done by the representatives of the province,[9] the *diputados* and *senadores*[10] elected by the province which is to become an Autonomous Community. The draft is sent to Parliament where it needs to be approved by the procedure of a *ley orgánica*. The *Estatuto de Autonomía* will, once approved, specify the powers of the Autonomous Community according to the maximum limits fixed by the Constitution depending on which type of procedure was followed.[11] The *Estatuto de Autonomía* is, therefore, a rule approved by Parliament, with special characteristics, and subject to the Constitution.

All the Autonomous Communities have legislative power by virtue of their respective *Estatuto de Autonomía*. The legislation produced by the Autonomous Communities' legislative power[12] can be in the form of *ley*[13] promulgated and published by the President of the Autonomous Community.[14] These dispositions are published in the Official Journal of the Autonomous Communities[15] and in the State or general Official Journal (BOE). The only difference between the *ley* of the State and a *ley* of an Autonomous Community is that if the Government challenges the constitutionality of legislation of an Autonomous Community, application of this legislation is suspended until the matter is resolved by the Constitutional Court.[16] The Autonomous Communities can also delegate legislative power to their Executive and so legislate in the form of *decretos legislativos*. Urgent legislation by *decreto-ley* is not possible as this possibility has not been established in any *Estatuto de Autonomía*. However, all the *Estatutos de Autonomía* mention the power to pass *reglamentos* (by the Executive of the Autonomous Community).

The idea of "autonomy" is based on a principle of equality between the rules of the State and the rules of the Autonomous Communities.

---

[7] This was the case of Madrid, today the Autonomous Community of Madrid.
[8] This was the case of Segovia.
[9] Members of the *Diputación* of each province.
[10] Members of Parliament, of the *Congreso* and *Senado* respectively.
[11] See Ignacio de Otto, *op. cit.*, pp. 259–63 for a detailed account of these procedures and in general of the whole topic.
[12] The Autonomous Communities have an "Autonomic Parliament" elected by the residents of the community. The best study on the autonomous communities is, S. Muñoz Machado, *Derecho Público de las Comunidades Autónomas* (1982 and 1984) Also E. García de Enterría, *op. cit.*, p. 279 *et seq.*
[13] Each *Estatuto de Autonomía* will determine the legislative initiative.
[14] In the King's name.
[15] *Boletin Oficial de La Comunidad Autonoma*.
[16] art. 340 LOTC and art. 161(2) CE.

The system works on the basis of the distribution of matters. Any rule of the system as a whole, including the State sub-system and autonomous sub-systems, is only valid if it has been made under the relevant and necessary authority. This would seem logical and straightforward enough, and it is. The problem, however, arises because the distribution of matters is not neat and clear cut. For each matter there can be a distribution of functions between the State and the Autonomous Community. A matter can be attributed to the Autonomous Community or the State "exclusively", in which case, whoever exercises the power over that matter can legislate and develop it with complementary rules. For example the Constitution says that the State has exclusive competence in respect of defence.[17] In such a case it is clear that no Autonomous Community can dictate any rules on the matter. On the other hand, the Autonomous Communities have the exclusive right to fix municipal limits in their territory and the State has no competence at all in such matter. However the distribution of authority between the State and the Autonomous Communities is often made according to issues concerning the same matter. For instance, the State will have legislative competence or power to regulate the matter and the Autonomous Community will have executive power over it; or the State will have competence over basic legislation and the Autonomous Community will have competence to develop further complementary legislation. This type of competence is called "shares competence" or "shared jurisdiction". The final way in which the division of legislative power can occur is in the case of "concurrent jurisdiction". In this case both the State and the Autonomous Community have the same, identical jurisdiction, to legislate over a certain matter.[18] In this case, when the Central State—or the federation, if it happens in a federal state—exercises its power to legislate over the matter, the legislation of the State will prevail over that of the Autonomous Community. This principle is established in article 149(3) of the 1978 Constitution.[19] Distribution of authority in the Spanish legal systems is either exclusive—to the State or to the Autonomous Community—or shared between these entities in different ways. To date the Constitutional Court has never had to use the rule in article 149(3) and has resolved every conflict between the State and the Autonomous Communities by applying the rules relating to the distribution of powers.

The last principle which it is necessary to mention in the context

---

[17] art. 149(1)(5) CE.

[18] This type of distribution is frequent in federal states see art. 72.1 *Ley Fundamental de Bonn*.

[19] The conflict is only of academic interest because the distribution of competences by the different *Estatutos de Autonomía* has not left any matter subject to concurrent powers of the State and an autonomous community.

of the relationship between the law of the State and the law of the Autonomous Communities is that the law of the Central State is supplementary to the law of the Autonomous Communities (article 149(2) CE). This principle complies with the initial aim of the system by recognising Autonomous Communities with a different degree of autonomy.

6. INTERPRETATION, APPLICATION AND EFFICACY OF THE LAWS

INTERPRETATION OF THE LAW

The application of the law by the judge for the resolution of a case brought before him is a complex intellectual activity by which the judge, even if he is deprived of the "power to create law", needs to analyse the facts of the case and apply to those facts a rule of law as indicated by the provisions on sources of law and their hierarchy. Before the judge can apply any of the sources of law he needs to be sure of the meaning of that particular rule of law. Sometimes this meaning will appear clear from the words of the text of the statute, but in other cases the meaning may not be clear at first, or it may not be clear whether that rule should be applied to the actual facts of the case. In this case the judge will have to proceed to interpret the rule of law according to the provisions of the Civil Code, which, in article 3, establishes the criteria for the interpretation of the different laws.

Interpretation is the search for the true meaning of the law. Every rule of law needs to be interpreted in order to be applied, not only legislation but also customs and general principles. It is, however, the interpretation of legislation[20] which is at issue most often due to its primacy in the hierarchy of sources.[21] Article 3 of the Civil Code indicates four ways of arriving at the meaning of the rule: literal, logical, historical and systematic. These different methods do not produce different types of interpretation; there is not a "literal interpretation" as opposed to, or different from an "historical interpretation". What article 3 of the Civil Code does is to establish an order to follow in order to arrive at the meaning of the rule of law.

In the first stage, when the judge is considering the application of a rule of law, he will look at the words used by the legislator, or in which

---

[20] In the wide sense explained above, including regulations and any other rule given by the State.
[21] Here the focus of study is on the interpretation of legislation.

the custom is expressed, and try to find the meaning of those words according to the usual sense of the word or, if it is a technical word, according to the technical meaning. In some cases, this will be enough. However, the task of interpretation never ends at this point because it is necessary to find the "spirit of the rule".[22] The "spirit of the rule", the *ratio legis*, is found by applying a logical or rational criteria in order to arrive at why that rule exists and at its true meaning. Closely connected with the logical interpretation is the systematic approach, by which the rule which is being interpreted is placed in relation with other rules governing the same legal institution in order to discover the principles informing that institution. The last of the interpretative guides given by the Code is the "historical element". This means that if, after the preceeding criteria have been applied, the meaning of the rule is still not clear, an investigation of the antecedents of the rule—since most rules of law are the product of a long evolution—may throw some light as to the purpose and sense to be given to the rule.[23] However, the value of the historical element is only relative, because article 3(1) CC *in fine* adds that the rules need to be interpreted according to the social reality of the time in which they have to be applied. It can well be the case that certain rules, for instance a particular statute, was passed a long time ago and it now needs to be interpreted according to the current social circumstances in a way which may be quite different from the original intention of the legislator or from previous interpretations given to the same statute in the past.[24]

Although the judge will be the person who most often is faced with the task of interpreting rules of law in order to apply these to the resolution of cases he is by no means the only possible interpreter. Traditionally there has been a distinction between different types of interpretation depending on the person performing it. It is common[25] to distinguish between "public" and "private" interpretation. Public interpretation is the interpretation made by any authority or agency of the State or Public Administration, for instance judges when applying the law—*interpretación usual* (usual interpretation)—or Parliament which can dictate a new law to clarify previous legislation—*interpretación*

---

[22] art. 3.1 CC *in fine*: "*Las normas se interpretarán según el sentido propio de sus palabras . . . atendiendo fundamentalmente al espíritu y finalidad de aquellas*". Also, STS of June 27, 1941.

[23] These antecedents can be more or less remote, for instance in the case of legislation the preparatory works or "exposition of motives" can be consulted. An investigation into historical or Roman law can help to understand some of today's legal institutions, or a comparative study of foreign codes, especially the French Civil Code due to its influence on the Spanish Codification.

[24] See in this sense, Rafael Ruiz Manteca, *Introducción al Derecho y Derecho Constitucional* (1994), p. 56.

[25] See R. Ruiz Manteca, *op. cit.*, p. 59; Castán Tobeñas, *op. cit.*, p. 489.

auténtica (authentic interpretation). Private interpretation is that done by individuals and it is also known as doctrinal interpretation. Its value depends on the prestige of the author and it is only indicative.

According to its effect, interpretation can be extensive or restrictive, depending on whether it extends or restricts the application of the rule of law to situations or cases that seem to be included or not included in the words.

THE ROLE OF "EQUITY"

The Civil Code, in article 3, mentions *la equidad* ("equity")[26] as an element to be considered when applying the law. *Equidad*,[27] according to Castán Tobeñas,[28] has two connected meanings. First, it means the adaptation of the rule of law to the circumstances of the actual case[29] and, secondly, it means the mitigation of the consequences of the rule of law in a particular case.[30] Equity is therefore a method of the application of the law. This method is, however, restricted as to its application by the courts. The Civil Code, in article 3, forbids the judge to base the resolution of a case exclusively in equity except when he is expressly so allowed.[31] In this sense, "equity" is not a source of law. The role of "equity" is much more restricted in Spanish law, and in general in all Civil law systems, than in English law.

Where "equity" has a role to play is in the application of the general principles of the law since it enables these to be adapted to the circumstances of the case.

EFFICACY OF THE LAWS: TERRITORIAL APPLICATION AND TIME-SPAN

The rules of law are limited in their application both in space and time. Usually, the laws given by a State are applicable only in the territory of that State[32]—including jurisdictional waters and air-space—since International Law recognises a State's sovereignty and the power to exclude the application of foreign laws in the national territory. There are two principles which govern the "spatial" application of the law: the

---

[26] "Equity" because it is not to be confused with what is understood as equity in English law. *Equidad*, in Spanish law, means justice.
[27] In order to avoid confusion the Spanish word will be used.
[28] *op. cit.*, p. 506.
[29] According to Greek concept of *epiqueya*.
[30] According to the Christian idea of *humanitas, benignitas* or *pietas*. See Castán Tobeñas, *op. cit.*, p. 506.
[31] See arts. 3(2) CC and 1154 CC.
[32] There are exceptions to this rule, but the study of this belongs to Private International Law.

principle of territoriality and the principle of personality. The principle of territoriality means that the law is only applicable in the territory of the State in which it was dictated and it applies to all people in the territory whether foreigners or nationals. Examples of territorial laws are criminal laws or laws relating to public security. The principle of personality, on the other hand, links the application of the law to people; certain laws are given for certain people and are applied to them wherever they are. The principle of personality of the law was common in primitive laws[33] and it was applied in the time of the Roman Empire. Roman citizens were subject to the *ius civile*, other inhabitants of the Empire to their own personal laws, and the relationships between people belonging to different groups was regulated by the *ius gentium*. Today's legal systems have a combination of both principles for the application of the law. Spanish law, adheres to the principle of territoriality of criminal and public order laws and recognises the principle of personality of the laws in aspects such as legal capacity or status of natural persons.

The question is particularly important in the Spanish legal system because, as has been previously explained, different systems of civil law co-exist. In private law, Spanish Civil law, as contained in the Civil Code, co-exists with different systems of *foral* law applicable in the historic territories. This phenomena is known as "inter-regional law" and the rules for the application of one or other systems of law are found in the Preliminary Title of the Civil Code.[34] Their application is governed by the principle of personality articulated according to the concept of *vecindad civil* (civil domicile). Article 4 CC determines the domicile of a person for this purpose and the consequence of being subject to the rules of the Civil Code or *foral* law for the areas in which these are different from the former.

The second question relating to the application of the rules of law makes reference to their life-span. Laws do not exist forever but change and are replaced by new rules. The laws start to have effect at the time when a law comes into force and ends when the law is repealed. Legislation comes into force from the time established by the legislation itself. A certain *ley* can state that it shall be applicable on the day following its publication in the BOE, or in three months or a year. If nothing is said the Civil Code in article 2(1) establishes that legislation will be applicable after a period of 20 days following its publication in the BOE. This period of 20 days is known as *vacatio legis* and the purpose of it is to give time to those who are subject to the law to become acquainted with its provisions before the law is applicable.

---

[33] See above, Chap. 1.
[34] arts. 13–17 CC.

Legislation ceases to be applicable for different reasons. The first one is when a particular *ley* is expressly repealed by later legislation (*derogación expresa*); or, when the contents of later legislation are incompatible with the contents of previous legislation[35] (*derogación implícita*). Only legislation can repeal legislation. The different rules should have at least the same position in the hierarchy of sources; for instance a *formal ley* cannot be repealed by an administrative regulation but only by another *ley*. In other cases a law can cease being applicable because it was dictated for a specific period only, or if the purpose of the law was to regulate a specific situation which has now disappeared. In these two cases some writers refer to *leyes temporales* (temporary legislation).

Closely connected with the questions of life-span of the laws is the problem of the "retrospective" or "non-retrospective" effect of the law; in other words, whether a new law has effect on situations created or existing before the new law was dictated. Article 2(3) of the Civil Code enunciates the general principle of non-retrospective effect of the law "unless something different is provided". The vague formula of article 2(3) reflects the reality of this problem of whether to apply a new law and its consequences to old situations or not. In principle, legislation is passed for the regulation of future situations but there are two considerations to take into account when choosing between the retrospective or non-retrospective effect of legislation: legal certainty and the changing social reality.

In effect, legal certainty would be hindered if individuals could not foresee the consequences attached to the legal relationships they enter into because at any time a new rule can be approved and this new rule can determine totally different consequences. The principle of legal certainty seems better guaranteed by establishing a system of non-retrospectivity of the law and this is indeed the principle applicable in areas such a criminal law or administrative law as stated in the Constitution.[36]

On the other hand, the need to adapt the law to the changing circumstances of social life can in some instances justify the retrospectivity of some legislation. This retrospectivity can have different degrees of applicability. The first degree is when the new law is applied only to those effects of a pre-existing legal relationship which actually occur after the entry into force of the new law. The second is when the new law is applied to effects of the pre-existing relationship which started before the new law was approved but which still have not finished. The

---

[35] For instance many laws approved during the dictatorship of General Franco were repealed in this way.

[36] art. 9(3) CE: "*Le Constitución garantiza . . . la irretroactividad de las disposiciones sancionadoras no favorables o restritivas de derechos individuales. . . .*"

third degree is when the new law is applicable to all the effects of the relationship annulling previous effects, and reshaping this legal relationship into a new one. This last case is extremely rare because of the serious consequences it has for legal certainty. It is generally associated with policy decisions such as those which happened after the Civil War when the *Ley de Matrimonio Civil*, approved during the Second Republic, and the *Ley de Divorcio* were declared null and void with retrospective effects and many people found themselves not "married" to their "spouses".

In order to smooth the transition for the applicability of a new law and avoid or minimise problems of retrospective or non-retrospective effect—since most legal relationships have a continuous duration—the laws establish particular rules known as "transitory law" or *disposiciones transitorias*, by which it is stated to which part of the relationship or to which effects each law, the old or the new, should be applied.

Chapter Three
Constitutional Organs of the State

1. THE CROWN

Spain, according to article 1 of the Constitution, is "a social and democratic State of Law" in which sovereignty rests on the nation and the political form of government is a parliamentary monarchy.[1] In a parliamentary monarchy the king is a separate organ from the executive, and the government is responsible to parliament as opposed to "pure constitutional monarchies" in which the king is the holder of the executive power and there is no provision for liability of the executive to parliament.

The 1978 Constitution drafted the main lines defining the physiognomy of the Spanish monarchy. However it is not possible to reduce the different forms of government to legal terms because within the framework of a constitution it is possible to find great varieties concerning the form of government. A clear example is provided by the United States, the history of which presents certain periods when Congress was prevalent, others, including the present, of presidential preeminence, and even times when it was possible to talk about a "government of the judges".[2] It is also important to note that the extent to which constitutional powers are exercised by the monarch will depend on external and political factors such as the system of political parties. In Britain, a classical example of a typical parliamentary monarchy, the intervention of the monarch in the formation of governments has been drastically reduced since the nineteenth century due to the rigid "Two-Party System", but this intervention would increase if this system of parties changed.[3]

---

[1] art. 1 CE *"España se constituye en un Estado social y democrático de Derecho . . . La soberanía nacional reside en el pueblo español . . . La forma política del Estado español; es la Monarquía parlamentaria."*
[2] Miguel Satrústegui. *Derecho Constitucional.* (Luis López Guerra y otros, ed. 1992), Vol. II p. 17.
[3] A. Hauriou, *Droit Constitutionnel et Institutions Politiques* (1974), pp. 465–8.

58 Constitutional Organs of the State

Functions of the King

The King of Spain is the Head of State.[4] The King is a constitutional organ of the State and his functions are defined by the constitutional text. As a constitutional organ the King is in a position of parity with all the other constitutional organs as none of them is subordinate to the others. As Head of State, on the other hand, the King enjoys formal primacy and higher dignities and honours.[5] He is also the symbol of the "unity and permanence" of the State. This function, which is common to Heads of State,[6] has an historical meaning since the monarchy has traditionally been a symbol of the territorial unity of a number of different kingdoms and territories in Spain.[7] The King stands in a position of neutrality, guaranteeing the regular functions of the institutions of the State.[8] He acts as a special type of arbitrator[9] and represents the State in international relations, signing international treaties and declarations of war or peace.[10] The powers of the King are at the service of State politics as directed by the Executive and authorised by the Parliament.

The King is also the head of the armed forces (article 62(h) CE) and guarantees the Constitution and the Constitutional order by carrying out the last step of the main acts of the State: he sanctions Acts of Parliament, the celebration of treaties, the convocation of referendum. As head of the armed forces his position is distinct from the military hierarchy because the King is in a position of institutional supremacy which has both a civil and a military character. This is crucial in times when the Executive is unable to govern because the orders of the King must be followed by the armed forces, according to military discipline.[11]

All the acts of the King as the Head of State need to be endorsed by a different constitutional organ, which will be held responsible for these.[12] The responsibility of the endorser extends to the content and formalities of the act except when the person endorsing the act has not participated in the procedure of production of the act; for example, when the President of the Government countersigns or endorses the

---

[4] art. 56(1) CE "*El Rey es el jefe del Estado . . .*".
[5] The Constitution itself starts with the Crown, before it defines the other powers of the State.
[6] See art. 5 of the French Constitution or art. 87 of the Italian Constitution.
[7] See, Chap. 1 and Miguel Satrústregui, *op. cit.*, p. 19.
[8] art. 56(1) CE "*El Rey arbitra y modera el funcionamiento regular de las instituciones*".
[9] Special, because sometimes his function is to impose the choice of the Congress for instance when he proposes a candidate for president in the absence of a majority party in Congress (art. 62(3) CE).
[10] arts. 63(2) and 62(3) CE.
[11] This aspect of the orders of the King was evident on the night of February 23, 1981 when an attempted coup was successfully aborted due to the intervention of the King.
[12] art. 64(2) CE "*De los actos del Rey serán responsables las personas que los refrenden*".

nomination of the members of the Constitutional Court proposed by Parliament, the President is only responsible for the formal requirements of the procedure.

2. LAS CORTES GENERALES (PARLIAMENT)

Parliament is the main institution of the State. As article 66 CE states, Parliament is the representative of the nation and its functions can safely be described as the main functions of the State: legislative (producing the main rules of the system), budgetary (authorising the expenses of the State) and of control of the Government. Parliament also authorises the international obligations of the State and proposes candidates for other constitutional organs such as the Ombudsman (*defensor del pueblo*).

In a democratic system Parliament is the forum where all the major decisions affecting society are taken and where the different political forces can express their views and give their consent or disapproval to the acts of the Government.

Freedom of Parliament is limited by the Constitution and the principle of national sovereignty. According to this principle, sovereignty rests on the nation and not with Parliament. Parliament is only a representative of the citizens and so it must seek their specific consent before taking important decisions, for example in cases of reform of the Constitution or the *Estatutos de Autonomía*. On the other hand the Constitution itself limits the freedom of Parliament when it legislates, and demands respect for the "fundamental rights and freedoms" recognised in the Constitution.[13] A further control on the legislative function of Parliament is provided by the Constitutional Court which supervises the adequacy of, and respect for the Constitutional order, by the different laws approved by Parliament.[14]

This system of control of the different organs of the State by other organs is typical of democratic societies and guarantees that there are no abuses of power by any of the organs of the State.

COMPOSITION

The Spanish Parliament has two chambers: *el Congreso de los Diputados* (The Congress of Deputies) and *el Senado* (The Senate).[15] According to

---
[13] See above, Chap. 1, p. 25.
[14] *Recurso ó cuestión de inconstitucionalidad*, arts. 27 and 37 LOTC. See below, p. 98.
[15] art. 66 CE.

the Constitution the bi-cameral system is a consequence of the recognition of the right to autonomy of the regions and nationalities (article 2 CE). The *Senado* is meant to be the chamber of territorial representation—such as is found in federal systems—while the *Congreso* is the chamber of popular representation. The members of each chamber are elected according to different electoral systems to reflect the different character and function of each chamber.

The Spanish bi-cameralism had been described[16] as "asymmetrical and uneven" because each chamber has a different function with powers which are exclusive to that chamber and in respect of which the other has no power at all,[17] which makes them asymmetrical; they are uneven, because the *Congreso* is in a position of clear superiority over the *Senado*, both in the relationship with the Executive and in the legislative proceedings whereby the *Congreso* can decide whether or not it accepts any modifications introduced by the *Senado*.

Due to the nature of Parliament as a deliberative organ with a large number of members, the Chambers are organised so as to achieve efficiency in the performance of their functions. The Chambers are organised by dividing their functions between "government agencies" and "functioning agencies". Each Chamber has a President, elected by the members of that Chamber at the beginning of a new Parliament, who co-ordinates the work of the Chamber and represents it when necessary. It also has a Board—*Mesa*—elected by the Members of Parliament, which is composed of the President of the Chamber, four Vice-Presidents in the Congress and two in the Senate, and several secretaries (article 30.2 *RC* and article 5.1 *RS*). The Board has administrative functions and in fact organises all the work of the Chamber. Together with these there is a *Junta de Portavoces*. This is a modern agency which reflects the reality of the political forces in Parliament. Each parliamentary group has a representative in the *Junta*. There is also a representative from the Executive, and it is chaired by the President of the Chamber.

How the Chamber actually works depends on the nature of the matter. The main decisions will be taken in a plennary session—*el Pleno*, by all the Members of the Chamber sitting to the right and left of the hemicycle according to political orientation,[18] or by different commissions—*Comisiones*—(article 75(1) CE). Since the normal functioning of Parliament nowadays would be impossible if every member had to give his point of

---

[16] M. Satrústegui. *op. cit.*, p. 69.
[17] The *Congreso* appoints the President (art. 99 CE) and ratifies *decretos ley* (art. 86 CE) while the *Senado* has exclusive powers relating to the autonomous communities.
[18] *i.e.* the denomination of groups of left and right.

view, because of the diversity, complexity and technicalities of modern regulations, the Chambers have a series of organs, called *Comisiones*, which study in detail the different proposed regulations and the technicalities involved therein. The draft legislation of these *Comisiones* is called *Dictamen* and this will usually be not only the basis of later discussion by the *Pleno*, but in general, very similar to the definitive text adopted. The *Comisiones* of the Chambers have full legislative power in most matters. They can definitively approve *proyectos ó proposiciones de ley* without the need for ratification or approval by the *Pleno*, the intervention of which is only necessary in particularly important matters such as modifications to the Constitution, international matters, *leyes orgánicas* and *leyes de bases*, and the approval of the general budget (article 75(3) CE).[19]

There are different types of *Comisiones*; usually each of them works in a delimited area which corresponds to a ministerial department of the Government, for instance, industry. These are called *Comisiones permanentes legislativas*. It is intended that these *Comisiones* reproduce the *Pleno* on a small scale and so they are composed of representatives of different parliamentary groups. They also have a president and a board. There are other types of *Comisiones* which are "special", and are created by the Chamber in order to study a specific matter, and which will be dissolved once this special project has been completed; a good example is the creation of the special commission for the investigation of party funding.

Members of Parliament of the same political ideology need to be grouped in what are called parliamentary groups. These groups represent a political ideology. If a member does not identify with any of these formations they integrate with what is called a "mixed group"—*Grupo mixto*—since it is compulsory to be integrated into a group. The minimum number of Members of Parliament for the creation of a parliamentary group is fifteen members for Congress and ten for the Senate. Members of the same party must all belong to the same group, otherwise artificial groups will be created in order to obtain greater voice and power. The function of these groups can be described as political on the one hand, because they either support or challenge the politics of the Executive; and technical on the other, because the different agencies of Parliament, *Juntas*, *Mesas* and *Comisiones*, will be created by the members of the different groups.[20]

---

[19] See for the requirements of these Chap. 2, pp. 21 and 38.
[20] For more information about parliamentary groups see: arts. 23–8 RC and 28–34 RS and J.M. Morales Arroyo, *Los Grupos Parlamentarios* (1990).

Status of Members of Parliament

Historically, democratic societies grant the chambers of Parliament and its members guarantees and privileges for the better performance of their functions. These are not rights of individual members of the Parliament but real rules of law which will be applied *ex lege* by the courts if the situation for which they exist arises. These prerogatives cannot, therefore, be renounced. There are two types of prerogative; the ones enjoyed by the Chambers (*Congreso and Senado*) and the ones enjoyed by their members. In the former group the most relevant is the power that each Chamber has to regulate its own functioning (article 72(1) CE). These regulations are known as *Reglamento*[21] and are the main source of law for the regulation of the activities of each Chamber.

The Constitution[22] specifies some of the main aspects of the functioning of Parliament, but due to the general character of the constitutional text the importance of the *Reglamentos* is crucial. A *Reglamento* is approved by the absolute majority of each Chamber, a procedure which guarantees protection of the interests of the minority groups. The *Reglamentos* are not *leyes* in the formal sense of the word because they are not made according to the legislative procedure[23]— they are not sanctioned by the King or published in the *BOE*; but they enjoy *fuerza de ley*[24] and are subject to the control of the Constitutional Court according to article 27(2) LOTC. The Chambers also have the power to approve their own budget for the exercise of their functions (article 72(1) CE) and they have "inviolability" which means that nobody can be held liable for the activities of the Parliament as such (article 63 CE).

Members of Parliament also enjoy different guarantees to ensure the best performance of their duties. These can be described as the *Estatuto de los Parlamentarios*, which includes the different prerogatives, guarantees and obligations attached to the condition of being a Member of Parliament. Included in these rules are certain duties; for example the incompatibility of being a Member of Parliament with certain other public positions (for instance it is not possible to be a judge and a Member of Parliament) in order to guarantee the independence of the office of the member and the obligation of accepting the Constitution (article 20(3) R and articles 11 and 12 RS).[25] Others are rights such

---

[21] There is a *Reglamento del Congreso* (of February 10, 1982) and a *Reglamento del Senado* (of May 25, 1982).
[22] arts. 73, 75.1, 1 76, 78, 79 and 80 CE.
[23] See below.
[24] STC 118/88, *Caso Roca*.
[25] See STC 119/90, *Caso Idígoras-Aizpurúa-Alcalde*.

as the protection, immunity and special jurisdiction of Members of Parliament. Members of Parliament are protected so that their declarations in the Chambers of Parliament do not attract negative consequences or legal sanctions. This protection covers any declaration made in Parliament, but excludes, for instance, opinions expressed by Members of Parliament outside any parliamentary activity.[26]

A different right of Members of Parliament is the right of immunity by which no criminal action can be brought against them as a consequence of their political activities. This latter right is very different from the former since it only extends to criminal actions. The immunity does not exclude criminal prosecution of a Member of Parliament but it aims to guarantee that any prosecution is not started for a political reason. It is given effect by establishing a procedure by which, before a criminal action is started against the member of one of the Chambers, a *supplicatorio* or petition must be made to the respective Chamber, which will then decide whether there is a political motivation or retaliation in starting the proceedings. If the Chamber thinks that there are no political reasons behind the action, it might authorise the action to proceed but at this point, the third prerogative arises. This is, that any criminal action against a member of Parliament will be heard and decided by the Supreme Court (article 71(3) CE). This is known as the "special jurisdiction" of *Diputados y Senadores*. The privilege of immunity has a clear political nature and it is not strictly a right of the individual member, because the Chamber might deny the possibility of prosecution even if the member asks for it to be permitted. This immunity of jurisdiction obviously does not cover cases in which the member of Parliament is caught in the flagrant commission of a crime.

Different in character, but related to the former, is the question of remuneration of Members of Parliament. In order to ensure that no economic factors would influence the political views of Members of Parliament and that every citizen has access to political activity it was necessary to provide Members of Parliament with an independent allowance.[27] Today the salary of Members of Parliament in Spain is fixed by the *Reglamento* of each Chamber (article 8(1) R and article 23.1 RS).

THE LAW-MAKING PROCESS

It has been stated that one of the functions of Parliament is the elaboration of laws. In parliamentary monarchies the legislative power,

---

[26] Compare STC 51/85 *Caso Castells* and STC 30/86 *Caso Casa de Juntas de Guernica*.
[27] It also establishes the definitive separation from a system of "imperative mandate" to pure representation.

or the capacity to make the rules of law that are to define the system, is vested in Parliament.[28] This does not mean that Parliament has the sole power to make laws because in modern societies, due to the complexity of the matters that need to be regulated, the Executive is increasingly producing rules through its own reglamentary power and by using the mechanism of "urgent legislation". However, even in those instances in which the Executive plays a leading role as to the volume of legislation, its activities of law-making are controlled by Parliament; either by *a posteriori* control and ratification of urgent legislation[29]; or by the principle of the hierarchy of sources, by which any *reglamento* produced by the Executive in the exercise of its legislative power must be subject to laws previously approved by Parliament (*leyes*) on the matter. Otherwise the laws made by the Executive (*reglamentos*), will be illegal and thus not applicable.[30]

Before describing the procedure of law-making, it is necessary to indicate who are the subjects, or entities, vested with what is called "legislative initiative". In other words, who can initiate or ask Parliament to produce a rule of law having the force of *ley*. Historically this power was linked to the question of who had sovereignty: the king, the government, parliament or the nation. Today the Spanish legal system, while recognising that sovereignty rests on the nation,[31] acknowledges a diversity of subjects with the power of "legislative initiative". Before considering these entities with "legislative initiative", it is important to point out that this is a preliminary stage to the legislative function of Parliament.

Article 87 of the Constitution vests the full ordinary legislative initiative in the Government, the Congress and the Senate. It also vests this power in the governments and assemblies of the Autonomous Communities (ap.2),[32] and, with some limitations (ap.3)[33] in the nation. All these five subjects have the power to initiate the law making process, but with important differences.

Since the Executive is in charge of national politics most of the proposals for legislation will actually come from it. The Constitution

---

[28] Even if the Executive can dictate rules of law—*reglamentos*—these are subject to the laws dictated by Parliament.

[29] See *Decretos leyes.*, Chap. 2, p. 37.

[30] See Chap. 2, p. 40.

[31] art. 1(2) CE. "*La soberanía nacional reside en el pueblo español.*"

[32] This is for a national law and different from the independent legislative power of the Autonomous Parliaments on matters within the powers conferred on them by their respective *Estatuto de Autonomía*.

[33] There is a requirement of 50,0000 signatures endorsing the proposal which can only affect matters which are not reserved to *ley orgánica*, international matters or the *prerogativa de gracia*.

accordingly vests full power to start the law-making procedure in the Government. The Executive will draft a "project of law"—*projecto de ley*—which needs to be approved by the Council of Ministers and then referred to Congress, which is the Chamber that starts the drafting of the laws, with an *Exposición de motivos* and all the antecedents, in order to facilitate the activities of Congress in elaborating the laws.

The Chambers of Parliament also have the power to initiate the law making procedure. The draft proposals—*proposiciones de ley*—must be endorsed by fifteen *diputados* or a Parliamentary group, and any antecedents and aims must be included. The Chamber then decides whether it wants to adopt the *proposición de ley* or not; if so, the law-making procedure starts. The approval of the Chamber as to whether the proposal of some of its members shall be followed is necessary because only the Chambers of Parliament have vested "legislative initiative" and not individual members or parliamentary groups. If the *proposición de ley* is presented in the Senate, once the Senate—as a Chamber—has decided to go ahead and endorsed the proposition, the draft proposal will be passed to the Congress for discussion. The Executive then, has an opportunity to give its opinion and eventually oppose the progress of a particular law if it affects certain matters.[34]

As regards the "popular initiative" or "citizen's initiative", the exercise of this is regulated by the LO 3/1984, of January 26,[35] which is fairly restrictive. First, the Constitution restricts the areas on which legislation based on "popular initiative" is possible.[36] Secondly, any project presented by the "popular commission" in charge of the project needs to be analysed and accepted by one of the *Mesas del Congreso*. If it is accepted, a period of six months begins to run during which it is necessary to collect 50,000 signatures supporting the project presented by the *comisión promontora*. If, after this, the project goes ahead the State will reimburse the expenses of authentication of signatures and of the publicity for the campaign. If the project fails, it is an expensive process which makes it difficult for certain groups/sectors of society to have access to this possibility. Some writers criticise this constitutional regulation as unduly restrictive.

The assemblies of the Autonomous Communities may demand that the Government and/or the Chambers of Parliament exercise their power(s) of legislative initiative.[37]

---

[34] The Executive can oppose legislative proposals which vary the national budget (art. 134 CE); or which contain measures contrary to a previous delegation of legislative power to the Executive (art. 84 CE).
[35] *Ley Orgánica Reguladora de la Iniciativa Popular* LO 3/1984 of March 26.
[36] arts. 87(3), 131 and 134 CE.
[37] See art. 87(2) CE.

As far as the ordinary legislative procedure is concerned the Constitution establishes the main lines, while the Chambers have the possibility of complementing and developing these guidelines in their own *Reglamento*. Draft legislation is examined first in the Congress and then in the Senate. The procedure starts with a discussion in the Congress where there are clear, differentiated steps. The first stage is the *fase de enmiendas a la totalidad* (period of amendments) during which the project or proposition can be totally rejected and substituted by a different one, by returning the text to the Executive or the Senate. These amendments to the whole of the proposal can only be presented by a parliamentary group and need to be discussed and approved by the *Pleno* (article 110(3), 126 and 127 RC). It is not possible to make a total amendment to a proposition coming from the Congress or from "popular initiative". The second stage is the discussion in the relevant commission, depending on the subject matter of the proposed text—*fase de comisión*. Here the amendments are studied and a report is prepared for a subsequent discussion in the plenary session. The last stage in the Congress is the plenary discussion and vote—*fase de pleno*—where it is decided which text is accepted, the original one, the amendment or an intermediate text.

After discussion in the Congress, the text goes to the Senate where, within a period of two months, the text must be approved, amended, or rejected. The procedure in the Senate is very similar to the discussion in the Congress: the text goes first to the commissions for discussion and is then referred to the plenary session for final approval. The Senate has the right of *veto*, *i.e.* the rejection of the text by absolute majority.

If the text is approved by the Senate, the new law is ready to be sanctioned by the King and published in the official journal and the legislative procedure ends. If the Senate, however, exercises its right of *veto* or introduces changes, the text must be returned to the Congress. It is in this situation that the superiority of the Congress is clearly apparent because even in the case of *veto* by the Senate, the Congress can approve the text by absolute majority. In the case of suggested amendments, these can be adopted or otherwise rejected by a simple majority, in which case the initial text can be approved after two months by a simple majority.

Before the draft discussed in the Chambers becomes a *ley*, there are some formalities it needs to comply with, namely to be signed by the King—*sanción* and *promulgación*—and its publication in the official journal.

3. THE GOVERNMENT AND THE PUBLIC ADMINISTRATION

THE GOVERNMENT

The executive power in modern monarchies is identified with the government and thus differentiated from the king. However, as has been pointed out by some writers,[38] there is a lack of historical and modern literature explaining the nature and function of modern governments. One reason for this, can be that the liberal division of powers concentrated on rationalising the exercise of power and subjection to the Law, thus giving Parliament preferential attention and leaving a block of differentiated and heterogeneous powers—which in absolute monarchies belonged to the king—grouped collectively as "executive power". This is why, in the early Constitutions, the government as such did not exist.[39] It was only when the evolution towards a parliamentary monarchy started to take place that the government, as a separate organ of the State, appeared.

In the British constitution the separation of the government as a separate organ started to emerge clearly with the electoral reform of 1832, when the enlargement of the electorate diminished the power of the Monarch in favour of Parliament, and therefore in favour of the Cabinet and the Prime Minister.[40] In the progressive consolidation of the parliamentary system the Cabinet exercises practically all of the powers of the Crown and the Monarch is an institution symbolising political unity, who can give advice and counsel, and should be kept informed, but does not designate the *Premier* or Prime Minister, as this is determined by the electorate. Because of the relationship between the electorate and the majority of the House of Commons, the British Cabinet effectively directs Parliament.

In Spain the Constitution clearly distinguishes the Government from the King. Article 98 states that the Government is composed of the President, Vice-Presidents, ministers and any other members determined by the law.[41] There are, according to the Constitution, certain essential members in the Government: the President and the Ministers. Together with these there is the possibility of having one or more Vice-Presidents and other members whose existence and functions will be determined

---

[38] See Antonio Torres del Moral, *Principios de Derecho Constitucional Español*, (1992), Vol. 2 pp. 159–61.
[39] The 1812 Constitution did not mention the Government because the executive power was vested in the King.
[40] A. Torres del Moral, *op. cit.*, p. 160.
[41] art. 98(1) CE: "*El Gobierno se compone del Presidente, de los Vicepresidentes en su caso, de los Ministros y de los demás miembros que establezca la ley*".

by the law.[42] In 1983 the LOACE[43] established fifteen ministerial offices and any variation of these must be passed by a law of Parliament. However, since 1985 the different *leyes de presupuestos* (general budget law) have altered this situation by conferring on the President the power to change the number, denomination and powers of the different ministers by *Real Decreto*, this is by a reglamentary disposition. This system has the advantage of having flexibility and speed, by which ministerial offices can be adapted to the changing circumstances of the nation.[44]

The Government is one of the central organs of the State. It has executive power and controls the direction of the national politics. The Government is a collegiate entity and functions as a *collegium*. At the same time each of its members has its own functions. It is usual to identify the Government with the Council of Ministers—*Consejo de ministros*—and when the Constitution refers to the Government as a collegiate entity this expression is used.[45]

The President

The President of the Government is a post which has its own characteristics which clearly differentiate the incumbent from other members of the Government. He is not a Prime Minister, in the sense that his position is not that of a *primus inter partes*, but he enjoys a pre-eminence and a power to direct the Government as a whole. Historically, the President was the only member of the Government who had *investidura parlamentaria* which meant that he enjoyed the initial confidence of Parliament. It is this parliamentary confidence on which the President bases his power. Other ministers are chosen by the President (article 100 CE) although all Ministers and the President are formally nominated by the King.[46]

The main function of the President is the direction of the Government and the co-ordination of the activities of its members. He also has other functions specifically designated in the Constitution, including

---

[42] Not necessarily by a formal *ley*, STC 60/86, *Caso RD ley de medidas urgentes de reforma administrativa*; a *reglamento* can, according to the main guidelines fixed by a formal *ley*, determine how many and which are the ministerial offices according to the needs and circumstances of each case.

[43] *Ley de organización de la administración central del Estado*; Ley 10/1983 of August 16.

[44] See Luis López Guerra, *op. cit.*, pp. 140–3.

[45] arts. 88, 112, 115, 116(2) and (3). Although in art. 116(2) uses both "Government and Council of Ministers" which has given rise to doctrinal discussion as to whether these two expressions should be identified or not. See Luis López Guerra. *op. cit.*, p. 145.

[46] The Ministers are appointed by the President and the President by Parliament (art. 99 CE).

the nomination and dismissal of Ministers, the petition of the King to preside over the Council of Ministers (article 62.9 CE), initiation of the *cuestion de confianza* (article 112 CE), the dissolution of Parliament "under his exclusive responsibility" (article 115(1) CE), and proposing the submission of a decision to popular referendum (article 92(2) CE). In most cases the President will consult the Council of Ministers[47] but the above can be called "acts of the President" because in the last instance they are dependent on his exclusive decision.

The President has the support of specific agencies in order to prepare and perform his functions. These organs are not necessarily ministerial departments and they are integrated in the "Presidency of the Government". These two agencies are the "General Secretary of the President" and the "Cabinet of the President". Both agencies are quite recent in Spanish political history and are regulated by reglamentary rules according to the general provisions of the LOACE.[48]

The Vice-President

Although the existence of one or more Vice-Presidents is optional according to article 98 CE, a Vice-President of the Government has been a constant presence in Spanish post-constitutional politics. The LOACE provides for the possibility of having more than one Vice-President and also regulates the main characteristics of his office. The Vice-President supports the President and substitutes for him in cases of illness, death or absence from the country. In practice his main function is the co-ordination of governmental action and planning. He also presides at the meeting of the General Commission of Secretaries of State.

The Ministers

The Ministers are the heads or directors of a section of the administration—ministerial departments. However, it is possible to have Ministers who are not the head of any department,[49] usually when it is necessary to resolve a specific task of a very specialised character and of such importance that it seems sensible to include it in the council of Ministers.

The position of Minister is both political and administrative since

---

[47] This is compulsory in the case of the *cuestión the confianza*.
[48] See above.
[49] "*Ministros sin cartera*" according to art. 4 of the *Ley de Regimen Juridico de la Administracion del Estado* of July 26, 1957 (*LRJAE*).

they are at the same time heads of a department of the Public Administration and members of Government. Ministers are chosen by the President and formally nominated by the King.[50] The President can decide on the termination of the office of Ministers. Their office will also end when the Government as a whole is dissolved, for instance in the case of new general elections or when Parliament withdraws its confidence from the Government.

Each Minister has a Cabinet as a support organ. The Cabinet is a political organ and its members are chosen by the Minister. Members of Government, like Members of Parliament, have a special status, rights and duties. The Constitution accepts the possibility of being Members of Parliament at the same time as Ministers,[51] but Members of Government are not able to have any other public office, nor practice a private profession or commercial activities. The *Ley de incompatibilidades de altos cargos* (L25/83) details the regime of incompatibility which extends even to the administration of their own estate if this conflicts with their ministerial duties. Members of Government enjoy criminal protection, and the Criminal Code specifies certain crimes against the freedom to exercise their functions by the Members of Government (articles 160, 161 and 163 CP). Members of Government also enjoy special jurisdiction since it is the Criminal Chamber of the Supreme Court which hears cases against the President and Members of the Government (article 102 CE). Another procedural particularity, established by the *L E Crim*, is that it is possible for them to give evidence from their office or residence or make any declarations to court in writing, instead of orally, in court.

An important duty of members of Government is the duty to keep secret any matter which could endanger the internal or external safety of the nation, even in judicial proceedings. In the case of Members of Government this provision extends to the deliberations of the Council of Ministers.

The functions of the Government

The Government, as previously pointed out, is not extensively regulated in the Constitution and so its functions need to be deduced from a variety of articles. Traditionally the Government has been associated with the executive power and its main function would be the execution of the laws previously approved by Parliament. However, this understanding of the division of powers does not reflect the reality of modern

---

[50] This is one of the "acts of the President". See above.
[51] art. 98 CE.

democracies in which the Government clearly does more than execute laws approved by Parliament. The functions of the Government can be divided into functions of political direction and executive functions,[52] since article 97 of the Constitution seems to differentiate between these.[53]

With regard to the political direction of the State, the powers and functions of the Government extend to the preparation of the political agenda which is explained by the President to the Congress when he demands a vote of confidence of Parliament (article 99(2)), the drafting of the general budget of the State (later approved by Parliament) and the general planning of the economy. Also included in the political functions of the Government are the exercise of legislative initiatives, the power to dictate *decretos-leyes* in cases of urgency and extreme need (article 82–85 CE) and the defence of the State.[54] Finally, the Government directs the external politics of the State.

In the exercise of its executive function the Government can legislate by "delegated legislation"[55] and dictate rules of law, *reglamentos*, subject to the *ley*—regulatory power. It also directs the Public Administration and ensures the effective performance of public services.

THE PUBLIC ADMINISTRATION[56]

While there is a clear separation between the King and the Government it is not so easy to differentiate the Government from the Public Administration. Theoretically the Government is the "directing mind" while the administration "the hand which executes".[57] The administration appears to be an entity subordinate to the Government, legally established and responsible for its activities. In practice there is continuity between the Government and the Administration because the Government "administers" and the Administration has a clear political dimension since all its senior positions are politically designated.

The State needs both personal and material means in order to perform

---

[52] Antonio Torres del Moral, *op. cit.*, Vol. 2, p. 168.
[53] art. 97 CE "*El gobierno dirige la política interior y exterior, la Administración civil y militar y la defensa del Estado. Ejerce la función ejecutiva y la potestad reglamentaria de acuerdo con la Constitución y las leyes.*"
[54] Because even if the King is the nominal head of the armed forces (art. 62(h)) it is effectively the Government which directs and controls the Military.
[55] See Chap. 2.
[56] It is not the object of this work to provide a detailed exposition of the constitutional regulation of the Administration. The major authority on the subject of Administrative law which should be consulted by anybody intending to approach the subject seriously is E. Garcia de Enterria, *Curso de Derecho Administrativo* (6th ed., 1993).
[57] A. Torres del Moral, *op. cit.*, p. 192.

the duties established by the Constitution. The instrument by which these functions are performed is the Public Administration. The Public Administration is a complex organisation whose function is to carry out the tasks of the State and whose activities are subject to particular rules, some of which are to be found in the Constitution and some in subsequent legislation.[58]

As a "social and democratic State" (articles 1 and 9(3) CE) the functions of the State are very complex since the State is present in different areas of activity, many more than in the original liberal State of the last century, when the State's main function was to guarantee individual freedoms and to provide minimum services such as the defence of the realm and the administration of justice. Although the Public Administration is the main instrument of the State in performing the duties and services imposed by the fundamental laws, it is not the only one. Sometimes the State employs private individuals or corporations to perform certain public services and sometimes the Administration provides services as a private organisation without exercising any public authority.

So far "the Public Administration" or "the Administration" has been referred to as an abstract entity connected to the State which is also an abstract entity. The concept of administration is abstract, but in practice there are different public administrations. The existence of a decentralised State in the form of a "State of Autonomies" has the consequence that there two different levels of administration: the central administration or the administration of the State as a whole, and the autonomous administrations for each of the Autonomous Territories. The central powers of the State have their own administration (*Administración del Estado*) through which they develop the functions reserved to them by the Constitution, and each of the Autonomous Communities has its own administrative organisation to perform its functions and powers (*Administraciones Autonómicas*). At a different level the Constitution recognises the autonomy of other territorial entities— *provincias* and *municipios*—for the carrying out of their functions and the protection of their interests (article 137 CE). Each of these provincial and municipal entities has its own administrative organisation (*Administraciones locales*).

Together with this territorial distinction of public administration there are other organisations with non-territorial foundations. These are dependent on a territorial administration but they enjoy separate legal personality. Amongst these non-territorial administrative entities some of them are based on a personal element, *i.e.* belonging to a professional

---

[58] Including not only formal *ley* but also *reglamentos*.

body (article 36 CE), and are called *Corporaciones Públicas*; others are created in order to perform specific public services—*Instituciones Públicas*; good examples are provided by the different institutions in charge of the health administration such as the National Institute of Health (*INSALUD*) or the National Institute of Social Security (*INSS*).

A third category of public administration, is that of the administrative bodies of the constitutional organs. Since each constitutional organ is independent from the others it is necessary to provide it with independent administrative support. Therefore there is an independent administration for Parliament, the judiciary, the Constitutional Court; all of these being totally separated from the administration of the State. The final example of independent administration is the electoral administration, the purpose of which is to "guarantee the transparency and objectivity of the electoral proceedings".[59]

The main principles of the organisation of the Administration are stated in the Constitution (articles 103–107 CE). They reflect the main ideas which inspire modern public administration as initially conceived during the French Revolution and subsequently modified by the requirements of the "Social State" in the second half of the twentieth century. The basic constitutional principle can be said to be that of article 103 CE: "... the Administration is subject to the laws".[60] Three points should be mentioned here: *a la ley y al Derecho* means that the actions of the Administration are subject to all the sources of law—the Constitution, statutes, by-laws and general principles of the law. The subjection is "total" and applies to all the areas of activity of the public administration. The action of the Administration is legitimate only when there is previous legal consent. As a consequence administrative activity is subject to the control of the courts both in the exercise of its "regulatory capacity" and in any other activity.[61]

Other principles governing the activities of the Public Administration are found in the Constitution. These are as follows: administrative activity must be objective[62] and neutral,[63] which means that even if the Administration follows the lines established by the Government its subjection to the law is a guarantee against arbitrariness; it must also be efficient, which is more a *desideratum* than a directly applicable principle; it must allow the participation of the citizens by guaranteeing access to

---

[59] art. 8(1) LOREG "*garantizar ... la transparencia y objetividad del proceso electoral*".
[60] art. 103(1) CE: "*La administración pública sirve con objetividad ... con sometimiento pleno a la ley y al Derecho*".
[61] art. 106 CE: *Los tribunales controlan la potestad reglamentaria y la legalidad de la accion administrativa, asi como el sometimiento de esta a los fines que la justifican.*
[62] art. 103(1) CE: "*la administración sirve con objetividad ...*".
[63] STC 77/1985, Caso LODE.

registers and documents of direct interest to any persons involved in the matter. Citizens also have the right to express their views before the drafting of general rules which might affect individuals.[64] The Administration is responsible for its activities; any damage caused as a consequence of any action of the Administration should be compensated for by the Administration (independently of any liability under contract or tort).

The Administration has the dual function of applying and executing the laws on one hand, and of being an instrument of the Government for the execution of governmental policies on the other. As a consequence a dual parameter must be applied to the control of administrative activity. Parliament, as the organ of control of the Government, controls administrative activity with respect to its political responsibility,[65] but control of the legality of administrative activity is left to other organs, some of which have a jurisdictional character—ordinary courts and the Constitutional Court—and others which have a dual or non-jurisdictional nature, such as the *Tribunal de Cuentas* and *Defensor del Pueblo*.

One of the main principles of the "State of Law" is the subjection of all the powers to the law. As such the Administration is subject to judicial review by the ordinary courts.[66] The Constitutional Court controls the subjection of the Administration to the Constitution in three main ways: first, by the *recurso de amparo*,[67] which is an extraordinary procedure for the protection of fundamental rights and civil liberties (Section 1, Chapter II, Title I CE) used when public powers have infringed one of these by their activities; secondly, by resolving conflicts of power between the Central State and the Autonomous Communities, thereby ensuring that both the acts of the Central Administration and the Autonomous Administrations are within the powers conferred by the Constitution and *Estatutos de Autonomia*; and thirdly, through the control by the Constitutional Court, on the request of the Government, of the constitutionality of regulatory dispositions dictated by the Autonomous Communities (article 161(2) CE).[68]

Other organs which control the Administration include the *Defensor del Pueblo*,[69] which is an agency designated by Parliament and responsible to it, the main function of which is to survey administrative activities so as to ensure that there are no violations of the fundamental rights

---

[64] arts. 105(a) CE and 105(b) CE.
[65] See above p. 59.
[66] See below "Administrative Courts".
[67] See below.
[68] As developed by Tit.V of the *LOTC*.
[69] The ombudsman, contemplated by art. 54 CE and regulated by the *Ley Orgánica* 3/1981, of April 6, "*del Defensor del Pueblo*" (Hereinafter, *LODP*).

recognised in Title I of the Constitution. The *Defensor del Pueblo* does not have executive power and so his activities are limited to persuasion and counselling. His supervision can be initiated by private initiative or *ex officio* and there are no limitations concerning nationality, age, sex or incapacity as to whom can demand this procedure. Any complaint must be signed by the person making it and the procedure is totally free and informal and does not require the assistance of an *abogado* or *procurador*.[70] The powers of investigation and inspection of the *Defensor del Pueblo* are wide and complemented by the obligation that public authorities have to provide any information, documentation and help which he demands. Only the Government, by a decision of the Council of Ministers, can decide not to disclose documents declared secret. Once he has finished his investigation the *Defensor del Pueblo*, because he lacks executive power, can pass the information and evidence obtained by his investigation to the Attorney-General in order to start criminal proceedings if he thinks that the facts amount to a crime (article 262 *LECrim* and article 25 *LODP*). He can also write to the administrative department against which the complaint was made, giving his view as to whether there has been a violation of a fundamental right and what steps should be taken in order to avoid it happening again. In this case the administrative authority is obliged to respond within a month, acknowledging receipt of the suggestions and specifying what measures will be taken in order to avoid further violations of the rights concerned. The *Defensor del Pueblo* can also make recommendations to the administrative authorities or Parliament if the case indicates that the implementation of legislation has produced unfair consequences for individuals. He will inform the party who started the complaint about the outcome of his work and produce an annual report to Parliament on his activities during the year, his conclusions and suggestions.

The last organ of control of the Administration is the *Tribunal de Cuentas* which controls the accounts of the State and the public finances in general. This special court has very specific jurisdiction and it is directly connected to Parliament and not to the judiciary. The members of the *Tribunal de Cuentas* have the same independence as judges.[71] The *Tribunal* is composed of 12 counsellors nominated by both Chambers of Parliament each of whom must be of recognised standing within the legal profession. The *Tribunal de Cuentas* has "jurisdiction" over any matter connected with the expenditure of public funds. Its "jurisdiction" ceases where the jurisdiction of administrative or criminal courts starts.[72]

---

[70] See Chap. 5.
[71] See below.
[72] See LO 2/1982, of May 12, *del Tribunal de Cuentas*, and for a more extensive and detailed

4. THE JUDICIAL POWER: COURTS AND COURT STRUCTURE

It is usual to refer to the French Revolution and the implementation by the revolutionaries of Montesquieu's classical theory of the division of powers[73] when starting an exposition of the judicial power in any contemporary society, especially if the legal culture of that society is so clearly influenced by the principles drawn from the French Revolution as the Spanish legal system is.

For the better understanding of the role of the judiciary in the structure of the different legal systems it is necessary to look back in history. Modern anthropology has established that in primitive societies the judge developed before the institution of the legislator.[74] Legal systems were created by the accumulation, and latter organisation and rationalisation, of case law. This was the situation in Roman law and accounts for the meaning of the term *iurisdictio*—the saying of the law. The judge, therefore, in the early stages of the creation of legal systems, appears to have had a major role in the production of rules of law. It was in the development of modern systems that the position of the "administration of justice"[75] changed and became centralised. In England this started in the twelfth century when itinerant judges gave judgement in the different courts in the name of the King, thereby starting the unification of legal customs and rules which became what is known as *common law*. In France the evolution started when the *Parlement* of Paris extended its jurisdiction to other territories,[76] and ended in the recognition of the supremacy of the King's justice as being more general and uniform than the "justice" of the different feudal lords. Later, the French Revolution, in order to avoid the concentration of powers in a sole organ and to guarantee the supremacy of Parliament as the expression of popular sovereignty, established the strict separation of powers and this idea has permeated contemporary legal thinking for a long time.

However, in the period between the two world wars the initial suspicion of the revolutionaries towards the judge was replaced, to a certain extent, by a suspicion towards the legislator and correspondingly, with a hope that the judge would correct any errors made by Parliament. It was

---

account, the collective work "El Tribunal de Cuentas en España", (Instituto de Estudios Fiscales 1982).

[73] Even if the motivation of Montesquieu and the French revolutionaries was quite different when implementing the division of powers, the judges were deprived of the "supralegality" they enjoyed in the last years of the absolutism.

[74] A. Torres del Moral, *op. cit.*, p. 251 referring to Max Weber's theory.

[75] Understood here as the role of the judges in administering justice in a concrete case.

[76] See C. Dadomo & S. Farran, *op. cit.*, 46.

during that period that the Constitutional Courts were created, with the function of controlling the validity of laws passed by Parliament, taking as a touchstone the Constitution itself.

Today, the tendency is to acknowledge that there is always a creative role involved in the application of the law which, combined with the power given to judges to control the legality of administrative action, and the constitutionality of the legal rules of the system, make some legal writers doubt the politically neutral role assigned to the judge.[77]

Having said that, constitutional states are organised according to the idea of the "material division of functions" and "formal division of powers".[78] The judicial power is exercised by the organs of the State, which according to the Constitution and other laws, have the function of resolving conflicts arising in the application and interpretation of the law.[79] These organs are judges—*jueces*—and magistrates—*magistrados*.[80] Judges are independent, irremovable, responsible and subject only to the Law (article 117(1) CE).[81] Only judges exercise the judicial power and although they rely on a variety of personnel in their service for the administration of justice (for example, judicial secretaries, officials, agents, forensic doctors[82]), these do not have judicial power and constitute what is called the "administration of the administration of justice"[83] in the sense of all the personal and material means at the service of the judge for the exercise of his judicial power. The difference between the "judicial power" and the "administration of justice" is important because it reveals the dual nature of the task of imparting justice. On one hand, it is a power of the State—the judicial power—on the other, it is a function, a public service. In this second sense the Executive is responsible for the functioning of this service in the same way as it is responsible for the defence of the State.

As one of the powers of the State in charge of the "jurisdictional function", the judicial power is unitary. The principle of "unity of jurisdiction" is important because there is only one judicial power in Spain.

---

[77] See A. Torres de Moral *op. cit.*, p. 254.
[78] According to the terminology used by J. Garcia Morillo in L. López Guerra y otros, ed., *op. cit.*, p. 223.
[79] art. 117 CE "*la justicia se administra . . . por jueces y magistrados, integrantes del poder judicial*".
[80] The term "magistrate" is used although it is not equivalent to the English "magistrate". In Spanish Law *magistrados* are a higher category of professional judges. The word "Judge" is used here to designate both *Jueces* and *Magistrados* unless a distinction is necessary.
[81] "*. . . independientes, inamovibles, responsables y sometidos únicamente al imperio de la ley*".
[82] See Chap. 4, p. 118.
[83] J. Garcia Morillo, in Luis López Guerra y otros ed., *op. cit.*, p. 255.

The division of the State into Autonomous Communities does not affect the unity of jurisdiction; Autonomous Communities have executive and legislative power but not judicial power. The courts situated in the territory of the Autonomous Communities are courts of the State.[84] All the courts are included in the judicial power (article 3(1) *LOPJ*). This unity of judicial power also excludes the existence of special courts (articles 26 and 117(6) CE) and any possibility of the Public Administration imposing punishment involving the deprivation of freedom. The only and relative exception to the unity of jurisdiction is the existence of a military jurisdiction (article 117(5) CE). This jurisdiction is limited to matters qualified as "military crimes" under the Military Criminal Code and to the special cases of state of siege, alarm or exception—*estado de sitio, alarma ó excepción* (*LOPJ* and article 9(2)). In any case, military jurisdiction is part of the judicial power.[85]

The judicial power is also "general" because the jurisdiction "extends to all the people, all the matters and all the territory" (article 4 *LOPJ*).[86] The only exception to this principle is the person of the King (article 56(3) CE) who enjoys special and total immunity; otherwise the judicial power has jurisdiction over any case involving any person, throughout the national territory. This obviously includes the Public Administration the activities of which are subject to the Law (article 103). This is different from the French legal system where, due mainly to historical reasons,[87] the administrative courts are separate from the ordinary courts. The only area of administrative activity which is not controlled by the judiciary is the evaluation of "opportunity of administrative action" because this evaluation is left to the Parliament.

Article 117(3) of the Constitution also states that the exercise of the jurisdictional function is *exclusive*, belonging only to judges, who must "judge and execute the judgements". The judge stands in a position of independence, in the sense that he is not subject to orders, directions or instructions by any other of the powers of the State, not even by other judges, and it is from this neutral position that he resolves conflicts between individuals or between individuals and the State.

ORGANISATION AND GOVERNMENT OF THE JUDICIARY

While the constitutional theory of the last century emphatically endorsed the independence of the Judiciary and the separation of powers,

---

[84] See below, *Tribunales Superiores de Justicia*.
[85] Indeed there is a "Military Chamber" in the Supreme Court. See below.
[86] "*la jurisdicción se extiende a todas las personas, todas las materias y todo el territorio español*".
[87] See Dadomo & Farran, *op. cit.*, p. 45.

for a long time judicial power was governed by the Executive through the Ministry of Justice. If the judge is to be neutral, subject only to the law, and independent of any other power in reaching his decisions, it is necessary to ensure that the personal position or professional future of judges is not left in the hands of the Executive. Otherwise, it would be easy to punish those members of the judiciary who, in applying the law, did not favour the political group in power. Conversely those judges seeking promotion would only need to ensure that their line of decision-making was sympathetic to the current government.

It was the French Constitution of the IVth Republic which first created a *Conseil de la Magistrature*,[88] an independent organ of government of the Judiciary. This has survived until today although it has lost some of its original functions. The Italian Constitution also established a similar organ, which inspired the legislator when creating the Spanish *Consejo General del Poder Judicial*. Portugal and Greece also have this type of organ, while in the United Kingdom and the United States the Executive retains authority over the organisation of the Judiciary.

The Spanish Constitution of 1978, in trying to guarantee the neutrality and independence of judges, created a special organ of government of the Judiciary called *Consejo General del Poder Judicial* (General Council of the Judiciary)[89] and supported this organ with a number of guarantees (article 122(2) CE). This organ is composed of 21 members, 12 of whom must be chosen from judges and eight from lawyers of recognised standing. The *ley orgánica* developing this constitutional provision—*Ley Orgánica 6/85 del Poder Judicial (LOPJ)*—establishes that the members of the CGPJ should be chosen by both Chambers of Parliament, in equal numbers, by majority of three-fifths. Once the members have been chosen they elect the President of the Supreme Court who will also be the President of the *Consejo*. Their mandate lasts five years and, with the exception of the President, they cannot be re-elected.

The main functions of the CGPJ are connected with the organisation of the Judiciary in the context of the nomination of judges, their promotion, sanctions and suspension from the exercise of their functions. In this sense the Constitutional Court has described the CGPJ as the "administration of the Administration of justice".[90] The *Consejo* does not have total discretion concerning these nominations and promotions, since most of these are carefully regulated by statute. The only discretion relates to the nomination of the presidents of the *Tribunales Superiores*

---

[88] A. Torres del Moral *op. cit.*, p. 284.
[89] The Spanish terminology will be retained and it will be referred to as the *Consejo* in this chapter or the *CGPJ*.
[90] STC 108/1986, of July 26.

de Justicia and the judges of the *Tribunal Supremo*. Even these must comply with previously stipulated conditions. The *Consejo* also inspects the *Juzgados y Tribunales*,[91] (articles 107(4), 348–77 *LOPJ*). It sends an annual report to Parliament about the situation, functioning and problems—if any—of the courts, and it has the capacity to submit reports about any proposed legislation affecting the Judiciary. Other functions are the capacity to nominate two of the members of the Constitutional Court[92] and it is consulted on the nomination of the *Fiscal General del Estado* (the Attorney-General).

The *CGPJ* has been criticised for being a highly political organ due to the procedure for selecting its members. This was changed from the original *LOPJ* of 1980, where 12 of its members were chosen by judges, to the election of its 20 members by Parliament[93] in the 1985 version.

CLASSIFICATION OF COURTS

The structure of the judicial power is organised according to three different and concurrent criteria: subject matter of the dispute, territory and hierarchy of courts. According to the subject matter of the dispute the jurisdiction is divided into four categories—*ordenes jurisdiccionales* (article 9(2) *LOPJ*): civil—for claims based on or related to civil or commercial issues; criminal—claims based on violations of the criminal code; social—claims based on or related to employment or social security; and administrative, for claims based on acts performed by the public jurisdiction. There is also a Military Chamber in the Supreme Court, *Juzgados de menores* and *Juzgados de Vigilancia penitenciaria*.

The national territory is divided for jurisdictional purposes into different areas (article 30 *LOPJ*): municipalities (*municipios*), judicial districts (*partidos judiciales*), provinces (*provincias*), Autonomous Communities (*Comunidades Autonomas*), and the whole of the national territory, over which two courts have jurisdiction, the *Tribunal Supremo* (Supreme Court) (article 123(1) CE and article 52 *LOPJ*) and the *Audienca Nacional* (National Court) (article 62 *LOPJ*). Most of these divisions coincide with the administrative division of the territory; the only exception is *partidos judiciales* which are based on a special jurisdictional concept and so need to be delimited by a special law (*Ley 38/88, de demarcación y planta judicial*, modified by the *Ley 3/92*).

---

[91] Courts. *Juzgado* is used to indicate a unipersonal court, while *Tribunal* is used for collegiate organs.
[92] See below p. 97.
[93] And therefore, by the different political groups.

The Judicial Power: Courts and Court Structure   81

Each territorial unit has a specific type of court. Municipalities have *Juzgados de paz*[94] (article 99(1) *LOPJ*), *partidos judiciales*, or one or several *Juzgados de Primera Instancia e Instrucción*[95] (article 84 *LOPJ*). Provinces have an *Audiencia provincial*[96] (article 80 *LOPJ*), *Juzgados de lo penal, lo social, de Vigilancia penitenciaria, de menores*, and will have *Juzgados contencioso administrativos*[97] when these are established (article 89 (bis) 90, 92 and 97 *LOPJ*). Each Autonomous Community has a *Tribunal Superior de Justicia* (article 152(1) CE and article 71 *LOPJ*); and there is a *Tribunal Supremo* and an *Audiencia Nacional* with jurisdiction over the whole territory.

Usually each court has its seat in the capital of the territorial unit to which it belongs, with the exception of the *Tribunales Superiores de Justicia*[98] which sometimes, according to the *Estatuto de Autonomía* of the community, have their seats somewhere different from the capital of the autonomous territory.[99] However, it is possible to establish Chambers, (*Salas*), of the *Tribunales Superiores de Justicia* in other localities depending on the volume of affairs and taking into consideration geographical circumstances. Also the *Audiencia Provincial* can open sections in places other than the capital of the province.

Hierarchically although each judge is independent and his decisions are not bound by any other court but only by the Law,[1] the organisation of the courts provides a system of appeals against the decisions of lower courts to higher courts and to the Supreme Court.

The Supreme Court

The *Tribunal Supremo* is the Supreme Court of the jurisdictional order (article 123 CE and article 53 *LOPJ*). It has jurisdiction throughout the national territory and it is based in Madrid. It is divided into five Chambers: civil, criminal, administrative, social and military.

---

[94] Justice of the Peace.
[95] First Instance Courts.
[96] Provincial Court.
[97] See below for an explanation of each of these courts.
[98] Superior Courts of Justice.
[99] Notwithstanding the fact that the *Tribunales Superiores del Justicia* are organs of the State in the Autonomous Community and that the Autonomous Communities do not have an independent judicial power.
[1] Although it is necessary to qualify this statement in respect of the effect of decisions of the Supreme Court. See Chap. 2, "*La Jurisprudencia*" and Chap. 5 and 6, *Recurso de casación*.

Composition

The Supreme Court is composed of a President[2] of the Supreme Court, a further five Presidents—one for each Chamber—the judges designated by law, a secretary, a Vice-President and other non-judicial personnel. The public prosecution is represented by the Attorney-General, and several other public prosecutors.

Jurisdiction

The Supreme Court has jurisdiction in civil, criminal, administrative, social and military matters. There are, consequently, five different Chambers which are in charge of the cases in each area.

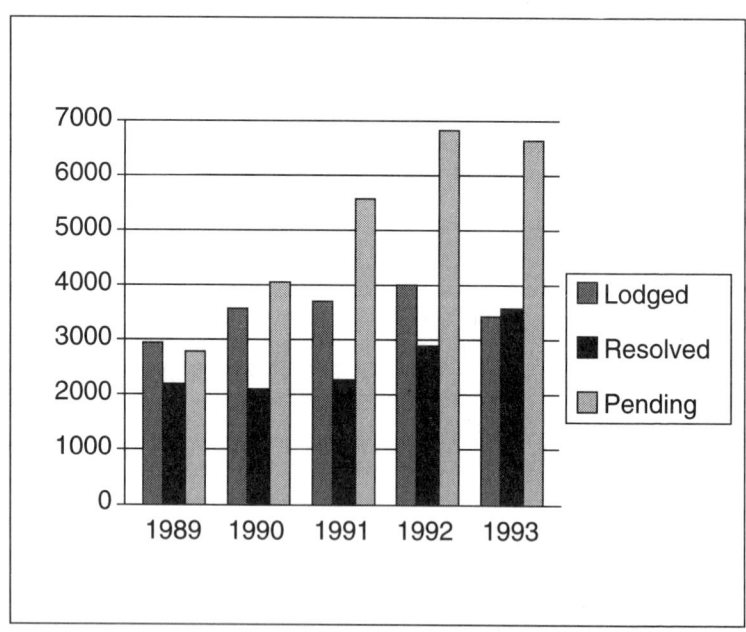

TRIBUNAL SUPREMO: CIVIL CHAMBER
Cases 1989–1993

Source: *Memoria del Consejo General del Poder Judicial*, Madrid, 1994.

---

[2] The President of the Supreme Court is also the President of the *Consejo General del Poder Judicial*. See above, p. 79.

Civil Chamber
The Civil chamber has jurisdiction over the *recursos de casación y revisión*, cases concerning the civil liability of the President of the Government, the Presidents the Congress, the Senate, the Supreme Court, the Constitutional Court, *Diputados* and *Senadores*, Members of the *Consejo General del Poder Judicial*, Judges of the Constitutional and Supreme Courts, Presidents and Judges of the *Audiencia Nacional* or of the *Tribunales Superiores de Justicia*, the Attorney General, high government officers, and petitions for the enforcement of foreign judgments.

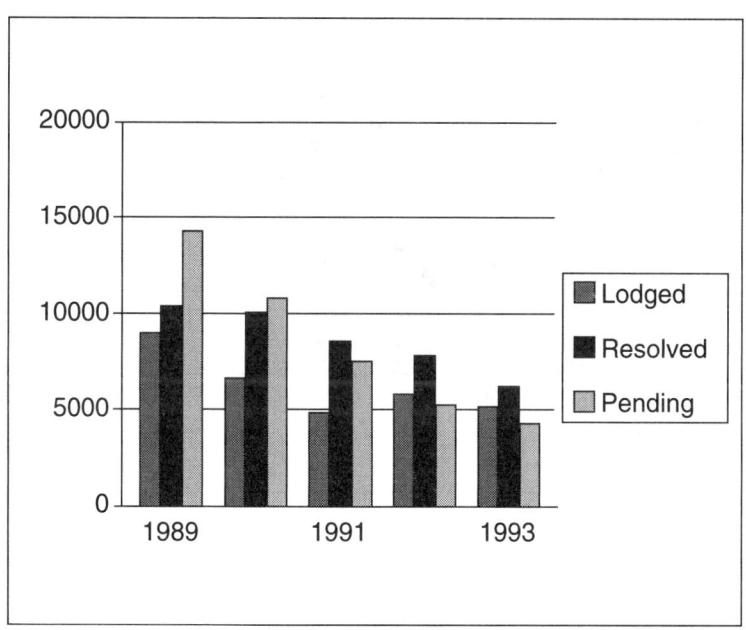

TRIBUNAL SUPREMO: CRIMINAL CHAMBER
Cases 1989–1993

Source: *Memoria del Consejo General del Poder Judicial*, Madrid, 1994.

Criminal Chamber

This has jurisdiction in all cases of *recursos de casación* and *revisión* against decisions of the *Audiencia Provincial* and *Audiencia Nacional* and criminal actions against any of the persons mentioned above for whom the Civil Chamber has special jurisdiction in civil matters.

TRIBUNAL SUPREMO: ADMINISTRATIVE CHAMBER
Cases 1989–1993

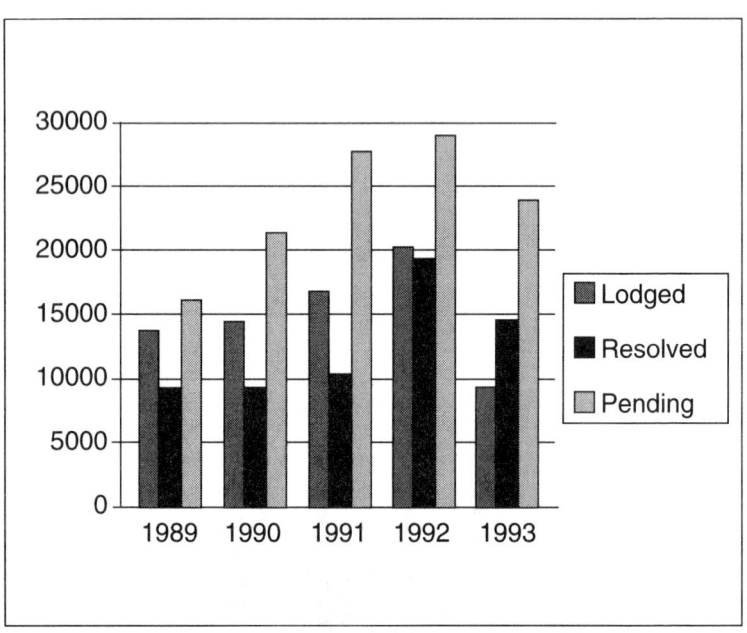

Source: *Memoria del Consejo General del Poder Judicial*, Madrid, 1994.

Administrative Chamber

The Administrative Chamber of the Supreme Court has sole jurisdiction in all cases of *recursos* against the decisions of the Council of Ministers, or against decisions of the *Consejo General del Poder Judicial*, or against decisions of the organs of Government of the Chambers of

Parliament and other high organs of the State. It also has jurisdiction on *recursos de casación* against decisions of the *Audiencia Nacional* and decisions of the *Tribunales Superiores de Justicia* relating to acts of the Autonomous Communities, and *recursos* against the resolutions of the *Tribunal de Cuentas*.

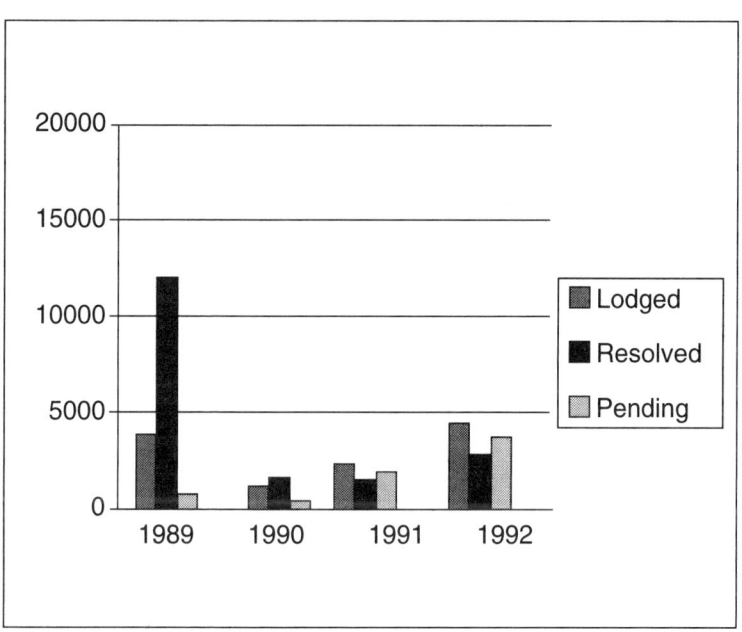

TRIBUNAL SUPREMO: SOCIAL CHAMBER
Volume of Cases 1989–1992

Source: *Memoria del Consejo General del Poder Judicial*, Madrid, 1994.

Social Chamber
 The Social Chamber has jurisdiction over the *recursos de casación* and *revisión* and any other extraordinary *recurso* as established by the *Ley de Procedimiento laboral* of April 27, 1990.

Military Chamber[3]

Recursos de casación and *revisión* against the resolutions of the *Tribunal Militar Central* and of the *Tribunals Militares Territoriales* are heard by this Chamber as are proceedings against high members of the military which are not disciplinary sanctions. Also heard are *recursos* in jurisdictional conflicts and petitions in error regarding the liability of the State established by the military jurisdictions.

There are also other organs in the Supreme Court such as the Chamber of Conflicts.

Audiencia nacional

This is a collegiate Court based in Madrid with jurisdiction in administrative, criminal and labour matters for the whole of the national territory.

AUDIENCIA NACIONAL: CRIMINAL CHAMBER
Cases 1989–1993

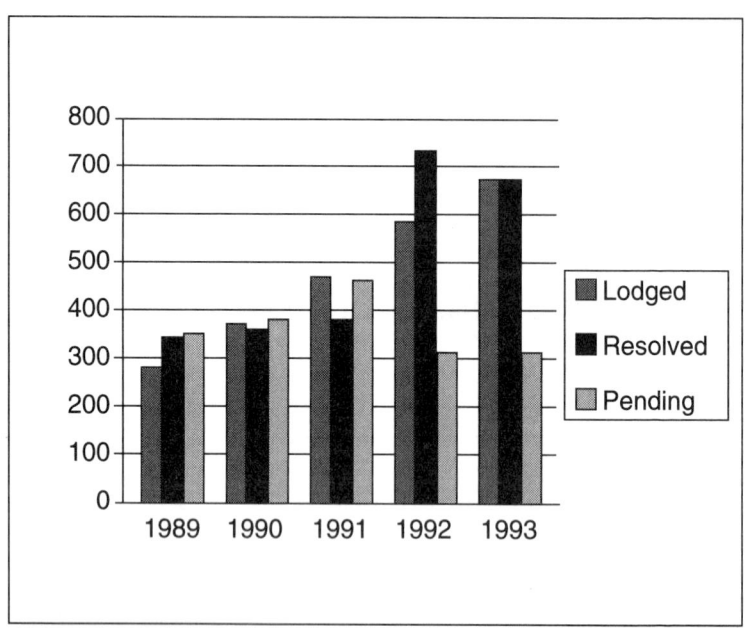

Source: *Memoria del Consejo General del Poder Judicial*, Madrid, 1994.

---
[3] Created by LO 4/1987.

Criminal matters

In criminal matters this court has jurisdiction in cases involving: crimes against the Crown, the high organs of the nation, or the government in the form of counterfeit and monetary crimes, drug trafficking, food and drugs crimes, crimes committed outside the national territory but which the Spanish courts are responsible for according to international treaties, terrorism, extradition of prisoners and *recursos* against decisions of the *Juzgados Centrales de Instrucción*.

AUDIENCIA NACIONAL: ADMINISTRATIVE CHAMBER
Cases 1989–1993

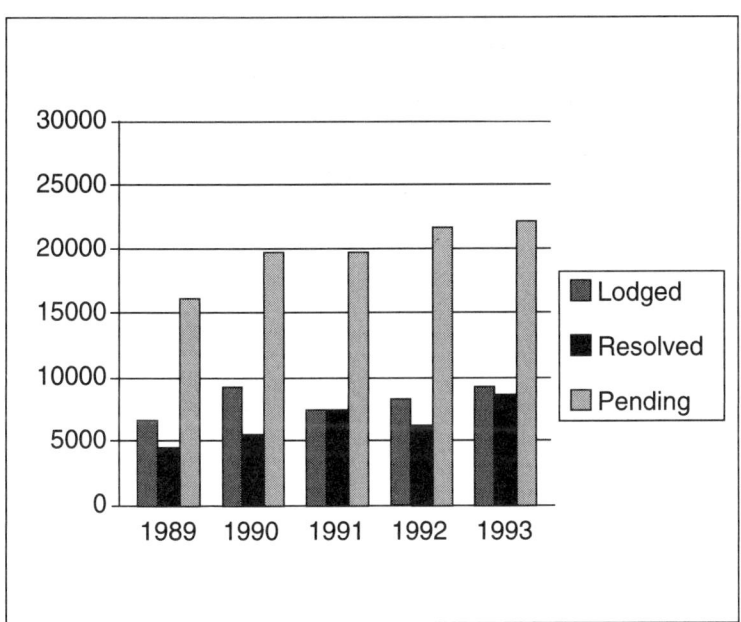

Source: *Memoria del Consejo General del Poder Judicial*, Madrid, 1994.

Administrative matters

In administrative matters it has jurisdiction over *recursos* against acts and decisions of Ministers and Secretaries of State.

AUDIENCIA NACIONAL: SOCIAL CHAMBER
Cases 1989–1993

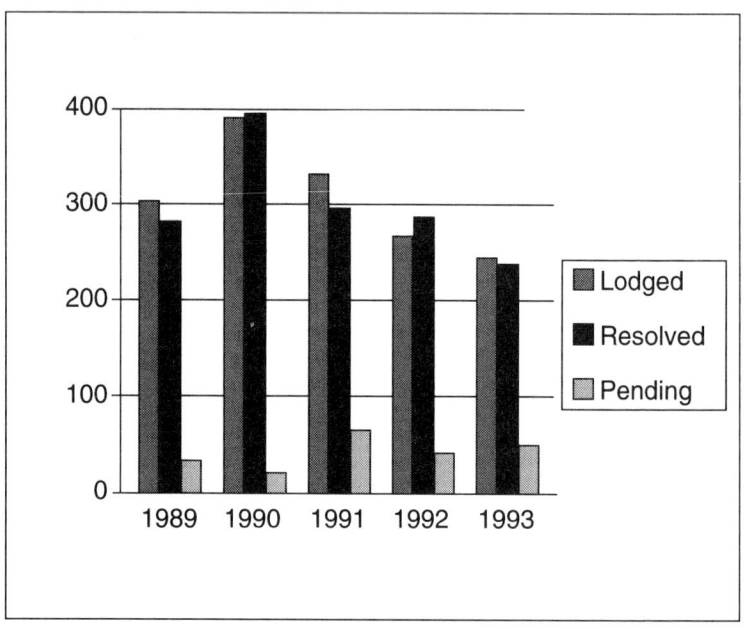

Source: *Memoria del Consejo General del Poder Judicial*, Madrid, 1994.

Labour matters

In labour matters it has jurisdiction over any dispute concerning collective bargaining agreements of national application.[4]

Tribunales superiores de justicia

These courts were created by the *LOPJ* of 1985 and have jurisdiction in civil, criminal, administrative and social matters in the territory of the Autonomous Community where they have their seat. They came into operation on May 22, 1989 and replaced the *Audiencias Territoriales* which had existed previously.

---

[4] From May 22, of 1989 when the *Tribunal Central de Trabajo* was abolished.

Jurisdiction

Civil matters

These courts have jurisdiction to hear: *recursos de casación* of decisions of courts within the territory of the Autonomous Community when the *recurso* is based on an infraction of rules of civil, *foral* or special law of the Community and when the *Estatuto de Autonomía* of the Community has delegated this jurisdiction to the *TSJ*.[5] They may also hear *recursos de revisión* based on rules of civil, *foral* or special law of that Community (article 73(b) *LOPJ*), actions for civil liability of the President or of Members of Government and Parliament of the Community—if the *Estatuto de Autonomía* does not confer jurisdiction on the Supreme Court—and civil liability of judges of the *Audiencia Provincial* having a seat in the Autonomous Community (article 73 *LOPJ*).

Criminal matters

The *Tribunal Superior de Justicia* has jurisdiction over all the actions provided for in the *Estatuto de Autonomía*,[6] and over both the *instruccion*[7] and judgment of actions against judges and *fiscales* in the exercise of their function, except when this is the responsibility of the Supreme Court.

Administrative matters

These courts have jurisdiction at first instance in the case of the *recurso contencioso-administrativo* against acts and dispositions of the organs of the administration of the State, where jurisdiction is not given to any other court. They also have jurisdiction to deal with *recursos contenciosos* against administrative rulings of the *Consejo de Gobierno* of the Autonomous Community where they have their seat, its President or *Consejeros*;[8] *recursos* against the organs of government of the Autonomous Parliament, and *recurso contencioso-electoral* against the decisions of the electoral administration concerning nominations of Presidents of local corporations.

As second instance courts they have jurisdiction to hear all the *recursos* against decisions of courts situated in the Autonomous Community in administrative matters.

---

[5] *Estatuto de Autonomia del Pais Vasco* (art. 14 LO 7/79), *Cataluna* (art. 19 LO 4/78), *Galicia* (art. 22 LO 1/81), *Murcia* (art. 35 LO 4/82), *Valencia* (art. 40 LO 5/82), *Aragón* (art. 29 LO 6/82) *Navarra* (art. 61 LO 13/82), *Extremadura* (art. 45 LO 1/83), *Islas Baleares* (art. 49 LO 2/83), all the other *Estatutos* expressly exclude this function.
[6] As an example, Cataluña gives jurisdiction to these courts to hear criminal actions against members of the Autonomous Parliament (arts. 26 and 31 LO 4/79).
[7] See below, Chap. 6.
[8] Equivalent to Ministers but at a regional level.

Social matters

Since 1989 the *TSJ* has replaced the *Tribunal Central de Trabajo*. At first instance, this court has jurisdiction to hear any dispute between employees and employers which falls outside the jurisdiction of a *Juzgado de lo Social*. At second instance they hear any *recursos* against decisions of the *Juzgados de lo social* based in the Autonomous Community and conflicts of competence between these courts. Article 7 of the *LPL* of April 27, 1990 also gives jurisdiction over the formation and recognition of trade unions and business associations, modification of their *estatutos*, protection of the right to belong to a trade union, collective conflicts and appeals against collective bargaining agreements with effects restricted to the territory of the Autonomous Community.

TRIBUNALES SUPERIORES DE JUSTICIA (ALL) Evolution of Cases 1989–1993: Percentage CIVIL & CRIMINAL, ADMINISTRATIVE AND SOCIAL CHAMBERS

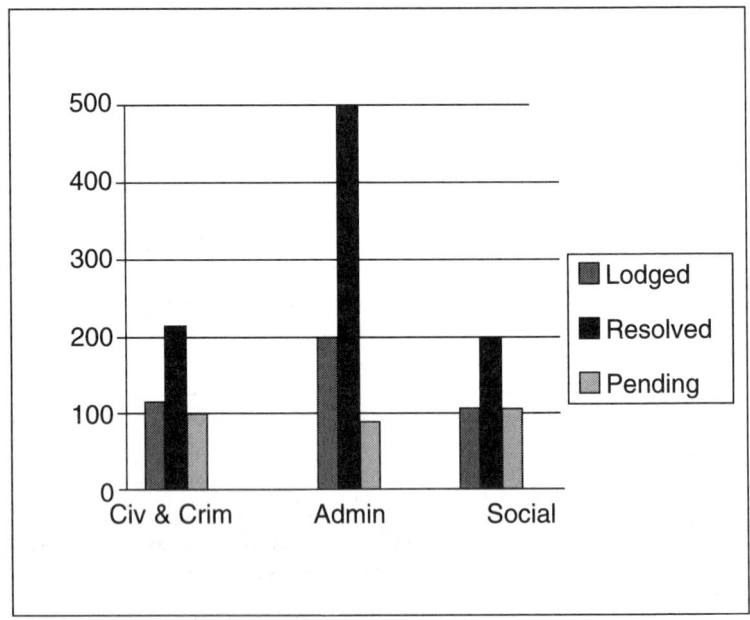

Source: *Memoria del Consejo General del Poder Judicial*, Madrid, 1994.

Audiencias provinciales

These are collegiate courts with jurisdiction in civil and criminal matters in the territory of a province.[9]

Jurisdiction

Civil matters

In civil matters these courts have jurisdiction to hear *recursos* against resolutions of the *Juzgados de Primera Instancia* of the province (article 82 *LOPJ*). They also have jurisdiction over conflicts of jurisdiction between courts situated in the province and in proceedings for the removal of judges from particular cases.[10]

Criminal matters

In criminal matters the *Audiencias* are mixed courts because they have jurisdiction to decide in the first instance on criminal proceedings concerning serious crimes—*delitos graves*—together with a significant appellate capacity.

According to article 82 *LOPJ*, as modified by the *LO* 7/88 of December 28, the *Audiencia Provincial* has jurisdiction in criminal actions not conferred on other courts, on *recursos* against criminal resolutions dictated by the *Juzgados de Instruccion y de lo Penal* in the province, *recursos* against resolutions of the *Juzgados de Vigilancia Penitenciaria* in matters relating to the enforcement of punishments in criminal cases, *recursos* against decisions made by the *Juzgados de Instrucción* in first instance proceedings for minor crimes, and *recursos* against decisions of the *Juzgados de menores*.

Juzgados de primera instancia e instrucción

These courts are composed of a single judge with jurisdiction in civil and criminal matters in a territory of a *partido judicial*. Their name, in theory, explains their jurisdiction; first instance in civil cases and *instrucción* in criminal cases. However, in practice, the jurisdiction of these courts extends beyond these matters because in civil matters they have jurisdiction to hear certain appeals and also for the enforcement of judgments; in criminal matters they actually decide some cases.[11] They have no jurisdiction in social or administrative matters.

---

[9] In Spain there are fifty-two provinces.
[10] *Recusacion de magistrados*.
[11] See Chap. 6, for an explanation of the different stages of the proceedings.

Since 1974 some of these courts have separated criminal and civil matters, creating *Juzgados de Primera Instancia* for civil matters and *Juzgados de Instrucción* for criminal matters. Moreover, in some places, such as Madrid, the *Juzgados de Primera Instancia* have specialised, creating *Juzgados de Familia* for family law disputes and special *Juzgados* for cases involving mentally handicapped people. All these courts are *Juzgados de Primera Instancia* in spite of their specialised nature.

Jurisdiction

Civil matters

In civil matters they hear and decide any case in which the amount of the claim is more than 8000 pesetas[12] and any other special proceedings.[13] They also hear all proceedings concerning matters regulated by special legislation, including matrimonial causes, civil proceedings for violations of fundamental rights, protection of the right to honour, privacy and personal image, bankruptcy, succession matters and, at second instance, appeals against decisions of the *Juzgados de Paz*.

Criminal matters

According to article 87 *LOPJ*, as modified by *LO* 7/88 the *Juzgados de Primera Instancia e Instrucción* carry out the stage of "instruction" of those cases in which the decision corresponds to the *Audiencia Provincial* and the *Juzgados de lo penal*.[14] They also have jurisdiction for the adjudication of minor offences, proceedings of *habeas corpus* according to the *LO* 6/84, appeals against resolutions of the *Juzgados de paz* within the territorial limit of their jurisdiction and jurisdiction to authorise searches of private dwellings.

Juzgados de lo penal

These unipersonal courts were introduced by the *LO* 7/88 as a consequence of the decision of the Constitutional Court[15] declaring unconstitutional the fact that the same court "instructing" or investigating a criminal case was the court giving the judgment.

These courts have jurisdiction in criminal matters within the territory of a province. According to article 14 *LECrim*, they have jurisdiction to

---

[12] Approximately £40.
[13] Such as *interdictos*, *juicios de retracto*, *juicio ejecutivo*, *alimentos provisionales*.
[14] It is important to emphasise the distinction between instruction and judgment in criminal proceedings. These are carried out by different courts in order to guarantee the rights of the citizen. See below, Chap. 6.
[15] STC of July 12, 1988.

judge crimes punishable with imprisonment of less than six years, with pecuniary sanctions or with any sanction not exceeding six years, and confiscation of a driving licence—whatever the period—and any minor offences committed in connection with crimes punished as mentioned above. In all these cases these courts apply the new *Procedimiento Abreviado*.[16] There are 143 *Juzgados de lo Penal* in Spain and they came into operation on September 15, 1989.

Juzgados centrales de instruccion

These courts were created by the *RD-Ley* of January 4, 1977, and they are *Juzgados de Instrucción* but with jurisdiction in the whole of the national territory. Their seat is in Madrid (articles 1 and 6 LO 7/88) and their composition is exactly the same as that of any other *Juzgado de Instrucción*. They carry out the "instruction stage" of cases which will be decided by the *Juzgado Central de lo Penal* or the *Audiencia Nacional*.

Juzgado central de lo penal

Created by the LO 7/88 the *Juzgado Central de lo Penal*, with its seat in Madrid and jurisdiction in the national territory, is the competent court for those matters which would be heard by the *Audienca Nacional* but are of less importance, that is, crimes for which the punishment is less than seven years imprisonment, pecuniary sanctions of any amount or withdrawal of a driving licence. The "instruction" for these cases is the same as to the *Juzgados Centrales de Instrucción*.

Juzgados de lo contencioso-administrativo

These courts have not yet been created. The idea of the *LOPJ* was to create one such court in each provincial capital to decide at first or only instance all administrative appeals. Until they are created the *Tribunal Superior de Justicia* of the relevant Community hears all cases concerning administrative matters.

Juzgados de lo social

These courts replace the old *Magistraturas de Trabajo* which were courts dependent on the *Ministerio de Trabajo y Seguridad Social*. Today the *Juzgados de lo Social* are proper jurisdictional organs with jurisdiction

---

[16] See below, Chap. 6.

in any matters related to employment contracts or social security obligations arising in the province for which they have jurisdiction.

Juzgados de vigilancia penitenciaria

These courts belong to the criminal order and are located in the capital of the province although it is possible to establish them in other localities. Their function is the enforcement of criminal decisions imposing loss of freedom and other security measures; they also safeguard the rights of prisoners.

Juzgados de menores

These juvenile courts are in charge of criminal offences committed by minors and the supervision of any educational or other measures imposed upon them.

Juzgados de paz

These are the only courts where the judge is a non-professional judge. Article 99 *LOPJ* declares that all the municipalities which do not have a *Juzgados de Primera Instancia e Instrucción* shall have a *Juzgados de Paz* with a *Juez de Paz* who performs his function gratuitously and who does not need to have any professional qualification. This "judge" is nominated by the Chamber of Government of the *Tribunal Superior de Justicia* from among the persons proposed by the respective *Ayuntamiento*.[17] They have jurisdiction over minor civil and criminal cases.

5. EL MINISTERIO FISCAL (THE PUBLIC PROSECUTION SERVICE)

Although the public prosecution service is not a part of the judicial power[18]—because the judicial function belongs exclusively to judges and magistrates—its function and activities are so closely connected with the judicial power that it is regulated under this title in the Constitution. The main function of the public prosecution is to "promote the cause of

---

[17] The *Ayuntamiento* (town hall) chooses a person from candidates who voluntarily nominate themselves.
[18] See J. Garcia Morillo, *op. cit.*, p. 247.

justice in defence of legality, of the rights of the citizens and of the public interest".[19]

The public prosecution is regulated by its own *Estatuto Orgánico*[20] by which it is given "organic autonomy in the Judicial power". It has its own resources and personnel and is organised according to the principle of "unity of action". All the members of the prosecution service are subject to hierarchical organisation with the Attorney-General at the top (articles 22, 25 and 27 EOMF). The Attorney-General (*Fiscal General del Estado*) is appointed by the Government (article 124 CE) because the public prosecution is a key function in the criminal policy of the Executive. Together with these principles of unity of action and hierarchy, the public prosecution is subject to the principles of neutrality and legality.[21]

The usual activity of the prosecution is to bring charges in criminal proceedings. However, in comparison with other countries, the public prosecution does not have the exclusive right of prosecution because this can also be started by the victim or by a third party by the mechanism of "a popular action" of article 125 CE.[22] The public prosecution also participates in other proceedings, such as proceedings before the Constitutional Court[23] where it has a separate office—*Fiscalía ante el Tribunal Constitucional*.

6. *EL TRIBUNAL CONSTITUCIONAL* (THE CONSTITUTIONAL COURT)

COMPOSITION AND FUNCTIONS

The Constitutional Court is one of the organs of the State. It is not included in the judicial power and it is only subject to the Constitution and to its own *ley orgánica* (LO 2/1979 of October 12 (LOTC)). Some writers[24] suggest that the Constitutional Court is a real "jurisdiction" in the sense that its decisions are made according only to the Constitution. However, it is important to distinguish this organ from the judicial power.

---

[19] art. 124(1) CE "*La función del Ministerio fiscal es promover la acción de la justicia en defensa de la legalidad, de los derechos de los ciudadanos y del interes público tutelado por la ley*".
[20] Ley 50/81: *Estatuto Orgánico del Ministerio Fiscal* (EOMF); developed by the RD 545/83.
[21] As with any other organ, including the Public Administration, it is subject to the Law (art. 103 CE).
[22] See below, Chap. 6, p. 168 *et seq*.
[23] See below.
[24] Pablo Perez Tremps, *op. cit.*, p. 254.

The origins of constitutional justice can be traced back to the famous American case of *Marbury v. Madison*,[25] in which Judge Marshall constructed the theory of judicial review of the law. It seemed quite logical that a system which recognised the supremacy of judicial decision through a system of precedent, should adopt such an approach, in contrast to continental Europe where the supremacy of the law as "the expression of popular will", as formulated by Rousseau was nearly a dogma. In its original formulation by the United States' Supreme Court in 1803, the control of constitutionality of legislation[26] was not only a power, but a duty of the judge. The judge was obliged to declare the law, and if two different laws were in conflict and one of them was in the Constitution, the judge had to respect the latter because this was hierarchically superior. This model is known as "diffuse control of constitutionality", because all the judges are responsible for controlling the legislation by refusing to apply any which is contrary to the Constitution. However, the judge does not have the power to derogate or declare legislation void, because this function belongs exclusively to Parliament. The system works well because the principle of precedent creates a special relationship between Acts of Parliament and case law, by which a statute has no other meaning than that which is attributed to it by judicial decisions.

In continental Europe it was only after the First World War that the idea of the supremacy of Parliament began to weaken in favour of the supremacy of the Constitution. Some writers[27] have pointed out that only when universal suffrage was introduced, did the fear of a more "democratic" Parliament, in which the majority might take decisions which were contrary to the interest of the dominant class, stimulate consideration of the introduction of a mechanism for controlling Parliament. This mechanism was the Constitutional Court. Without endorsing this approach the first models of constitutional courts in Europe can be found in the Czech and Austrian Constitutions of 1919 and 1920 which followed the ideas of K. Kelsen regarding constitutionality. According to Kelsen the Constitution provides only rules and mandates to Parliament and not directly applicable rules. The Constitution is applied through Acts of Parliament and these, in turn, are applied by judges in their decisions. It is then necessary to establish an organ outside the judiciary to control the adequate compliance of Acts of Parliament to the Constitution. This organ, the Constitutional Court, has a function of negative legislator because when it declares that a

---

[25] (1803).
[26] *Leyes* and dispositions on the same hierarchical level.
[27] Antonio Torres del Moral, *op. cit.*, pp. 381–2.

statute is unconstitutional it rejects it from the system. In this respect the Constitutional Court shares legislative power with Parliament. This model has been followed in Europe only as far as there is an organ responsible for the control of constitutionality of legislation but most of the European Constitutional Courts—the Spanish, Italian, and German—have elements of both models.

In Spain the first Constitutional Court appeared in the Constitution of 1931, which created a *Tribunal de Garantias Constitucionales* (Court of Constitutional Guarantees). When the draftsmen of the 1978 Constitution met to draft Title IX, they all agreed on the need to establish an organ to control the legislative and also that this organ should be independent of all the other powers of the State, partly because this was the model followed by other countries with a similar legal culture,[28] and partly because there was reluctance to leave the control of constitutionality in the hands of a judicial class mainly drawn from the period of dictatorship.[29]

The Constitutional Court is a real jurisdiction neither dependent on, nor incorporated in the judicial power. Its main function is the interpretation of the Constitution (article 1 *LOTC*) and in doing this it plays a key role in the distribution and organisation of the powers of the State. The Constitutional Court controls the exercise of the legislative power by Parliament, ensuring that any legislation approved by Parliament which is contrary to the Constitution is declared null and void. However, it is not only Parliament that is controlled by the Constitutional Court; the Executive and the Judiciary are also subject to the control of constitutionality over their activities, exercised through the procedure of the *recurso de amparo*.[30]

The Constitutional Court is composed of 12 Members, four of whom are chosen by Congress, four by Senate, two by the Executive and two by the *Consejo General del Poder Judicial*. Judges of the Constitutional Court are selected from lawyers, judges, civil servants and university professors with more than 15 years experience and "recognised professional standing". All the Members need to belong to the legal professions. Their mandate is for nine years, which means that they do not necessarily coincide with the period of the legislature and so are not chosen by a given majority in Parliament at the time. For the election of the Members of the Constitutional Court a qualified majority of three-fifths is required in order to ensure a consensus of the main political

---

[28] It is important to remember the influence of the German Constitution of 1949 in Spanish public law.
[29] Pablo Perez Tremps, in Luis López Guerra, ed., *op. cit.*, p. 254.
[30] See below.

forces. The Members of the Constitutional Court are subject to very similar principles as those of judges and magistrates; they are independent, cannot be removed (article 159 CE) and their tenure of office is incompatible with the exercise of any other trade, profession or public office (article 159(4) CE). The difference between judges and Members of the Constitutional Court is that judges cannot be members of any political party while Members of the Constitutional Court may be.[31] They also enjoy the benefit of "special jurisdiction" by which any criminal action against them will be heard by the Criminal Chamber of the Supreme Court.

The Members of the Constitutional Court elect their President— by majority—and their Vice-President. The work is organised by the President who also represents the institution.

The function of the Constitutional Court as the supreme interpreter of the Constitution can be summarised as follows: control of the constitutionality of the rules with *fuerza de ley*[32] (articles 161(1)(a) 163 and 95 CE); protection of the fundamental rights and freedoms recognised in articles 15–30 of the Constitution (article 161(1)(b) CE); control of the constitutionality of the legislation of the Autonomous Communities (article 161(2) CE); guarantee of the territorial distribution of power between the State and the Autonomous Communities (article 161(1)(c) CE); and control of the distribution of power among the different organs of the State (article 59(3) LOTC).

In order to perform these functions most effectively the Constitutional Court organises itself in three different ways: in Sections (*Secciones*), in Chambers (*Salas*) or in full (*Pleno*). The Chambers, each of which has six Members and is presided over by the President or by the Vice-President, have jurisdiction to hear the *recurso de amparo*. The different sections decide on the admissibility of different cases and each of them is composed of three Members.

THE DIFFERENT PROCEDURES OF THE CONSTITUTIONAL COURT

El recurso de inconstitucionalidad[33]

This procedure is established in order to control the constitutionality of the rules with *fuerza de ley*. These are not only rules approved by Parliament (*leyes* in the formal sense) but also *Estatutos de Autonomía, decretos leyes, decretos legislativos, Reglamentos* of the Chambers of Par-

---

[31] They cannot, however, have any executive position on the political organisation.
[32] See above, Chap. 2.
[33] "Appeal of unconstitutionality" against rules with *fuerza de ley*.

liament and international treaties (article 27(2) LOTC) and rules of the Autonomous Communities equivalent to those mentioned. The Constitutional Court has expressly ruled out any competence to control the derivative law of the European Community[34] even if this is directly applicable because the parameter of control is Community Law itself and not the Constitution and it is up to the European Court of Justice to effect any control. With respect to any legislation approved prior to the Constitution, the problem can be looked at from a double perspective; first, any subsequent legislation derogates previous legislation and in this case the judge has to apply the latter rule on the matter; secondly, an issue of the hierarchy of sources should be resolved by recognising the superiority of the Constitution. From this second perspective the Constitutional Court will have to decide whether or not there is a conflict. In one of the earliest decisions of the Constitutional Court,[35] it was decided that a mixed approach should be adopted to control the position of pre-constitutional legislation: the judges can automatically refuse to apply the rule that they understand has been abrogated by the Constitution or, if they have any doubt, they can demand a ruling from the Constitutional Court.

The *locus standi* for starting a *recurso de insconstitucionalidad* is restricted by article 162(1) CE to 50 *Diputados*, 50 *Senadores*,[36] the President of the Government, the Ombudsman, the Government of the Autonomous Communities or the Legislative Assemblies of the Communities.[37] The *locus standi* of the *Defensor del Pueblo* seems to be associated with his role of protecting of fundamental rights,[38] although there is a wide spectrum of laws which can directly or indirectly affect these fundamental rights.[39]

An appeal of unconstitutionality must be initiated within three months following the publication of the legislation which is being contested in the BOE.[40]

---

[34] STC 64/1991, *Caso APESCO*. See Chap. 2, p. 36.

[35] STC 2/81, *Caso Ley de Bases de Régimen Local*.

[36] In order to protect the rights of the minoritary groups in Parliament who can thereby contest actions of the majority.

[37] Against rules "affecting their autonomy" (art. 32(2) LOTC) not only in the sense of revindication of powers taken by the State through its legislation but also in cases in which the legislation of the State affects any of the interests of the Community, STC 56/1990, *Caso Ley Organica del Poder Judicial II*.

[38] P. Perez Tremps, in L. López Guerra y otros, ed., *op. cit.*, p. 269.

[39] STC 150/1990, *Caso Recargo del tres por ciento*.

[40] If it is an appeal against legislation of an autonomous community which is published both in the BOE and the Autonomous Community Journal the period starts to count from the date of the first publication. ATC 597/1990, *Caso Ley asturiana de caza*.

Procedure

An appeal is started by any of the persons/organs with *locus standi* by means of a written complaint specifying the law which is being challenged and the reasons for the complaint. If the Constitutional Court accepts the case—which is decided by one of its sections—it will pass a copy of the complaint to Congress, Senate and to the Government or to the organs of the Autonomous Communities, if the rule which is being challenged was passed by one of those Communities. If these organs consider it appropriate they can put forward any arguments which they believe to be pertinent.

The decision of the Constitutional Court will be effective from the day after its publication in the *BOE* (article 164 *CE*) and the effect will be the nullity of any law declared to be "unconstitutional". Nullity, strictly speaking, means that the legal provision has never existed. However, article 40 of the *LOTC* modifies the effects of this nullity, by providing that it will not affect those decisions which are *res iudicata*, except when the application of the law resulted in the imposition of criminal or administrative sanctions which would not have been imposed had the law not existed. Also, the Constitutional Court itself has sometimes modified the effects of the declaration of "unconstitutionality" by limiting the period of applicability, if the circumstances of the case so demand.[41]

The decisions of the Constitutional Court are binding on all the powers of the State (article 38 *LOTC*) and have full *erga omnes* effects. There are no appeals against these decisions and it is not possible to start new proceedings in the Constitutional Court based on the same legal provision once a decision has been given. This effect of decisions of the Constitutional Court has resulted in some writers including Constitutional Court decisions amongst the sources of law. Without entering into a doctrinal discussion about this, it is important to note that these decisions are not *case law* in the strict sense of the word, given the peculiar nature of the Constitutional court.[42]

La cuestión de inconstitucionalidad[43]

According to this second procedure it is possible to control the constitutionality of a legal provision when a judge, in the course of judicial proceedings, believes that the rule he has to apply to decide a case may be unconstitutional (article 35(1) *LOTC*). Doubt about the con-

---

[41] STC 45/1989, *caso I.R.P.F.*
[42] See Chap. 2.
[43] Question of unconstitutionality.

stitutionality of a rule can be brought either by the parties or by the judge himself, in any type of proceedings. If that doubt arises, the judge, will first, try to interpret the rule in a way which is compatible with the Constitution. If he cannot do so, he will request an interpretation from the Constitutional Court once he has heard the parties to the proceedings and the *Ministerio Fiscal*. The procedure in the Constitutional Court is very similar to the procedure for *recurso de inconstitucionalidad* and the decision will have the same effects.

Control of International treaties

This control has a different nature from the two previous procedures because it is consultative. The control occurs prior to the signature of the treaty and its purpose is to determine whether the terms of the international treaty will in any way be contrary to the Constitution. If this is so, the Constitution will need to be modified (article 95 CE) before the treaty is signed and ratified, otherwise the treaty should not be entered into. Both Parliament and the Government have the right to initiate consultation (article 78(1) *LOTC*). The only case to date in which this mechanism has been used has been in relation to the Treaty of the European Union.[44]

Once the Treaty has been ratified and has become a rule of the legal system it is possible to challenge the constitutionality of any of its provisions by way of either a *recurso* or *cuestión de inconstitucionalidad*.[45]

Recurso de amparo

This procedure, directed at the protection of rights and freedoms recognised by the Constitution, is the last of the internal appeals available to a citizen for the protection of such rights and freedoms.[46] Whilst, in principle, the protection of such rights comes within the jurisdiction of the ordinary courts,[47] this procedure is extraordinary and is only used as a last resort. It is only justified when judicial intervention has proved inefficient, because the object of the *recurso de amparo* is protection

---

[44] *DTC* of 1 July, 1992, *caso Tratado de la Union Europea*.

[45] See Chap. 2, p. 35.

[46] It is possible to appeal to the European Court of Human Rights if the person believes that any of these rights has been violated.

[47] The Constitutional Court has repeated its subsidiary character on the protection of fundamental rights several times.

against any act of public power[48] which violates any of the following rights: article 14 CE (principle of non-discrimination), articles 15–19 CE (fundamental rights and public freedoms) and article 30(2) CE (right to military objection). As a consequence of the subsidiary character of this procedure, several requirements need to be met in order to be able to start such an appeal. The main requirement is that all ordinary procedures for the protection of the right invoked have been exhausted (article 43(1) and 44(1) LOTC). These procedures will vary depending on the origin of the violation, the organ which is responsible, the time and occasion and so on. It is important to note that article 53(2) CE provides a special and summary procedure for the protection of the same rights which can be pleaded in *amparo*[49] and it will always be necessary to have previously exhausted this procedure.

The right to commence proceedings rests with any natural or juridical person who was party to the proceedings (article 46(1)(b)) and who claims a legitimate interest, the Ombudsman and the Attorney General.

The time limit to start the procedure of *amparo* varies. In the case of acts or omissions of the judicial power (article 44 LOTC) the period is twenty days from the date of notification of the judicial decision; in the case of acts of the legislative organs of the State or of the Autonomous Communities[50] it is three months from the date when the act becomes definitive;[51] against an act of the Executive—State and Autonomous Communities—or the Public Administration, it is twenty days from the date of notification of the judicial decision concerning any previous judicial proceedings.

Procedure

The procedure consists of two stages; the first stage, admission, involves of an examination of all the legal requirements, limitation periods or the existence of a previous decision by the Constitutional Court on the same matter (article 50 LOTC); the second stage is the actual procedure in which the public prosecutor and the parties are present and can formulate any statements they think are applicable.

---

[48] This has been interpreted quite flexibly allowing *amparo* against acts of entities such as TVE which has a mixed public and private nature; STC 35/1983, *Caso Hermanos Bengoechea v. TVE*. The criteria to apply is whether there has been an exercise of *imperium*, that is public power, or not.
[49] *Procedimento Preferente y Sumario para la protección de derechos fundamentales*. See above.
[50] These acts do not include legislation approved by the Parliament of the Autonomous Assemblies.
[51] If there is an administrative procedure available, for instance in cases of internal administration, it is necessary to exhaust this and any available judicial proceedings first.

EL TRIBUNAL CONSTITUCIONAL (THE CONSTITUTIONAL COURT) 103

After this the *Sala* hearing the case will make a decision.

The decision can have several effects. If it admits the claims of the plaintiff, the most obvious consequence is the declaration of nullity of the act or resolution against which the appeal was initiated, and the recognition and reaffirmation of the right or freedom claimed by adopting whatever measures are necessary.

Conflictos de competencias[52]

In this type of procedure the Constitutional Court will rule on the distribution of powers, determined by the Constitution and the *Estatutos de Autonomía* between the State and the Communities, or between different Communities, when a disagreement regarding the exercise or the extent and method of the exercise of one of these powers arises.[53]

The only organs with capacity to initiate this procedure are the Government—of the State—and the executive of the different Autonomous Communities (article 62 and 63 LOTC). There is a difference in the position of the Central Government and the Autonomous Governments. The former is in a position of superiority because it can either start the proceeding in the Constitutional Court when it is believed that an Autonomous Community is acting outside its powers, or demand the annulment of the disputed act or disposition of the Autonomous Community (article 62 LOTC). If it is the Autonomous Community which considers that the Central Government is acting outside its powers it is always necessary first to make a request to the State (article 63 LOTC). The time limit to effect the request to the State or the Community, or to start the proceedings if it is the Central Government which is initiating these, is two months from the date of publication of the act or law complained of. If there has been no response within one month or if this is negative, then, the procedure can be started in the Constitutional Court. The difference in position between the Central Government and the Autonomous Community is reflected in the fact that there will be an automatic suspension of a legal provision of the Community for a maximum period of five months (article 161(2) CE), while any legal provision of the Central State can only be suspended by the Constitutional Court once it has considered the possible prejudicial

---

[52] Conflicts of power between the State and the Autonomous Communities or between the Autonomous Communities themselves (art. 161(1)(c) CE and Tit.IV LOTC).

[53] The conflict can be positive, when more than one Community or both the State and an Autonomous Community exercise a power; or negative, when none of them exercise the power.

effects of such an application, until a definitive ruling is made (article 64(3) LOTC).

The procedure of the Constitutional Court consists of an analysis of the allegations of both parties and giving a decision determining to whom the power belongs according to the Constitution and the *Estatutos de Autonomia*. The Constitutional Court will also determine what action is necessary to restore the initial positions of the parties which have been altered as a consequence of the law dictated outside the competence of one of the executive powers.

Conflictos de atribuciones[54]

This type of procedure was introduced by the LOTC, Chapter II, Title IV article 10(b) according to article 161(1)(d) CE: "The Constitutional Court has jurisdiction ... in any other matter according to the Constitution or the Organic Laws".[55] The object of this procedure is the resolution of any conflict between the organs of the State—the Executive, Parliament and the Judiciary—as to the powers that each of them enjoy and the exercise of those powers. It can only be commenced when one of these powers considers that one of the others has invaded its sphere of influence. The capacity to initiate the proceedings rests with on the Executive, the Congress, the Senate and the General Council of the Judiciary (article 59(3) LOTC). The organ which believes another organ has invaded its powers must communicate this to the "intruder", demanding the withdrawal of such intrusion. If the organ which has been requested refuses on the grounds that it has acted within its powers, then it is possible to initiate the procedure in the Constitutional Court, which will hear both powers and make a decision confirming the attribution of the disputed power and any *ultra vires* activity null and void.

There is a special type of *conflicto de atribuciones* in respect of the powers of the *Tribunal de Cuentas* regulated in article 8 LOTC which is identical to any other resolution of a conflict of powers.

---

[54] Conflicts between the Constitutional Organs of the State concerning the extent and exercise of their powers.
[55] "*El tribunal constitucional tiene jurisdicción ... las demás materias que le atribuyan la Constitución ó las leyes orgánicas*".

Chapter Four
The legal professions

1. INTRODUCTION: LEGAL EDUCATION IN SPAIN

It is necessary to have obtained the title of *licenciado en derecho*[1] in order to practice any legal trade in Spain.[2] This is obtained after completing the approved course of studies in a Law faculty. The study of law has recently been changed after nearly half a century[3] and today the old programme of studies of 1953 co-exists with the new programme, which is being gradually implemented in the different faculties. According to the old programme, everybody aiming to obtain the title of *licenciado en derecho* had to follow a compulsory programme consisting of the study and corresponding examinations of 25 compulsory law subjects, covering virtually all the branches of law. Today, the new programme is designed to offer some compulsory subjects for all universities (*materias troncales*), some compulsory subjects for each university, and some optional subjects. Each subject, according to the new plan, carries a certain number of credits and in order to obtain the title of *licenciado* the number of credits will vary from 350 to 400 depending on the University. The major innovations of the new programme were introduced in order to attain some kind of homogeneity with legal education in Europe and include the introduction of a compulsory subject called "Institutional Community Law"[4] and a *Practicum*, which is intended to offer some integrated

---

[1] Equivalent, to a certain extent, to Bachelor in Law but with certain differences because the course of studies is longer and more comprehensive than the English equivalent and amounts to a qualifying degree.
[2] Alegría Borrás, *Legal Education and Training in Tomorrow's Europe* (paper presented at a conference on Legal Education in Europe, Metz, October 1994).
[3] *Real Decreto* 1497/1987 of November 27, about "General principles common to study programmes for obtaining of official degrees in Universities" and 1424/1990 of October 26, "Principles concerning the study of programmes tending towards the obtaining of the title of *licenciado en derecho*".
[4] In the old plan of studies there was no subject called "European Community law", although the study of the institutions of European law was included in different topics—public law II, public international law and administrative law—mainly with references to substantive law where appropriate in the other subjects.

practice of law—although the content of this has not yet been developed by the different universities.

The assessment of students falls within the discretion of each university according to article 27.1 of the LO 11/1983 of August 25. There is no compulsory final exam; usually there is one final exam for each subject to be held in June of the academic year, with the possibility of resitting the examination up to a maximum of five times. Exams are oral or written depending on each department and usually each student goes through a combination of both written unseen papers and orals in the course of his degree.

Many students commence law studies in Spain but usually only a percentage complete them. The study of law in Spain is not regarded as the main step to becoming a practising lawyer,[5] in contrast with England where the majority of law students aim to become solicitors or barristers, but rather as a means of gaining a solid legal foundation in order to engage in a diverse range of legal professions or in industry or business. The term "legal profession" has, therefore, a much wider meaning than in England because not only does it refer to barristers or solicitors but to all those professionals who, holding a law degree, have any kind of involvement with legal matters. It includes: judges, *fiscales*, civil servants in different departments of the public administration, *abogados*, corporate lawyers, *procuradores*, judicial secretaries, notaries and public registrars.

It is important to note that it is not possible to practice any legal profession without the title of *licenciado en derecho* which can only be obtained by following the course of studies described above. There is no provision or possibility for graduates from other disciplines undertaking any type of "conversion course"—such as, for instance, the "Postgraduate Diploma in Law" in England—in order to qualify to start any legal profession.[6]

After obtaining the title of *licenciado en derecho* the new graduate has different possibilities if he wishes to pursue a legal career. He can register with a *Colegio de Abogados* and become a practising lawyer.[7] He can prepare for some of the public competitions in order to become a judge, a public prosecutor, a notary, a registrar or a civil servant. He can work for business or industry or engage in postgraduate studies.

Postgraduate studies in law[8] are divided into two main types; those relating to obtaining a doctorate in law and those which lead to other

---

[5] Indeed only a small percentage of law graduates became *abogados en ejercício* despite the automatic qualification they obtain.
[6] Compare with the survey on the education of solicitors in England in "Solicitors in private practice" New Law Journal (1992) pp. 833–4.
[7] See below.
[8] art. 31 *et seq*. LO 11/83 of August 26.

diplomas. Doctoral studies are regulated by the government and are delivered by the different departments of law faculties. Their aim is to provide specialisation of knowledge and training in research techniques. Studies are divided into a series of taught lectures and seminars and the presentation of a thesis on a legal topic under the approval and supervision of a university department or a scientific body, e.g. the *Consejo Superior de Investigaciones Científicas*.[9] Each department has discretion to accept students for postgraduate courses. It is usually the director of the department who makes the selection, taking into account the marks obtained during the university degree and/or any other relevant experience. When a student is accepted by a department, he is appointed a tutor who must hold a doctorate and be a member of that department. Once the student has obtained a "certificate of competence" issued by the department and submitted a thesis which is evaluated by a five-member jury, he will be allowed the title of Doctor in Law. The title of doctor is required in order to become a university lecturer either in the category of *Profesor Titular de Universidad* or *Catedrático de Universidad*.

2. *ABOGADOS*[10]

It has been pointed out by Almagro Nosete[11] that the increase in the number of laws and the application of these rules to increasingly complicated cases were the historical factors which originally led to the creation of professional courts and the need to have professionals, familiar with the complications and technicalities of the law, to stand for the rights of the parties demanding justice. This was how the *abogados* (*patroni, defensores, causidici o vozeros* in historic law) and *procuradores*, originated.

The complete defence of the parties in Spanish law consists of an *abogado* and a *procurador*. First, the profession of *abogado* will be considered and then, the role of the *procurador*.

The profession of *abogado* is a liberal and independent profession dedicated to the advice, conciliation and defence of public and private interests through the application of legal science and technique.[12] Only *abogados* can carry out the legal defence of the parties.

---

[9] High Council of Scientific Research.
[10] The term *abogados* or lawyers will be used throughout since this does not translate as either solicitors or barristers but indicates a combination of both.
[11] J. Almagro Nosete, *Instituciones de Derecho Procesal*, Tomo I (1993), p. 132.
[12] art. 8 of the *Real Decreto* 2090/1982 of July 24, by which it is approved the *Estatuto General de la Abogacía* (EA).

The denomination of *abogado* applies to a *licenciado en derecho* belonging to a *Colegio de Abogados* as a practising member, who has a professional address and professionally exercises the right of defence and direction of the parties in all types of litigation, or gives legal advice outside any proceedings.[13] *Abogados* are organised into public law corporations called *Colegios profesionales*,[14] and it is a necessary requirement to be incorporated to one of these Bars in order to practice as an *abogado*.[15] It is possible to be a member of a *Colegio de Abogados* as a non-practising lawyer if all the requirements for incorporation are met. However, according to article 9 RD 20980/1982 only practising lawyers can be called *abogados*. There are 84 *Colegios de Abogados* in Spain, one in each provincial capital and the rest in major towns. In principle it is only possible for the members of a *Colegio* to litigate in the courts in the district of each *Colegio de Abogados*, except in the case of appeals, for which it is not necessary to be a member of the *Colegio* where the appellate court has its seat. It is sufficient to present a certificate of membership of the *Colegio* of origin and to present this certification to the Dean of the new *Colegio*, who will authorise the *abogado* to practice in the courts of this area. The *abogado* will become assimilated, in terms of discipline and protection, to the members of the recipient *Colegio*.[16] The co-ordination of the different *colegios* corresponds to the *Consejo General de la Abogacía Española*. There are 97,432 *abogados* registered in the eighty-four *Colegios de Abogados*; of these, 79,490 are practising members and 22,942 are non-practising members.[17]

The following requirements must be complied with in order to become a member of a *Colegio de Abogados*. It is necessary to have Spanish nationality or nationality of any country of the European Community,[18] to have reached majority, to hold the title of *licenciado en derecho*, not to have any criminal record preventing the exercise of the profession, to pay the registration fee,[19] to join the *Mutualidad General de Previsión de*

---

[13] art. 9 RD 2090/1982 of July 24 and art. 436 *LOPJ*; see also F. Rámos Méndez, *Derecho Procesal Civil I* (1992), p. 116–20.
[14] Similar to a certain extent to the English Bars.
[15] art. 9 RD 2090/1982 of July 24, and art. 439(2) *LOPJ*.
[16] art. 22 RD 2090/1982 of July 24.
[17] According to the information provided by the *Colegio de Abogados* of Madrid.
[18] The extension to nationals of other states which are members of the European Community was brought into effect by the RD 147/1991 of February 15, in order to adapt Spanish legislation to art. 52 of the European Community Treaty, by which nationality cannot be a reason for restricting access to the legal professions. In any case this requirement can be dispensed with if all the others are complied with for nationals of non-EEC states.
[19] The amount varies from one *Colegio* to another, usually depending on the size and importance of the City; for instance in Madrid it amounts to 120,000 pesetas (approx. £600) while in other smaller cities it can be reduced to 50,000 pesetas (£250).

la Abogacía, and to obtain a licence of economic activities.

Advocacy is a liberal profession in the sense that the *abogado* gives a service without any subjection to the person to whom the service is given. It is also an intellectual profession because it encompasses the application of legal science, and it is independent because the *abogado* is only subject to the moral, deontological and technical demands of his profession.[20]

They are some circumstances in which the exercise of advocacy is forbidden. These are: any physical or mental disability which, by its nature or circumstance makes it impossible to carry out the defence of private interests; suspension or disability due to a judicial decision or disciplinary sanctions imposed by the *Colegio de Abogados*. The exercise of advocacy is also incompatible with the posts of: President of the Government, Minister, Secretary of State, Subsecretary, Director General and high positions of the public administration, *procurador*, judge, public prosecutor and judicial secretaries, Secretary of the *Consejo General de Poder Judicial*, and any other public post which expressly forbids. It is also impossible to act as *abogado* in a case where the judge is a member of the family of the *abogado* within the second degree of consanguinity. Civil servants can practice advocacy although they cannot act in cases in which the Ministry or Department where they are posted is involved.

Lawyers cannot advertise their services to the public or give free advice in professional magazines or newspapers without the authorisation of the *Junta de Gobierno* of the *Colegio* to which they belong, subject to disciplinary sanction. They are subject to a "Code of Ethics and Conduct"[21] by which they are not allowed to intervene in any case in which the defence was initially given to a colleague, without express consent.

There are no compulsory training periods to be completed in order to become an *abogado* in Spain,[22] although in practice most graduates will either join a course of legal practice in schools sponsored by the Bars or join a law firm in the unofficial category of *pasante*.[23] This situation has been an issue for a long time and during the last Congress of Spanish Lawyers (Palma de Mallorca, 1989), it was decided that law graduates

---

[20] Almagro Nosete, *op. cit.*, p. 132.
[21] The *Consejo General de la Abogacía* adopted, in September 1989, the "Code of Ethics for European Community Lawyers" approved in Strasbourg on October 28, 1988 by the Council of Bars and Law Societies of the European Community.
[22] The equivalent to a training contract in England is called "*pasantía*" in Spain.
[23] Which roughly means "trainee" but due to the lack of regulation amounts in many cases to abuses by the law firms both as to the length of time for which one is considered to be a "trainee" and to the remuneration during this period, which varies from nothing to £400 a month. In this respect it would be preferable to establish some regulation of the *pasantía* and make it a compulsory stage.

should receive practical and technical training with a final assessment of the skills acquired, before exercising the profession of *abogado*. However to date no steps have been taken to implement these aims. There are no requirements for the continuous training for *abogados*, although in practice the different Bars organise courses and seminars in various legal areas of current interest.[24]

The main duties of *abogados* are connected with their function of legal defence. *Abogados* collaborate with the administration of justice by defending the legal interests they represent. They have duties towards their clients, their colleagues and the courts. Their remunerations are not subject to any fixed fee and they enjoy the benefit of a special proceeding for the payment of their fees regulated by article 12 of the *LEC*.[25] The *Colegios de Abogados* publish indicative guidelines about legal fees, but each *abogado* is free to fix these. However, it is forbidden to fix the fees as a percentage of the amount obtained in the proceedings—*pacto de quota litis* or contingent fees (article 56(1) *EA*).[26] This prohibition also extends to the so-called *pacto palmario*, by which the *abogado* obtains a fee superior to the one originally fixed if he wins the case. The respective *Colegio de Abogados* will sanction any of these practices.

All practising lawyers belonging to a *Colegio de Abogados* have a duty to give free legal advice to those entitled to legal aid.[27] This is called *turno de oficio*. Also, in criminal cases outside the scope of legal aid, all the *abogados* have the duty to defend any person who so requests. If the services are given to somebody entitled to legal aid, the State will compensate the *abogado* for his services; if the person to whom services are given is not entitled to legal aid the duty solicitor has the right to demand payment on his normal terms from the beginning of the case. For important criminal cases,[28] there is a special *turno de oficio* available to those *abogados* with at least five years experience.[29]

Article 10 of the *LEC*[30] prescribes the compulsory intervention of *abogado* in all types of proceedings except in acts of conciliation, oral proceedings, acts of voluntary jurisdiction or the adoption of urgent measures. In all other cases the signature of an *abogado* is a requisite to

---

[24] See B.M. Cremades, "La formación continua del abogado" *La Ley*, October 12, 1993.
[25] The *abogado* and also the *procurador* can, if their client refuses to pay, present a note with their fees to the court which will order enforcement of the debt.
[26] The prohibition originated in Roman and canon law and was introduced by the Historic Law in Spain: *Fuero Real*; *Las Partidas* and *Novísima Recopilación*; it was later forgotten by the *LO* of 1870 but reintroduced by the *Estatuto de la Abogacía* of 1946.
[27] art. 57 of the *EA*. See also Chap. 5, "Legal Aid", p. 155.
[28] Those for which the punishment can be of six or more years imprisonment.
[29] art. 58(3) *EA*.
[30] *Ley de Enjuiciamiento Civil* of 1882.

the acceptance of the claim by the court. In criminal proceedings the assistance of an *abogado* is compulsory.

Spanish law firms—*bufetes*—are usually specialised. They are much smaller than English law firms although there is a tendency in big cities to establish larger practices. There is no differentiation between associates and partners, although in practice, there is a hierarchy between different *abogados* of the same firm, especially in larger ones, based on experience and professional standing. The *Estatuto de la Abogacía* makes provision for what are called *despachos colectivos*.[31] *Despachos colectivos* are formed by a maximum of twenty *abogados*, all of whom must be members of the same *Colegio*. They are based on the collaboration of all members in every case and shared liability. These *despachos* are organised in partnership and have their own regulations which must be authorised by the *Colegio de Abogados*. The members of any of these *despachos colectivos* can not have an independent professional address. A *despacho colectivo* is different from the situation in which several lawyers share the same premises with individual practices and no collaboration or shared liability.

EUROPEAN COMMUNITY LAWYERS

The Treaty of Rome—articles 59 and 60—recognised the free rendering of services and unrestricted establishment for professionals of the different Member States of the Community. The Directive 77/249, which established the basis for the implementation of this right, was adopted in Spain by the *Real Decreto* 607/1986 of March 21, and the *Real Decreto* 1062/1988[32] of September 16. In order for a European lawyer to exercise the free rendering of services in Spain it is required that he is qualified for the exercise of advocacy in the country of origin, that he is introduced to the president or dean of the *Colegio de Abogados* where he intends to render the service and that he co-operates with a lawyer registered with the local *Colegio de Abogados*. There is a limit on the number of appearances in the Spanish Courts for such a lawyer, which cannot be of more than five in a year for collegiate courts and ten for unipersonal courts and administrative offices.

As to the freedom of establishment, recognised in article 60 of the Treaty of Rome, the Community has adopted a system of recognition of university-level degrees. The Directive 89/48 recognising university degrees was introduced in Spain by the *Real Decreto* 1665/1991 of

---

[31] Collective offices.
[32] Which introduced the modifications of the Directive 77/249 based on the decision of the European Court of Justice of February 25, 1988.

October 25. This established that degrees can be recognised in two ways: by an examination in the country in which the lawyer wants to be established or by acquiring professional experience in that country. For law degrees the country where the lawyer wants to establish his practice has a choice as to which system should be adopted. Spain has adopted the system of an aptitude test; once this is passed the lawyer can be incorporated into one of the Spanish *Colegios de Abogados*.

3. *PROCURADORES*

Procuradores are lawyers who represent[33] the parties in court and other official departments through a power of attorney given by the person requiring their services. They also collaborate with the *abogado* through the reception and communication of documents received by the court. Their profession is defined as a liberal and independent profession and is regulated by the *Estatuto General de Procuradores de los Tribunales*, approved by *RD* 2046/1982 of June 30, and the *RD* 1030/1985 of June 5, by which their fees are fixed. *Procuradores* are organised in *Colegios de Procuradores*, which are public law entities governed by the *Consejo General de Ilustres Colegios de Procuradores de los Tribunales de España*. In order to register in one of these *Colegios* it is necessary to have Spanish nationality, to have reached the age of majority, to hold the title of *licenciado en derecho* and to have obtained the title of *procurador*, which is given by the Ministry of Justice once applicants have fulfilled the other requirements. They also have to pay the required fee and join the *Mutualidad de Previsión de los Procuradores de los Tribunales de España*; deposit a bond and swear an oath to the Court where they are intending to practice.

The intervention of *procurador* is compulsory in civil proceedings with the exception of those proceedings mentioned in article 3 *LEC*.[34] In criminal proceedings their intervention is always compulsory.

In order to act as a *procurador* it is necessary to have a power of attorney—*poder suficiente*—given by the client, which enables the *procurador* to act as the legal representative of the client. Historically, the client approached the *procurador*, gave him a power of attorney and advanced some money for starting the proceedings, leaving to the *procurador* the choice of the *abogado*. Today the practice is different because clients approach their *abogados* first and usually these appoint a *procurador*.

---

[33] As distinct from *abogados* who advise and defend their clients.
[34] See above for cases in which the intervention of *abogados* is not compulsory.

Procuradores are subject to similar incompatibilities as *abogados* and they have civil, criminal and disciplinary responsibilities in the exercise of their profession. Since the distinction between *abogados* and *procuradores* does not exist in all E.C. countries, the E.C. regulations for freedom of establishment and rendering of services apply to both these professionals.

4. REPRESENTATION AND DEFENCE OF THE STATE: *ABOGADOS DEL ESTADO*

The representation and defence of the State, its constitutional organs and the Administration, corresponds to the *Cuerpo de Letrados del Estado*.[35] In some cases it is possible to give the legal defence of the State, or organs mentioned above, to a private practitioner specially designated for this task (article 447(1) *LO* 6/1985 of July 1).

This body of lawyers is dependent on the Ministry of Justice and it is composed of legal professionals who hold a law degree and join this body by passing a competitive examination consisting of both theoretical and practical exercises on legal matters. These lawyers represent the State and the Administration in all legal proceedings and also advise the Autonomous Communities.[36]

5. *JUECES Y MAGISTRADOS*

Access to a judicial career is based on a distinction between three types of judges[37]: *Magistrados del Tribunal Supremo*,[38] *Magistrados*[39] and *Jueces*[40] (article 299 *LOPJ*). All members of the judiciary are covered by these categories including civil registrars. With the exception of the *Jueces de Paz*, who are appointed by the *Consejo General del Poder Judicial* following a proposal by the municipal authorities, all other judges and

---

[35] Apto 1,4 of the *DA* 9 of the *Ley* 23/1988 of June 28, changed the name to *Letrados de Estado* from *Abogados de Estado*".
[36] They are regulated by *Ley* 30/1984 of August 2—*ley de reforma de la función pública*; *RD* 2169/1985 of November 27, and *RD* 849/1985 of June 5.
[37] Alegría Borrás, *op. cit.*, p. 10.
[38] Judges of the Supreme Court.
[39] Judges sitting in higher courts.
[40] All other judges; used in general to designate both *Magistrados* and *jueces*.

magistrates hold a law degree. *Jueces de Paz* have very limited functions in minor civil and criminal cases.[41]

There are two ways of becoming a judge, either by passing a competitive examination[42]—*turno normal*—set by the *Centro de Estudios Judiciales*, taking the courses and final examination also set by the *Centro de Estudios Judiciales*, or by selective competition amongst lawyers of recognised standing with at least six years of private practice. For each four places, three are reserved for the *turno normal* and one for an applicant selected by competitive entry. The entrance exam consists of three different examinations. Failure of one of them leads to exclusion. Two of the examinations are theoretical and one is practical. The examinations cover General Theory of the Law, Constitutional Law, Civil Law, Criminal Law, Commercial Law, Administrative Law and Civil and Criminal Procedure. Once the examination has been passed and the candidate has completed the course offered by the *Centro de Estudios Judiciales* and its assessment requirements, the *Consejo General del Poder Judicial* can award the title of Judge.[43]

There are three ways of becoming a *Magistrado*. A third of the places are filled by the judges who are highest in the hierarchy, a third by way of competitive examinations amongst judges, and a third is reserved for practising lawyers of recognised standing with at least 10 years of professional experience.

There are two ways in which to become a *Magistrado* of the Supreme Court.[44] For each five posts, four are filled by those members of the Judiciary who have held the position of magistrate for at least 10 years and have been members of the Judiciary for at least 20 years. The candidate for the fifth post is elected from among lawyers of recognised standing with at least 20 years of practice in the area of law of the chamber of the Supreme Court to which they are appointed.[45]

The continual training of judges is actively organised by the *Consejo General del Poder Judicial* with provincial and local training schemes, and is adapted to the needs of the members of the Judiciary. This training is voluntary.

Judges enjoy a special status in order to guarantee the proper performance of their duties in administering justice. They are independent, irremovable and subject only to the law (article 117 CE). Their independence must be respected by all citizens and public powers. If a judge feels that his independence is being threatened he will inform the *CGPJ*

---

[41] See sections on *Juicio Oral* and *Jueces de Paz* in Chap. 5.
[42] For which it is necessary to hold a law degree.
[43] Alegría Borrás, *op. cit.*, p. 10.
[44] The highest post in judicial hierarchy.
[45] These Chambers are civil, criminal, administrative or social.

who will then take the necessary measures. The independence of judges, which is necessary for the rightful application of the law, is also guaranteed by establishing two procedures by which a judge can be required or voluntarily abstain from resolving a case due to personal or professional connections with the parties involved or with the subject-matter. These are known as *abstención* and *recusación* and are regulated in article 219 LOPJ.

Judges can be held civilly, criminally and disciplinary responsible in the exercise of their functions and are subject to a strict regime of incompatibilities in order to guarantee their independence in the application of the law. Judges can only be dismissed, transferred, suspended or forced to retire according to the terms provided by law. The independence of judges from other powers, especially from the Government, is achieved by providing the judiciary with a system of self-government: the *Consejo General del Poder Judicial*.[46] Judges in Spain are anonymous in the sense that they do not enjoy the publicity that they do in England. Decisions are not published with the name of the judge. However, a recent phenomenon has appeared in Spanish society mainly linked to the big scandals of political corruption which have shocked public opinion. This is known as the *superjueces*[47] by which certain judges, mainly the ones of the *Audiencia Nacional* in charge of special crimes and political corruption, have become national heroes and are well known by the public due to extensive media coverage of notorious trials, in particular the ones involving Members of Parliament and Government.[48]

Together with the judges and magistrate members of the judicial career, there are also other judges known as *jueces temporales*. These temporary judges are not members of the Judiciary although they can give judgments. Temporary personnel are divided between *Magistrados Suplentes* and *Jueces de Provisión Temporal*.

The *Magistrados Suplentes* are appointed in exceptional circumstances when it is impossible to appoint a *Magistrado de Carrera*[49] (article 200 LOPJ). They are selected from among the members of a list drafted by the CGPJ. The office of *Magistrado Suplente* is an honorary post, even if remunerated. These can only be selected from those who fulfil the requirements to enter the Judiciary, with preference being given to persons who have performed judicial or academic functions in the past.[50]

---

[46] See above, Chap. 3, p. 79.
[47] Literally "Super-Judges".
[48] Names of judges like Baltasar Garzón, Marino Barbero, Marinas, Ana Ferrer, are common knowledge as public opinion follows big cases of political corruption due to the extensive media coverage.
[49] This is a professional judge, a member of the Judiciary.
[50] It is common to appoint university professors specialised in the area that the *Magistrado Suplente* has to cover.

The *jueces de provisión temporal* are appointed by the *Tribunal Superior de Justicia*, giving preferences to those who are doctors in law, who have passed the competitive exams for other legal careers,[51] or who have had academic experience. They can be nominated for a year with the possibility of extension for a further year. The post is remunerated.

6. SECRETARIOS JUDICIALES

In the second rank of importance according to their function in the administration of justice and just below judges, are the *Secretarios Judiciales*.[52] This body of law graduates is in charge of running the courts and has the task of directing the *Oficina Judicial* and organising the proceedings.

Secretarios de Justicia hold a law degree and have passed a competitive entry examination and a course organised by the *Centro de Estudios Judiciales*. They are attached to the Ministry of Justice[53] and assist the judges in the administration of justice. They are subject to a similar regime of incompatibilities as judges, with the exception that secretaries can participate as candidates in local elections.[54]

Their functions fall mainly under the heading of assisting judges in the function of administering justice. They have custody of all documentation, depositions and any objects connected with the judicial proceedings; they keep all books and records of the judicial activities of the Court; they also practice all notifications and communications related to the proceedings. The *Secretarios Judicales* are in charge of the *Oficina Judicial* and exercise direct control over all the auxiliaries[55] of the judge. As is the case with judges, *Secretarios Judiciales* are subject to civil, criminal and disciplinary liability.

7. FISCALES[56]

Fiscales, according to the Constitution are in charge of upholding the law and ensuring the application of justice by defending the rights of

---

[51] For instance Civil Servants.
[52] Court Clerks. Their status, functions and duties are regulated by the *LOPJ* arts. 472 to 483 and RD 429/88 of April 29, approving the *Reglamento Orgánico de Secretarios Judiciales*.
[53] They are, therefore, a part of the Public Administration compared to judges who are ingrated within the Judicial Power.
[54] From which judges are precluded.
[55] See below.
[56] Public Prosecutors.

citizens, the public interest and the independence of the courts (article 124 CE[57]).

The *Ministerio Fiscal* has independent means for the performance of these functions. It operates through different agencies.[58] The most important authority of the *Ministerio Fiscal* is the *Fiscal General del Estado* nominated by the King and elected by the Government following consultation with the *Consejo General del Poder Judicial*.[59]

In order to be a member of the *Carrera Fiscal*, it is necessary to hold a degree in law and to pass a competitive entry examination very similar to the examination which must be passed by judges. Their place in the hierarchy, honours and remuneration are similar to those of judges and they are subject to the same civil, criminal and disciplinary liability and have the same rights of independence and irremovability.

Within its main function of "upholding the law and ensuring the application of justice" the *Ministerio Fiscal* intervenes in a variety of proceedings. It is in charge of the civil and criminal actions arising as a consequence of the commission of a criminal offence, intervenes in all proceedings concerning the civil status of natural persons and in the defence of the legality in proceedings involving those subject to guardianship, ensuring respect of their rights. It also intervenes in proceedings of the Constitutional Court[60] and in any proceedings involving the infringement of fundamental rights of citizens. Recently its functions have been expanded in criminal proceedings by the LO 7/88,[61] which confers limited capacity for investigations on the public prosecution, beyond its traditional function of guaranteeing the rights of the suspect and the victim and the application of the law.[62]

---

[57] art. 124 CE: "El Ministerio fiscal ... tine por misión promover la accion de la justicia en defensa de la legalidad de los derechos e los ciudadanos y del interés público tutelado por la Ley, de oficio o a petición de los interesados, asi como velar por la independencia de os tribunales y procurar ante estos la satisfacción del interés social".
[58] These agencies are: *el Fiscal General del Estado, el Consejo Fiscal, la Junta de Fiscales de Sala, la Fiscalía del Tribunal Supremo, la Fiscalía de Tribunal Constitucional, la Fiscala de la Audiencia Nacional, las Fiscalías de los Tribunales Superiores de Justicia de las Comunidades Autonomas, las Fiscalias de las Audiencias Territoriales.*
[59] See Chap. 3, p. 95.
[60] *ibid.*
[61] See Chap. 6.
[62] See Chap. 3, p. 95 and Chap. 6, p. 160.

8. AUXILIARY PERSONNEL IN THE ADMINISTRATION OF JUSTICE

OFICIALES, AUXILARES Y AGENTES[63]

There are other civil servants within the Ministry of Justice whose work supports that of judges, magistrates and public prosecutors in the administration of justice. These are the *oficiales, auxiliaries* and *agentes*. They are in charge of the day to day running of the courts or agencies to which they are attached and their functions are administrative. They do not need to hold a law degree and they are civil servants of "Grade B" or "C" depending on whether they have primary or secondary education. Entry is by means of a competitive examination.

POLICÍA JUDICIAL

The judicial police is not a separate body from the general police but includes all those members of the police force who are directly under the orders of the courts and the *Ministerio Fiscal* (article 126 CE). According to the *LOPJ* (article 443 to 445) the functions of the judicial police can be summarised as providing assistance to the courts of justice and the *Ministerio Fiscal* in the investigation of crimes and the search for criminals. This is a duty of all members of the police force but the judicial police specifically assist the courts in any situation which requires the use of force or public coercion.[64]

OTHER TECHNICAL AUXILIARIES OF THE ADMINISTRATION OF JUSTICE

These are professionals from different disciplines who assist the courts in their role of administering justice. The common feature of all of them is that they are experts in different areas of knowledge at the service of the administration of justice. Some of them are civil servants and others are independent professionals.

Forensic doctors have a wide input in criminal cases. They determine the time and causes of death and give a report in all cases involving offences against physical integrity. They are appointed by the State.

Doctors of the Civil Registry provide reports for all those cases concerning the civil status of individuals, for instance in the ascertainment of birth or death.

Translators and interpreters make official translations of foreign docu-

---

[63] Officials, auxiliaries and agents.
[64] For more detail see Chap. 6, pp. 167 *et seq*.

ments and verify private translations. They also provide an interpretation service when one of the parties to the proceedings requires this.

The Institute of Toxicology, which is part of the Ministry of Justice, provides all the required information in this area (article 505 *LOPJ*).

The National Institute of Medicine and Security in the Workplace, advises the Social Courts on specific areas related to security and hygiene in the workplace.

9. CIVIL SERVANTS

The highest category in the civil service, Grade "A", is open only to graduates including, but not exclusively, law graduates. A large proportion of the graduates holding a title of *Licenciado en Derecho* will prepare for the competitive exams in order to become civil servants, partly due to the difficulties in securing employment nowadays. This category of higher civil servants includes diplomats who must pass a competitive examination requiring a university degree and perfect knowledge of at least two foreign languages. The subject matter of this examination covers topics of law and politics, current affairs and general knowledge. A large proportion of the members of the Diplomatic Service are, in fact, law graduates. After passing the examinations the successful candidate must take a course in the *Escuela Diplomática* and obtain a certificate of completion. After that they become members of the diplomatic corps and enjoy all the related privileges and dignities. They can take postings abroad and occupy one of the posts at the Ministry of External Affairs.

Certain bodies of the administration do require a degree in law; these are the *Cuerpo de Letrados del Tribunal Constitucional*, *Letrados de las Cortes* and *Abogados del Estado*.

10. NOTARIOS

Notarios are legal professionals whose function consists in conferring authenticity on documents by which the parties effect different legal transactions. This function is exclusive to them and the documents drafted by them enjoy a presumption of authenticity; that is, their content is presumed to be the truth unless falsity is proved in the corresponding criminal proceeding.

The profession of *notario* has a dual nature in Spain. On one hand, *notarios* have a delegated power from the State and they perform a public service—the authentication of documents. In this respect the number of notaries is *numerus clausus*, their fees are fixed and they are subject to various rules of conduct and competence which assimilates them to civil servants. On the other hand, *notarios* are liberal professionals who exercise an independent activity giving advice[65] to the parties on the drafting of private documents. However, even when providing legal advice *notarios* have a very different role from *abogados* since they are impartial and do not act on behalf of any of the parties. What a *notario* attempts to do is to explain the legal consequences of the documents that the parties want to have drafted.

Notarios are dependent on the Ministry of Justice and belong to professional bodies—*Colegios de Notarios*—presided over by the *Consejo Superior del Notariado*. The *Consejo Superior del Notariado* is at the head of all the notaries' associations and performs a function similar to that of the *Consejo General de la Abogacía*, that is, it represents the interests of notaries, drafts guidelines for practice and liaises with other legal bodies. *Notarios* are independent in the exercise of their functions and are subject to civil, criminal and disciplinary liability in the same way as any other legal professionals.

The delegation of powers from the State means that the principle of freedom of establishment of articles 52 *et seq.* of the *TCEE* justifies the application of the exception contained in article 55 *TCEE*.

In order to be awarded a *Notaría* (the office of a *notario*) it is necessary to hold a degree in law and to pass a competitive examination, traditionally regarded as being very difficult both in terms of the actual examination and as regards the tough competition for the few places of *notario* available. Once the examination has been successfully passed the new notary will be asked to deposit a bond or security and will be granted a licence and appointed to a specific office. There are three types of *Notarías* depending on the population of the town where the *notario* has been appointed.

The functions of *notarios* are regulated by the *Ley del Notariado* of May 28, 1862 and the *Reglamento Notarial* of June 2, 1994 (modified by *RD* 1209/1984 of June 8, and *RD* 1728/1991 of November 29.

Since the concept of authentic documents or "public faith" is unknown to common law lawyers, this concept may be explained by the function performed by the *notario* throughout the legal system. Legal certainty, in the sense of the possibility given to citizens to foresee the consequences of their acts, is of foremost importance in civil law systems.

---

[65] *Notarios* can give legal advice in any area. However, they are precluded from exercising the representation and defence of clients in courts, which is reserved for *abogados* and *procuradores*.

This is achieved by a variety of means including the establishment of the sources of law, the principle of legality, the publicity of the laws, the subjection of the judge to the established sources and, as Rodriguez Pinero[66] suggests, by the existence of professionals—*notarios*—who prevent conflicts by conferring certainty on the documents that they authorise. In conferring authenticity to documents notaries must comply with several requirements.

Public documents are those authorised by a *notario*, they are presumed to represent the truth and, therefore, they can constitute *títulos ejecutivos*.[67] This is achieved by subjecting the activities of notaries to certain principles.[68] The first of these is the principle of "authorship of the document". The *notario* drafts the document once the parties have declared their intentions and the parties later express their agreement with the document.[69] These documents are drafted according to the principles established in notarial regulations (*Ley del Notariado* and *Reglamento del Notariado*), that is, according to article 147 of the *Reglamento Notarial*, by listening to each of the parties, giving legal form to the intentions of the parties and informing each of them of the consequences of what is being drafted. In doing all this the *notario* is impartial. Whilst *abogados* advise their clients and protect their interests, notaries, given their dual public and private function, act in the interests of both parties and the Law. Once a document has been drafted, the notary keeps the original which becomes a "Protocol" from which he can issue a copy to the parties if they so request. The *Protocolo Notarial* is secret—article 274 of the *Reglamento Notarial*—and the possibility of obtaining copies is carefully regulated in order to avoid forgeries, alterations or obliterations and even loss of the document.

The intervention of a *notario* is required by law in a number of transactions: transfer of real estate, constitution of companies, donations between spouses, contracts determining or altering the economic consequences of marriage, mortgages, creation of easements and declaration of heirs (article 1280 CC).

---

[66] In Vol. "*La fé pública*", *Jornadas organizadas por el Ministerio de Justicia y el Consejo Superior del Notariado*, Madrid, 1994; cited by A. Gomez-Martinho Faerna, "*La situación y la organización del notariado en los paises miembros de la Union Europea*" LA LEY, n. 3775, (May 9, 1995).
[67] They are "enforceable". See Chap. 5.
[68] See Jose-Maria de Prada, "*La forma de los actos jurídicos privados y la seguridad jurídica*" *Seminario sobre Seguridad Jurídica* (1990); cited in detail in Augusto Gomez-Martinho Faerna, *op. cit.*, p. 2.
[69] art. 1216 CC, art. 1 of the *Ley del Notariado* and art. 2 of the *Reglamento del Notariado*.

THE LEGAL PROFESSIONS

```
                    ┌──────────────┐
                    │ PROCURADORES │
                    └──────────────┘
                           ↑
                    ┌──────────────┐
                    │  PRACTICE    │
                    │   OF LAW     │
                    └──────────────┘
                      ↑       ↓
                    ┌──────────────┐
                    │   ABOGADOS   │
                    └──────────────┘
                      ↑
┌──────────┐        ┌──────────────┐        ┌──────────┐
│ DEGREE   │───────→│    ENTRY     │───────→│ DIPLOMATS│
│  IN LAW  │        │ EXAMINATION  │        └──────────┘
└──────────┘        │      +       │        ┌──────────┐
                    │   TRAINING   │───────→│  CIVIL   │
                    └──────────────┘        │ SERVANTS │
                      ↓       ↓             └──────────┘
                                            ┌──────────┐
                    ┌──────────────┐        │ NOTARIES │
                    │     Ph D     │        └──────────┘
                    └──────────────┘        ┌──────────┐
                           ↑                │ JUDGES & │
                    ┌──────────────┐        │PROSECUTORS│
                    │ POSTGRADUATE │        └──────────┘
                    │   STUDIES    │
                    └──────────────┘
                           ↓
                    ┌──────────────┐
                    │  MASTERS &   │
                    │   OTHERS     │
                    └──────────────┘
```

Chapter Five
Civil procedure

1. GENERAL CHARACTERISTICS

INQUISITORIAL AND ADVERSARIAL PROCEEDINGS

There are two models of procedures in legal and comparative history: inquisitorial and adversarial proceedings. In the inquisitorial model the judge controls the proceedings and the parties passively await a decision of the judge. Inquisitorial proceedings are written—as a guarantee of protection for the parties from the great powers of the instructing judge— and secret. They are usually open to review by a different court. Adversarial proceedings, on the other hand, are based on the existence of a duality of parties who stand in a position of "contradiction". These parties are in control of the proceedings from beginning to end and can terminate the proceedings at any point by amicable settlement. The judge is a spectator—though a qualified one—of the activity of the parties. The choice between a procedure based mainly on one or other model depends primarily on the subject-matter of the dispute, although the history of different legal systems has an undoubted influence. In most cases, however, the actual proceedings have elements of both the inquisitorial and adversarial models.

Together with these two models there are two main principles according to which judicial proceedings can be organised: the "dispositive principle" (*principio dispositivo*) and the "principle of officiality" (*principio de oficialidad*). In all proceedings inspired by the "dispositive principle" there are two parties in a position of "contradiction"; these parties have full powers over their substantive and procedural rights. The plaintiff[1] brings proceedings against the other party, the defendant.[2] Both plaintiff and defendant have equal rights of audience and equal opportunities for the protection of their rights; they can present any evidence they think relevant and have the right to end the proceedings because these are only an instrument for the protection of substantive rights that can be disposed of at any time.

---

[1] In Spanish the plaintiff is called *actor* or *demandante*.
[2] *Demandado*.

In proceedings inspired by the "principle of officiality" the judge is under the obligation to initiate the proceedings, ensuring compliance with all the necessary requirements and carrying the proceedings through to a conclusion. Whilst, in order to implement the "dispositive principle", it is necessary to have a procedure based on the adversarial model, it is not strictly necessary to have an inquisitorial procedure in all proceedings inspired by the "principle of officiality". This is the case in Spanish judicial proceedings, which are inspired by both the "officiality" and "dispositive principle" and which incorporate elements of the inquisitorial and adversarial models.

Spanish civil proceedings are adversarial and mainly based on the "dispositive principle" according to which the partes are in control of the proceedings, however, there are some elements derived from the "principle of officiality" especially since the reform of the *Ley* 10/1984, by which the judge has to ensure *ex officio* that he has jurisdiction (article 74 *LEC*) and that the right type of proceeding has been started (article 694 *LEC*). If not, he can declare the proceedings null (article 240(2) *LOPJ*).

Spanish criminal proceedings, while based on the "principle of officiality", incorporate elements of both inquisitorial and adversarial proceedings. In the standard criminal procedure[3] there is an initial stage—*sumario ó fase de instrucción*—which is clearly inquisitorial, written and secret; the judge has wide powers of investigation although this judge is different from the judge giving the judgment. The second stage of the proceedings—*fase de plenario ó juicio oral*—is, however, oral, public and contradictory. In criminal proceedings the subject-matter of the proceedings is beyond the control of the parties. The judge can, and must, start the proceedings *ex officio* once there is enough evidence of the commission of a crime. Even in the second stage, or *juicio oral*, the parties do not have the power to terminate the proceedings[4] because the Public Prosecutor has the obligation to prosecute in all cases prescribed by law.

ORALITY AND WRITTEN PROCEEDINGS

Article 120 of the Spanish Constitution states that "the proceedings will mainly be oral".[5] This general provision is complemented by article 229(1) *LOPJ* which contains a similar declaration.[6] If Spanish judicial

---

[3] The *Juicio por delitos graves*, see below, Chap. 6, p. 166.
[4] See below, Chap. 6, p. 158.
[5] art. 120 CE: "*El procedimiento será predominantemente oral, sobre todo en materia criminal.*"
[6] art. 229(1) *LOPJ*: "*las actuaciones judiciales serán predominantemente orales, sobre todo en materia criminal, sin perjuicio de la documentación*".

proceedings are examined both statements seem to be a declaration of intention which can indeed guide the legislator in future reforms but little more, because most Spanish proceedings are written.[7] What the Constitution seems to indicate is that proceedings should be public, and publicity has historically been connected with orality. Article 24 CE recognises the right to a "public hearing" as a guarantee for the defendant without precluding that some activities may be carried out in secret, if necessary, for the security of one of the parties or society.

2. SOURCES OF CIVIL PROCEDURE

The main source of civil procedure in Spain is the *Ley de Enjuiciamiento Civil (LEC)* of 1881; this regulation has been criticised by some writers[8] because it was basically constructed around the long and mainly written "common procedure" of Spanish historical law.[9] However, despite numerous reforms it is still applicable. The main reform to the *LEC* is the *Ley 34/1984* of August 6, by which it was intended to start the transformation of Spanish civil proceedings towards a more modern model, adapted to the changes in circumstances and social demands. Other modifications were introduced by the *Ley 10/1992* of April 30 *de Medidas Urgentes de Reforma Procesal*, which was mainly directed at better resourcing of the administration of justice and had minor consequences for the regulation of the different civil proceedings.

Together with the *LEC*, the basic law on civil—and any type—of procedures, is the *Ley Orgánica del Poder Judicial, LO 6/1985* of July 1 which has important provisions affecting the organisation of the Judiciary and principles of procedure. This has been developed by the *Ley 38/1988 de demarcación y planta judicial* and the *RD 122/1989* of February 3.

3. INTERNATIONAL JURISDICTION OF THE SPANISH COURTS

Jurisdiction is the authority which a court has to decide matters that are litigated before it or to take cognisance of matters presented in a

---

[7] Only in employment litigation is there a clear prevalence of orality.
[8] See J. Almagro Nosete, *op. cit.*, pp. 34 and 35.
[9] See above, Chap. 1, p. 11.

formal way for its decision.[10] From the point of view of anybody considering starting judicial proceedings, the first question which should be asked is: does the court have jurisdiction? When considering the international jurisdiction of the Spanish courts, the question of whether or not the Spanish Courts have jurisdiction to hear a specific matter is the first step in order to determine the appropriate court in which lodge the case.

In principle each country is free to decide which cases its courts are going to be competent to hear and to decide. This is a matter to be regulated by domestic law. However, even if each country is free to decide virtually any case litigated in its courts, it does not mean that this is the best option in terms of policy because it might be inappropriate to overload the courts with cases which have little or no connection with the country. Different countries have approached the question of international jurisdiction following different policy principles; England, for instance, has a wide scope of international jurisdiction by which the courts of England and Wales are competent to hear and decide virtually any case served on a defendant present in England: "whoever is served with the King's writ and can be compelled consequently to submit to the decree made is a person over whom the courts have jurisdiction".[11] Courts in other countries, for instance France, have international jurisdiction in any case involving a French national.[12] The Spanish law on international jurisdiction was substantially changed in 1986 with the establishment of a system based on the Brussels Convention[13] criteria on international jurisdiction.

To some extent it seems only good sense to limit jurisdiction to those cases in which an eventual decision can be executed in the national territory. This is why different countries impose upon themselves certain limits in the exercise of jurisdiction by their own courts. These limits are usually established in two ways, by international bilateral or multinational Conventions and by domestic rules of private international law on jurisdiction. Together with this, it is important to add the exceptions to the jurisdiction of a country's courts imposed by public international law in the form of "immunity from jurisdiction" for Heads of State and diplomatic personnel. This exception is specifically made in the *LOPJ* article 21(2). This immunity from jurisdiction covers foreign states—*par in parem non habet imperium*—although in public international law there is a distinction between acts of the state as a state and its com-

---

[10] Mozley & Whitley's *Law Dictionary* (10th ed., 1988).
[11] *John Russell & Co Ltd v. Cayzer, Irveine and Co Ltd* [1916] 2 A.C. 298 at 302, HL.
[12] Art. 14 of the French Civil Code.
[13] Brussels Convention on Jurisdiction and Enforcement of Judgements in Civil and Commercial Matters 1968. See below.

mercial acts as a private person.[14] The most important treaties concerning the immunity of foreign personnel are the Vienna Convention on Diplomatic Relations 1961, the Vienna Convention on Consular Relations 1963 and the Convention on Special Missions 1969.

The most important multilateral agreements limiting the jurisdiction of the Spanish courts are the Warsaw Convention on International Air Transport 1929, the Geneva Convention on Carriage of Goods by Road 1956, the Convention Relating to the Arrest of Sea-Going Ships of 1952, and the Brussels Convention on Liability for Oil Pollution Damage of 1969. These conventions confer jurisdiction on a certain state to hear and adjudicate certain matters and so deprive all other member states which are signatories to the convention of any jurisdiction.

Spain is also party to a large number of bilateral agreements on jurisdiction, the main object of which are to facilitate the execution of decisions in the two countries which are signatories to the treaties by establishing rules on international jurisdiction.[15]

However, and without diminishing the importance of any of these conventions, the most important convention in terms of international jurisdiction is the Brussels Convention of September 17, 1968 on International Jurisdiction and Recognition of Decisions in Civil and Commercial Matters (hereinafter Brussels Convention or BC), and the Lugano Convention which is a parallel convention to the Brussels Convention, between EC/EFTA countries.[16]

It is possible to suggest that the world is now divided into two groups of countries as to jurisdictional effects (in the international context): those countries which are party to the Brussels and/or Lugano Conventions and those which are not. In certain circumstances in civil and commercial cases (article 1 BC),[17] the Brussels and Lugano Conventions substitute the national private international law rules on jurisdiction. These circumstances are, namely when a defendant is domiciled in a state which is a member to the Convention, in certain exclusive jurisdiction areas (article 16 BC), and in jurisdiction agreements with some connecting factors (article 17 BC). If these connecting factors are not

---

[14] See amongst others M. N. Shaw, *International Law* (1991) pp. 430–80 for a detailed study on immunities from jurisdiction in public international law.

[15] There are bilateral treaties with France: *Convenio de 28 de mayo de 1969*, with Colombia: *Convenio de 30 de mayo de 1908*; with Italy: *Convenio de 22 de mayo de 1973*; with Germany: *Convenio de 14 de Noviembre de 1983*; with Austria: *Convenio de 17 de febrero de 1984*; with Czechoslovakia: *Convenio de 4 de mayo de 1987*; with Israel: *Convenio de 30 de mayo de 1989*; with Mexico: *Convenio de 17 de abril de 1991*.

[16] See Peter North, *Private International Law* (12th ed., 1992) pp. 180–1.

[17] See Case 29/76, *LTV v. Eurocontrol*: [1976] E.C.R. 1541 and P. North, *op. cit.*, pp. 286–8, as to the meaning of civil and commercial matters.

present or if the country is not a party to the Conventions it is up to the law of any country to decide when and in what circumstances they are going to hear and decide a case.

The *LOPJ* 1985 sets out in detail, in article 21–5, the matters over which the Spanish courts have international jurisdiction. The general rule is that Spanish courts have jurisdiction over persons domiciled in Spain and/or where there is submission to the Spanish courts (article 22(2) *LOPJ*). Submission can be express, that is, by agreement to submit any dispute to the Spanish courts, or tacit, by the parties appearing and contesting the case on its merits. Regardless of the above criteria, Spanish courts retain exclusive jurisdiction over matters involving real rights, incorporation, validity and dissolution of companies domiciled in Spanish territory, the validity of entries on public registers, the recognition and execution of foreign judgments and arbitration awards (article 22(1) *LOPJ*). In these instances of exclusive jurisdiction, the nationality or domicile of the parties is totally irrelevant; also, because this competence is exclusive, no decision affecting these matters which is given by a foreign court will be enforced in Spain.

Spanish courts also retain jurisdiction over matters such as contracts made in Spain (between Spaniards, between foreigners or between Spaniards and foreigners) or when Spain is the place of performance of the contractual obligation; in extra-contractual obligations, when the tort was committed in Spain or both author and victim have their habitual residence in Spain; in succession matters when the deceased had his last domicile in Spain or immovable property in the country (article 22(3)).[18]

In criminal matters Spanish courts have jurisdiction over all crimes committed within Spanish territory and over specific crimes committed by Spanish citizens abroad. In administrative matters Spanish courts have jurisdiction over claims involving acts performed by the Spanish public administration. In labour matters, the labour courts protect worker's rights and so different rules apply from ordinary civil cases. Jurisdiction is decided on the basis of the place of performance of the contract of employment. If both employer and employee are Spanish and the contract is performed abroad the Spanish court retains jurisdiction.

The Spanish courts will examine their own international jurisdiction *ex officio* and abstain when they are lacking it, especially in cases in which exclusive jurisdiction is given to the courts of another country by virtue of an International Treaty,[19] but also when the criteria of

---

[18] See the long list of connecting factors of art. 22(3) *LOPJ* which can be compared *mutatis mutandis* with the "special jurisdiction" of arts. 5–15 of the Brussels Convention.

[19] art. 19 Brussels Convention and art. 19 Lugano Convention.

article 22 *LOPJ* are not present. Otherwise it is up to the defendant to challenge the international jurisdiction of the Spanish courts; if he does not, he must submit to the court (article 22(2) *LOPJ*). If the defendant wants to challenge the jurisdiction of a Spanish Court, he must do so by applying for a stay of the action on the basis of lack of jurisdiction; the procedure is called *declinatoria internacional*,[20] and it must be done at the time of appearance and before contesting the case on its merits, otherwise the defendant implicitly submits to the jurisdiction of the court.

4. COURTS OF FIRST INSTANCE IN CIVIL PROCEEDINGS

Once it has been decided that the Spanish Courts have jurisdiction to hear and decide the case, it is necessary to determine which court will be the court with jurisdiction over that specific matter. This is mainly done according to the subject-matter of the dispute (*jurisidicción por razón del objeto*) and the claim of the plaintiff.

According to the subject matter of the dispute the case will be decided by one of the four "jurisdictional orders": civil, criminal, administrative or social.[21] The judge is under an obligation to examine his own jurisdiction on the basis of the subject matter of the claim and to refuse jurisdiction if it belongs to a court of a different "order". The parties cannot "give" jurisdiction to judges of a different order.[22] If the judge fails to realise his lack of jurisdiction according to the subject matter, the parties can exercise the "exception of lack of jurisdiction" (article 533(1) *LEC*). Together with this, both parties—or the public prosecutor in cases in which his intervention is prescribed by law—can challenge the jurisdiction by means of a "conflict of jurisdiction" (article 43 *LOPJ*), at any time during the proceedings. This is decided by a different judge who will, once he has heard the parties and examined the case, require the judge who is currently hearing the case to abstain if he believes that the case must be decided by a different order of courts. If both judges disagree as to whether there is a lack of competence they must refer the matter to the Supreme Court, where a special "Chamber of Conflicts"[23]

---

[20] Similar to the *declinatoria* for lack of territorial competence (see below), and accepted by the Supreme Court in its decisions of STS of July 1, 1897, confirmed by STS of February 22, 1960 and STS of May 30, 1961 as the appropriate procedure for challenging questions of international jurisdiction.
[21] See above, Chap 3, p. 80.
[22] art. 9(6) *LOPJ*: *"la jurisdicción por razón del objeto es improrrogable"*.
[23] art. 42 *LOPJ*, *Sala de Conflictos*. This special chamber is composed of the President of the Supreme Court and two judges; one for each *orden* in conflict.

will determine which type of court shall decide the case (article 42–8 LOPJ).

The second problem of jurisdiction regards the choice of higher or lower courts within one "jurisdictional order", that is, which of the civil courts, for instance the *Juzgados de Primera Instancia e Instrucción* or the *Tribunal Superior de Justicia*, has jurisdiction to hear at first instance a particular claim. This is determined by the type of proceedings which are applicable for the resolution of the dispute. In civil matters this will normally depend on the amount of money of the claim although there are some cases in which knowledge of a specific matter means that the dispute will be allocated to certain courts regardless of the amount of the claim. For instance, a decision concerning the enforcement of arbitration awards falls under the *Jueces de Primera Instancia*,[24] as does the enforcement of foreign decisions once they have obtained the *exequatur*[25] regardless of the amount of the arbitration decision or foreign judgment (article 958(II) LEC).

Due to the nature of the case, the Supreme Court has jurisdiction over civil and criminal suits brought against members of Government, members of Parliament and magistrates (article 56(2) LOPJ). The *Tribunales Superiores de Justicia* have jurisdiction over civil and criminal cases involving members of the autonomous government or parliament (article 73(2)(a) LOPJ), and the *Audiencia Nacional* over matters of particular national interest such as crimes against the Crown, currency counterfeit and extradition proceedings.

If there is no provision that a case should be heard by a specific court because of the subject-matter, then, the determination of the type of judge who will hear the case at first instance depends on the amount of money of the claim (*la cuantía del litigio*). The relevant amount is what the plaintiff asks for in his petition. This amount will determine two different but connected issues; first, it will determine the type of proceedings (article 484–6 LEC): proceedings for larger claims—*juicio de mayor cuantía*,[26] for lesser claims—*juicio de menor cuantía*,[27] *juicio de cognición*,[28] or oral proceedings—*juicio verbal*.[29] Secondly, it will determine the type of judge of first instance. In

---

[24] art. 31 *Ley de Arbitraje*.
[25] *Exequatur* is the procedure by which a foreign judicial decision is equated to a Spanish decision and so can be enforced by the national courts. This procedure is regulated in arts. 951–6 LEC and the applicable jurisdiction corresponds to that of the Supreme Court.
[26] art. 483 LEC: claims over 160 million pesetas (£80,000).
[27] Claims over 800,000 pesetas and under 160 million pesetas.
[28] Claims from 8,000 to 800,000 pesetas.
[29] Minor claims up to 8,000 pesetas.

principle the judges of first instance (*Jueces de Primera Instancia*) hear of all proceedings in which the value of the claim is above 8,000 pesetas. The Code of Civil Procedure (*LEC*) establishes detailed rules for the calculation of the *cuantía* when this is unclear (article 489 *LEC*).

Once the type of judge and the type of proceeding has been determined, it is necessary to choose among courts of equal rank but with jurisdiction over different parts of the national territory. This question is perceived by the legislator as a secondary problem and so freedom is given to the parties to choose a particular forum. Territorial competence has a dispositive character (it is *prorrogable* in the words of the *LEC*, article 54), and thus parties might submit by agreement or by appearance to any court having "objective jurisdiction". Otherwise the Spanish Civil Procedure Act lists a series of criteria applicable to the different types of cases: for example, in suits regarding contractual obligations court of the place of performance of the obligation has jurisdiction; in suits regarding rights over personal or real property the domicile of the defendant is relevant (article 52 and 63 *LEC*). The only exceptions to the principle that the parties have freedom to choose the forum are: in landlord and tenant disputes, when the courts where the property is situated have jurisdiction (article 121 *LAU*); in matrimonial proceedings, when it is the court of the conjugal domicile (Disp. Adic. 3, *Ley* of July 20, 1980); in damages arising out of road traffic accidents the courts of the place where the accident happened (Disp. adic 1, *LO* 3/89 of July 29), and in cases concerning patents and trade marks the judge of first instance will be the judge of the *Tribunal Superior de Justicia* of the Autonomous Community where the defendant has his domicile (article 125(2)—Patent law and article 40—Trade Marks law).

The last question concerning venue relates to the court having jurisdiction to hear appeals against the decision of the competent court of any other matters relevant to the litigation.[30] This includes questions concerning which court is competent to execute the decision. All these matters are referred to as "functional competence"—*competencia funcional* (article 533 *LEC*). The rules of "functional competence" can be found scattered throughout the Code of Civil Procedure.[31]

---

[30] For instance conflicts of jurisdiction, see above.
[31] See arts. 55, 733 and 919 *LEC*.

132 Civil Procedure

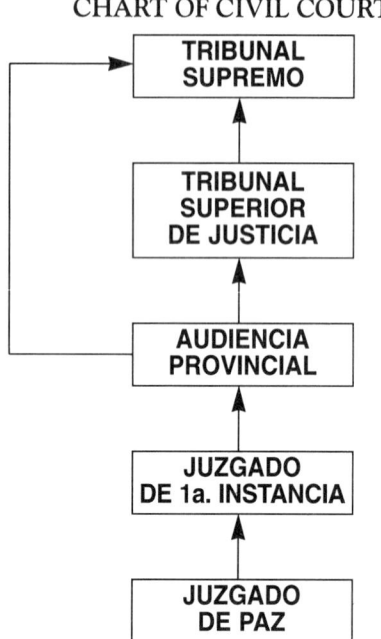

CHART OF CIVIL COURTS

Note: The arrows indicate the system of appeal to higher courts.

5. Main civil proceedings

While it would be impossible to describe each of the civil proceedings available under Spanish Law in detail, the main types available and the general lines of these will be mentioned.

PROCEEDINGS FOR PROVISIONAL REMEDIES

Medidas Cautelares, or provisional remedies, are those which provide provisional relief to the plaintiff until the case is fully decided in court. The type of provisional remedies proceedings available is of paramount importance when planning litigation in a foreign country. It would be of little or no help to the owner of a right, if the law acknowledged the existence of that right and was prepared to defend and protect it but, due to the unavoidable length of time that judicial proceedings take, it could not do so until the enjoyment of the right was impossible. Provisional remedies are so important because they provide immediate and fast relief to the person whose right is being infringed, without prejudicing the innocence or guilt of the defendant which will be established and if necessary condemned after the plenary procedure has taken place.

The main types of provisional measures are:

Interdictos (Injunctions)[32]

These are restraining orders involving the possession of real estate. There are four types in Spanish law (article 1621 LEC): an interlocutory injunction granting possession—*interdicto de adquirir* (article 1633–50 LEC); an interlocutory injunction restraining or restoring possession—*interdicto de retener o recobrar* (article 1651–62 LEC); orders against new construction—*interdicto de obra nueva* (article 1663–75 LEC); or orders for the repair or demolition of a building which is in a dangerous condition—*interdicto de obra ruinosa* (article 1676–85 LEC).

Interdictos are summary proceedings in which the court deals with factual situations that need a prompt response. They are conducted under the oral procedure: *Juicio Verbal*.[33]

Medidas cautelares (Precautionary measures)

The main function of these measures is to ensure the eventual enforcement of the judicial decision. The main measures can be divided into the following categories:

(i) Embargo preventivo (Attachment): Article 1397–1418 LEC.

This proceeding can be used in respect of cash debts or debts in kind, and it aims to limit the debtor's freedom to dispose of his assets before the outcome of the main proceedings thereby frustrating the enforcement of the final judgment. To obtain the order of "attachment" the presentation of documents proving the existence of the debt is required, and the debtor must fall into one of the following categories:

a) he must be a foreigner nor naturalised in Spain; or
b) a Spanish national or foreigner not resident in Spain and without any fixed domicile, immovable property, or a commercial address where the court order of enforcement could be served; or
c) even if he does not fall into categories (a) or (b) has disappeared from his domicile without leaving an address where he can be contacted (article 140 LEC).

---

[32] arts. 1631–85 LEC.
[33] See below p. 146.

Before giving the order of attachment the judge can demand a deposit from the plaintiff in order to cover any damages caused by the attachment to the defendant.

(ii) *Aseguramiento de bienes litigiosos* (Attachment of the property in litigation): article 1419–27 LEC.

These proceedings are designed to ensure judicial intervention in the administration of property which is the object of litigation. These proceedings can only be used when the ownership of mines, woods, agricultural exploitations or industrial plants, is being discussed, and can be initiated before, at the time of, or after the commencement of the main action. The judge deciding the main action will be the one who will order the intervention in the administration of the property. The defendant can give a deposit in order to avoid this.

(iii) *Medidas cautelares innominadas* (Non-specific precautionary measures): article 1428 LEC.

These are discretionary measures which the judge can adopt if he feels this is appropriate in the circumstances submitted for his consideration. These measures can be demanded before, at the time of, or after the commencement of an action *in personam*. This latter is an action asking the defendant to do, not to do, or to deliver specific goods. If these measures are demanded before the commencement of the action this must be started within the eight days following the grant of the measure otherwise the measure granted will become ineffective and the plaintiff will be order to pay damages and costs. The defendant, can challenge the grant or need for such measure and, if he considers it convenient, provide a security or guarantee in order to avoid its implementation.

Miscellaneous

Other measures can include deposit or seizure in real actions against movable property, preventive annotations in the property register in actions against immovable property, suspension of corporate resolutions, etc.

DECLARATIVE PROCEEDINGS

Ordinary declarative proceedings apply to the resolution of most civil and commercial matters. The type of proceeding is determined by the value of the claim or the subject matter of the action. Most of these are decided by the judges of first instance with the exception of very minor disputes which are decided by the *Juez de Paz*.

After the modification made to the *LEC* by the *Novela* 34/1984, there are in Spain four types of ordinary declarative proceedings: *juicio de mayor cuantía*,[34] *juicio de menor cuantía*,[35] *juicio de cognición*[36] and *juicio verbal*.[37] Traditionally the *juicio de mayor cuantía* was the main ordinary civil procedure, having the most detailed regulation in the LEC and with a supplementary character for other proceedings on those points not specifically regulated. However, the aim of the 1984 modification to the laws of civil procedure was to abandon the primacy of the *juicio de mayor cuantía*, which is a lengthy and formalistic procedure, and to resolve the majority of cases by the procedure of the *juicio de menor cuantía*, which is much less formal but still offers the same guarantees for the resolution of disputes. This is achieved by increasing the *cuantía* for each type of procedure.

El juicio de mayor cuantía

This was for a long time the standard procedure in civil proceedings. It originates in the common procedure of medieval times and it has Roman, germanic and canon law elements. Today, with the increase in the amount of the claim effected by the *Ley 34/1984*, only cases where the amount of the claim is superior to one hundred and sixty million pesetas,[38] and cases concerning honorific rights are heard by this procedure.

The *juicio de mayor cuantía* is divided in four main stages: *fase de alegaciones* (allegations), when the parties plead the facts and the applicable law. This includes the filing of the complaint, the answer, the reply and the rejoinder; *fase de prueba* (evidence), when the parties propose and present evidence in order to prove the truth of the facts pleaded; *fase de conclusiones* (conclusions), when the parties establish their respective understanding of the facts upon evaluation of the evidence presented; and *fase de decisión o de sentencia* (decision) when the judge arrives at a decision.

Fase de alegaciones (Allegations)

La demanda (The complaint)

All civil proceedings in Spain commence by a writ. The *demanda* can be *declarativa* (declarative) if what is sought from the court is a dec-

---

[34] Major claims proceedings.
[35] Lesser claims procedure.
[36] Difficult to translate, this procedure is used for smaller claims than the *juicio de menor cuantía*.
[37] Oral procedure.
[38] Approx. £800,000.

laration about the existence, creation, modification or extinction of a legal relationship, or a declaration obliging the defendant to do or not to do something; or the *demanda* can be *ejecutiva* (enforceable) when the request of the plaintiff is for the enforcement of a declarative judgment or for the seizure and sale of the defendant's assets as a way of compensation for the defendant's unperformed obligation. In this second case the plaintiff must present a *titulo ejecutivo*[39] together with his *demanda*.

This first document, the *demanda* or writ of complaint, must comply with several requirements both formal and substantive. Formally, it must contain a heading consisting of a generic invocation to the judge to whom the complaint is addressed, the full names of the plaintiff and his *procurador* and the name and address—if known—of the defendant, or as much information as possible in order to identify him,[40] an exposition of the facts—*fundamentos de derecho*—and a *petitum* or claim to the courts stating what relief is sought. It is also important to enclose a statement by which it is submitted that the *procurador* has a legally sufficient power of attorney. These documents should be presented in as many copies as there are parties to the trial, they should be drafted in Spanish or in any other of the official languages (Catalan, Euskera, Gallego) and the trial can proceed in any of these languages if none of the parties object to this. If one party objects, all documentation and proceedings must be translated into Spanish. Foreign documents should be translated into Spanish, preferably by a sworn translation as if this is not done the defendant might challenge the accuracy of the translation and delay the proceedings. If some of these requirements are not complied with the defendant can file a dilatory exception for defect of formalities.

Once the action has been filed any limitation period is interrupted and the presumption of good faith ceases to have effect (for instance in cases concerning possession in good faith). Also the subject matter of the claim becomes *lis pendens* and no other proceedings can be started in a different court involving the same parties and the same cause of action.

Service on the defendant

Once the *demanda* has been filed and the court has accepted jurisdiction, the complaint is served on the defendant within three working days along with a summons to appear at the proceedings on a certain

---

[39] See below, enforcement of judicial decisions and *juicio ejecutivo*.
[40] A nickname or alias would be enough if the real name is unknown.

date—*emplazamiento*.[41] This date will never be less than nine days from the date of receipt and may be longer if problems of distance or communications affect the defendant.[42] Service is effected either by personal service on the defendant's domicile, by registered mail with acknowledgment of receipt or by publication of *edictos*, by public notice in the *Diario de avisos* and the Official Journal of the province (article 260–71 LEC). Service on a defendant who is outside the jurisdiction is effected according to the procedure set forth in international treaties on the matter.

The *emplazamiento* is important because it is one of the requirements of the principle of contradiction *audiatur et altera pars* and, if it is not properly observed, can give rise to *recurso de casación*[43] and *recurso de amparo* for violation of article 24(1) CE.[44]

La contestación a la demanda (The response)

Article 530 LEC gives the defendant twenty days from the day of his appearance in court to answer the *demanda*. At this point the defendant can do three things: not appear, appear and contest the *demanda* or appear and challenge any of the requirements of the proceedings by way of a dilatory exception.

If the defendant does not appear before the court at the relevant time, the court will consider that the *demanda* has been answered and will carry out the proceedings in default of the defendant's presence.[45] All subsequent communication will be made by publication in Court—*notificación en estrados*, with the Court Clerk reading aloud in the presence of two witnesses who will sign the record along with him. The fact that the defendant does not appear does not mean that he admits the plaintiff's claim and so does not result in an automatic judgment. In fact, the defendant can appear at any stage in the proceedings and in certain cases even have these re-opened after judgment has been given.[46]

If the defendant does appear, this does not automatically mean that he submits to the jurisdiction of the court, because he can file a dilatory exception—*excepciones dilatorias*—challenging some or all of the requirements of the process. These exceptions must be filed before the time for

---

[41] arts. 525 LEC for the *Juicio de mayor cuantía*; arts. 681 and 682 LEC for *Juicio menor cuantía*, and arts 38 and 39 *Decreto de 21 de noviembre de 1952 por el que se desarrolla la Base decima de la Ley de 19 de julio de 1944 sobre normas procesales aplicables en la justicia municipal* for *juicio de cognición*.
[42] art. 526 LEC, this period can be extended to a maximum of one day for each 30 km.
[43] See below.
[44] The Constitutional Court understands that the Court may "adopt any measure necessary to guarantee the presence of the defendant" STC of June 3, 1987, extending beyond mere formalities, STC of November 3, 1987.
[45] The defendant is declared *en rebeldía*.
[46] *Recurso extraordinario de revisión*, art. 773 LEC. See below.

the answer has expired.[47] The exceptions are of paramount importance if for instance the defendant challenges the international jurisdiction of the court, because if the exception is not duly filed at the right time, the defendant will be deemed to have submitted according to article 22 LOPJ. These exceptions can be of two types: procedural and substantive and are *numerus clausus* according to the LEC. The dilatory exceptions are: lack of jurisdiction—*falta de jurisdicción o competencia* (article 533(1) LEC);[48] lack of personal or procedural capacity of the plaintiff—*falta de personalidad del demandante* (article 533(2) LEC), or lack of representation when this is necessary; defects in the power of attorney of the plaintiff's *procurador* (article 533(3) LEC); lack of personal or procedural capacity of the defendant—*falta de personalidad del demandado* (article 533(4) LEC)[49–50]; *lis alibi pendens* (article 533(5) LEC); lack of formalities or defects in the *demanda* (article 533(6) LEC); non-exhaustion of administrative remedies prior to the judicial process (article 533(7) LEC). To these it is necessary to add the agreement to submit to arbitration according to the *Ley* 36/1988 of December 5 (article 23 LA) and the *cautio iudicatum solvi* (article 534 LEC), by which, when the plaintiff is a foreigner and the defendant is Spanish, the defendant can request the deposit of security from the plaintiff to cover eventual costs incurred in litigation and damages; the defendant has to prove that, in the country of origin of the plaintiff, a similar measure is applied to Spanish plaintiffs.[51]

These dilatory exceptions must be raised in the first six days of the period given to the defendant for the response and they interrupt the proceedings[52] until they are resolved. If they are not proposed within this time the defendant can include them in his answer to the *demanda*, in which case they do not suspend the proceedings (article 536(2) and 542(1) LEC). Once these exceptions have been formulated they are

---

[47] Within the first six days of the 20 days given to the defendant to contest the *demanda* in the *juicio de mayor cuantía*.

[48] Which can be lack of international jurisdiction, lack of jurisdiction by reason of the object (conflict between an ordinary or special jurisdiction), by reason of the subject-matter (between criminal and civil jurisdiction), lack of territorial jurisdiction (article 79 LEC), or lack of functional jurisdiction.

[49–50] When he lacks the character or representation with which he has been sued.

[51] The Supreme Court has always been very restrictive in the application of the requirement and today the scope of this exception is very limited due to the existence of several bilateral and multilateral treaties on the matter. The most important of these treaties is the Hague Convention of 1905, modified by the Hague Convention of 1954 (ratified by Spain in 1961) which suppresses the requirement of *cautio iucatum solvi* for nationals of all the countries which are signatories to the Convention.

[52] This is only for the *juicio de mayor cuantía* (art. 535.1 LEC); for all the others these are included in the response.

passed to the plaintiff during the next three days and resolved by incidental proceedings (article 537 LEC). If the judge accepts one or several of these exceptions and they were raised before the response, the proceedings will be suspended until the defect has been made good. It is possible to appeal against a decision on the existence of one of these exceptions (article 538(3) LEC). If the exceptions were raised at the same time as the response they will be resolved in the main decision and the appeal will be against this.

The defendant can, of course, appear and contest the case on its merits. The *contestación a la demanda* is the procedural expression of the principle of equality of the parties[53] and the constitutional right of defence of article 24(1) CE. The *contestación a la demanda* is symmetrical to the *demanda* itself (article 540 LEC)[54] and it must contain all peremptory pleas, dilatory pleas not previously raised and, if applicable, a counterclaim (*demanda de reconvención*). If the defendant in his response not only denies the facts alleged by the plaintiff or their legal effects or both, but he also raises new facts, two things can happen: one those new facts constitute a substantive exception to the plaintiff's claim, or two they are an independent claim—a counterclaim.

If they constitute a counterclaim this will be a new action which will be decided in principle in the same proceedings provided the judge originally in charge of the case is competent (this means competent by reason of the subject matter of the counterclaim as well as that of the original claim). There is no requirement for the counterclaim to have any connection with the original claim although it will usually do so.[55] The counterclaim, once it has been established, has the same effects of *lis alibi pendens* as any other *demanda* and it is not possible for the original plaintiff to start new proceedings based on the facts of the counterclaim.

The last of the possible responses of the defendant is acceptance of the facts and their consequences as expressed in the *demanda*. This is called *allanamiento* and can be done orally or in writing provided it is express. However, it cannot be done in certain types of procedures, for instance it is impossible in proceedings not governed by the dispositive principle, such as proceedings relating to the civil status of natural persons[56] when the rights are not renounceable or when the public interest or the interest of third parties is involved.[57]

---

[53] See above, "Principles of procedure".
[54] "*El demandado formulará la contestación en los términos prevenidos para la demanda*".
[55] The only limit is that the judge must have jurisdiction based on the subject matter; arts 542(3) and 689 LEC and art. 46 of the *Decreto* of November 21, 1952.
[56] A resolution of divorce would, for instance, be impossible.
[57] As in criminal proceedings.

Réplica y dúplica (Reply and rejoinder)

This stage exists in order to give the plaintiff the opportunity to express his view and position regarding the new facts alleged by the defendant in his counterclaim. In the *juicio de mayor cuantía*—procedure for large claims—the plaintiff has to respond within a period of 10 days (article 546 *LEC*) to the allegations made by the defendant in his response. If the plaintiff does so the defendant is given a further opportunity—*dúplica* (rejoinder)—to contest the reply by virtue of the principle of equality, by which both parties must be given the same procedural opportunities in order to protect their rights or positions. In the *juicio de menor cuantía* if the defendant presents a counterclaim the plaintiff is given a period of 10 days to reply to this. In the *juicio de cognición* the counterclaim is served on the plaintiff who has to respond within three days (article 45 *Decreto* of November 21, 1952). In oral proceedings, because of the concentration of the proceedings on one act, there is no need to grant special periods. If the plaintiff waives his right to reply the defendant's right to rejoinder is precluded.

Both reply and rejoinder have to be filed in writing and contain: a definitive statement of the disputed facts and the applicable law; a definitive statement of the claims and exceptions formulated in the complaint and the answer—an express admission or denial of facts stated which are prejudicial to the party (since silence or an evasive answer may amount to *ficta confessio* (article 583 *LEC*) that is, admission of the facts); an accessory petition, either for judgment to be entered or for evidence to be taken (article 549(2) *LEC*). If the parties do not request that evidence is taken, it is understood that they renounce this stage (article 547(3) *LEC*). It is not possible at this stage to modify the facts, applicable law, claims or exceptions previously alleged unless something critical happens subsequent to the filing of the complaint or the answer.

Fase de prueba (evidential stage)

Evidence is a procedural activity the purpose of which is to persuade the judge of the veracity of the facts alleged (article 578 *LEC* and article 1215 *CC*). Only disputed facts are subject to evidence—*thema probandi*. Facts admitted by both parties, confessed by any of them, or simply notorious, need not be proved. However, it is not only facts that have to be proved because sometimes legal aspects need to be established by evidence, for instance, foreign law[58] (which the judge is not obliged to know) customs[59] and commercial usages.

---

[58] The judge has the obligation to apply the choice of law rule but the person invoking foreign law needs to prove its content (art. 12 CC).

[59] art. 1 CC and see Chap. 2, p. 41.

MAIN CIVIL PROCEEDINGS   141

Petition
Only the parties can request the judge to admit evidence in the proceedings. This should be done at the time of the reply and/or the rejoinder. If the parties are not exercising their rights of reply and rejoinder they need to request the admission of evidence in three days. In *juicios de menor cuantía* the admission of evidence should be requested as accessory relief in the writs of complaint and response. The judge will then decide whether he admits evidence or not; if he refuses to admit evidence it is possible to exercise a *recurso de apelación*.

Commencement and terms
Usually a proposal must be made within 20 days from receipt of the decree admitting evidence and presentation of evidence or practice of evidence must take place 30 days thereafter. These terms can be extended at the judge's discretion, especially if evidence is to be taken outside Spain—customarily three months are granted to take evidence in another European country and four months if evidence is to be taken elsewhere in the world. The party who requested the admission of evidence has to provide and present it.[60]

Weighing up of evidence
Certain types of evidence, namely public documents and admissions of facts made under oath, carry legal weight—*prueba tasada*—and the judge must not undervalue them, otherwise this would be a ground for a *recurso de casación*[61] (article 1687 LEC). In all other cases the judge is free to evaluate the evidence, although this does not mean that he is entitled to act unreasonably.

Means of evidence
According to article 578 LEC the parties may rely on the following means of evidence: confession at trial, public documents,[62] private documents and letters, official books of trade, expert testimony, judicial inspection and witness testimony.[63]

Pre-trial discovery
The parties are under no obligation to provide evidence before a trial, however Spanish procedure provides certain pre-trial practices aimed at

---
[60] This is known as *carga de la prueba*, or burden of proof.
[61] See below, p. 148.
[62] For the value and weight of public documents see Chap. 4, pp. 119–121
[63] For a detailed explanation of all these see, among others, F. Ramos Méndez, *op. cit.*, pp. 556 to 634.

obtaining some types of evidence before the trial. The judge can order this evidence to be provided or not, at his discretion. A general practice is the presentation of movable property in cases in which the plaintiff is seeking the recognition by the court of his ownership rights. He can request the prospective defendant to present movable property to the court in order to identify this. The court will then allow him to remain in possession but will make him aware of the need to preserve it in its current state. The plaintiff can also request the attachment of the property[64] if the conditions for this are met. There is also the possibility of requesting the exhibition of documents between heirs, partners or joint owners of property. This can be demanded by any person claiming to be a co-heir, co-partner or joint owner.

The burden of proof

The burden of proof (*carga de la prueba*) has two meanings, one procedural and the other substantive. In procedural terms the party who seeks the performance of an obligation must prove it existence, while the party who wants to prove that the obligation does not exist must prove its non-existence. The substantive burden of proof refers to the duty that the party who alleges a fact has to prove it. The plaintiff therefore, has to prove all constitutive facts[65] while the defendant will have to prove any mitigating circumstances; in Spanish law these are divided between *hechos impeditivos* and *hechos extintivos*. The former are those facts which make the performance of the obligation impossible, even if the obligation still exists; the latter are facts which wipe out the obligation, for example payment of the debt.

Presumptions

Experience teaches that certain consequences usually follow certain acts. Presumption, according to Hardy Ivamy[66] is "that which comes near, in greater or less degree, to the proof of a fact". Presumptions are established by the legislator and they are usually based on rules of experience. Legal presumptions can be absolute—*iuris et de iure*—when they do not admit counter-evidence (for instance, a person under 16 is not criminally responsible) or relative—*iuris tantum*—when they can be rebutted by counter-evidence (for example, the presumption of good faith in respect of possession of article 434 CC).

---

[64] *Embargo preventivo*, see above.
[65] Constitutive facts are those on which the obligation is based, for example the contract on which a debt originates.
[66] *Mozley & Whiteley's Law Dictionary* (1988) p. 355.

Main Civil Proceedings 143

Fase de conclusiones (conclusive stage)

Once the evidential stage has been concluded the judge must arrive at a decision. Before he does so the parties have a final opportunity to intervene by representing their conclusions in the light of the evidence submitted (article 667 LEC for the *juicio de mayor cuantía*, and article 701 LEC for the *juicio de menor cuantía*. The judge, once the evidence has been presented, will order that this should be included in the record and will give an original copy to each party for them to prepare their conclusions.

Escritos de conclusiones (Writs of conclusions)

In principle it is possible for the parties to choose whether to submit their conclusions orally or in writing. If they choose to do so in writing they present a writ of conclusions (*escrito de conclusiones*); if they prefer to do so orally they will proceed to the public hearing (*vista pública*).

In the *juicio de mayor cuantía* if none of the parties asks for a *celebración de vista pública*, that is, for oral conclusions within a period of three days, the judge will pass the record to the parties for them to prepare their writs of conclusions—*escrito de conclusiones*—within a period which can vary from ten to twenty days. Each party submits a clear and concise statement of the facts in writing, a brief summary of the evidence sustaining or rebutting each fact, an evaluation of the other party's evidence of each fact, and a clear statement of whether the applicable law alleged in the complaint, the answer, reply or rejoinder is supported in whole or in part (article 670 LEC). These writs of conclusions will be attached to the record and a copy given to each party (article 671 LEC). The judge will then, declare the proceedings to be *listo para sentencia*.[67]

If both parties request a public hearing the judge must grant one. If only one party demands this, the judge has discretion as to whether or not to grant it taking into account the importance of the litigation. Conclusions are always oral in the *juicio de cognición* and the *juicio verbal*.

Diligencias para mejor proveer (Conclusion of the proceedings by the judge)

After the parties have presented their conclusions and before the judge gives the judgment he can request further evidence to be presented in order to clarify some of the facts. This is not contrary to the dispositive principle, because the judge should not, and cannot,[68] supplement the lack of evidence caused by the parties. What he can do is to order further evidence (*diligencias para mejor proveer*) to be provided on those points

---
[67] Which literally means "ready to be decided".
[68] STS of June 30, 1977.

already raised and put forward as evidence by the parties, but which, for whatever reasons, was not presented, or even if presented failed to clarify the facts[69] (article 340 *LEC*).

La sentencia (The judgment)

Once all the conclusions have been presented and/or the judge has effected his own *diligencias para mejor proveer*, the judge issues an order declaring the case closed. This is served on the parties together with the summons for judgment—*citación para sentencia*.

The judgment must be in the form prescribed by article 248(3) and article 4 *LOPJ*, containing an exposition of the facts (*antecedentes de hecho*), proved facts, applicable law (*fundamentos de derecho*), and the decision (*fallo*). It must also indicate whether the judgment is or is not definitive—*firme*—and the possible appeals, stating the judge with jurisdiction to hear these appeals and the period in which it is possible to appeal.

As to its content, the judgment must adequately meet the petitions of the parties—it must be *congruente*—and respect the principles of *Iudex iudicare debet secundum allegata et probata partium*[70] and contradiction which inform civil procedure. Article 359 *LEC* specifies that judgments must be clear, precise and congruent with the petitions of the parties and must decide all the points raised by these.

Once a judgment has been given its main effect is of *res iudicata* (*cosa juzgada*). This means two connected but different things: first, that no other proceedings can be started on the same matter between the same parties, and that the decision must be respected in latter judgments dealing with connected issues (*cosa juzgada material*) and secondly, that the decision of the court cannot be changed or reviewed after the period for bringing a *recurso* has elapsed.

Juicio de menor cuantía

Since 1984 this has been the most widely used type of ordinary civil proceedings. The denomination "lesser claims" is rather unfortunate because at present not only all cases for which the *quantum* is superior to 8,000 pesetas and inferior to 160 million pesetas[71] are decided by this type of procedure, but also any other case in which it is impossible to fix the quantum, *ie.* proceedings of filiation, paternity or maternity, capacity

---

[69] See F. Ramos Méndez, *op. cit.*, p. 649.
[70] The judgment of the judge must be according to the allegations and evidence presented by the parties.
[71] Approximately £40 and £800,000 respectively.

and civil status of natural persons and any other for which there is no special type of proceedings determined by the law.

The *juicio de menor cuantía* can also be divided into five major stages.[72]

(i) *Fase de alegaciones* (Allegations)

The proceedings start with the issue of the writ (*demanda*)[73] which is served on the defendant. The defendant has 20 days to appear and answer[74] the *demanda*. In his answer he must file all dilatory and peremptory exceptions and he can also make a counterclaim. There is no reply or rejoinder.

(ii) *Formalización del objeto litigioso* (Stating the grounds for litigation)

Three days after the answer to the *demanda* both parties must appear in court where the judge will first ask the parties whether they want to reach an agreement and so end the proceedings. If they do not agree and wish to continue the proceedings the judge will hear each party in turn. The parties, without substantially altering what they said in their initial complaint and answer, can explain or rectify minor errors and request the presentation of evidence.

(iii) *Fase de prueba* (Evidential stage)

Evidence is presented if any of the parties so requested in the same way as in the *juicio de mayor cuantía*. If none of the parties has requested the presentation of evidence the judge must reach a decision in the next five days. The period for the presentation of evidence is 20 days which can be extended a further 10 days.

Conclusiones (Conclusions)

After the submission of evidence the parties can submit their conclusions within a period of 10 days; it is also possible to have a public hearing if all the parties so request.

Sentencia (Decision)

The judge will give his decision in the ten days following the writs of conclusions presented by the parties. This decision can be appealed.

---

[72] Only the differences within the *juicio de mayor cuantía*, will be indicated.

[73] With the same requirements as in art. 532 LEC.

[74] There is only one period for both appearing and answering the complaint. Compare with the *juicio de mayor cuantía*, above, pp. 136–138.

Juicio de Cognición

This procedure is not regulated in the *LEC*, but in the *Decreto* of November 21, 1952, as modified by article 29 of the *Ley 34/1984*. There is not much justification for having yet another type of procedure and it is very likely to disappear. With the elimination of the *Jueces de Distrrito*, the *juicio de cognición* is applied by the *Juez de Primera Instancia* in cases in which the quantum of the claim is over 80,000 pesetas and under 800,000 (article 486 *LEC*).

The main difference in this proceeding is that the period for answering the complaint is reduced to six days and there is the possibility of answering orally if the defendant agrees with the claim in the complaint; if not the defendant must respond in writing. After the response a major difference is the existence of an oral hearing where the parties can ratify or rectify points made in their written allegations and request the presentation of evidence. In this oral hearing the plaintiff has the opportunity to answer some of the exceptions alleged by the defendant in his answer. If one of the parties disagrees with the facts alleged by the other the judge must accept the presentation of evidence within a period of no more than 10 days. The presentation of evidence if followed by a public hearing after which the judge must reach a decision within three days.

El juicio verbal

This type of proceeding is for the resolution of civil cases in which the *quantum* is under 80,000 pesetas. It is applied by the *Jueces de Paz* in cases in which the quantum is under 8,000 pesetas and by *Jueces de Primera Instancia* in cases ranking from 8,000 to 80,000 pesetas.

Although predominantly oral, as its name indicates, this proceeding starts by way of a written complaint with fewer requirements than the ones necessary to start other types of proceedings (article 720 *LEC*), since it is only necessary to state the name, address and occupation of plaintiff and defendant, and the date and the nature of the claim. This is because once the proceedings begin the plaintiff has the opportunity to develop his claim. After this, the proceedings take place in a public hearing where the parties orally express their positions and present any appropriate evidence. If the plaintiff does not appear at the oral hearing it amounts to waiver and he will be condemned to pay costs and damages to the defendant. If the defendant does not appear the proceedings are carried on in default.

6. RECURSOS (APPEALS)

The main appeals available in civil proceedings are: *recurso de reposición* (motion to set aside), *recurso de súplica* (petition for reconsideration), *recurso de queja* (petition in error), *recurso de apelación* (ordinary appeal), *recurso de casación* (cassation appeal) and *recurso extraordinario de revisión* (extraordinary appeal for review).

Recurso de reposición

This is an ordinary *recurso*, against interlocutory decisions made by an unipersonal court, which will be decided by the same judge who gave the judgment which the party seeks the revocation of, and its substitution by a new one (article 373–9 LEC).

Recurso de súplica

This is the equivalent of the *recurso de reposición* against the interlocutory resolutions of a collegiate court. It also an ordinary *recurso* and therefore non-devolutive, that is, resolved by the same court which gave the original judgment (articles 401–405 LEC).

Recurso de queja

This appeal is devolutive, that is, decided by a court other than the court which gave the judgment. It is instrumental because it seeks the preparation of another appeal. There are two types of *recurso de queja*. The first, against resolutions of first instance judges denying the admission of the *recurso de apelación*, should be addressed to the *Audiencia* or court which has functional jurisdiction to hear the *recurso de apelación* (article 398(1) LEC); the second, against the decisions of the *Audiencia*, transmits the case to the *Tribunal Supremo* or *Tribunales Superiores de Justicia* for a *recurso de casación* (article 1697 LEC).

Recurso de apelación

This is an ordinary appeal, devolutive, against any definitive judgment and resolutions of dilatory exceptions and incidents by which the court *ad quem*, examines the correctness and regularity of the decision made by the court *ad quo*. It can have two different effects: it either suspends, or does not suspend, the execution of the judgment (article 381–9 LEC).

Recurso de casación

This is an extraordinary appeal, in the sense that it is not possible in all cases. Only some judicial resolutions have access to the *recurso de casación*, based on the grounds fixed by the *LEC*. However, it is clearly a jurisdictional appeal, although it originally had a political meaning, having been established as an instrument to enforce respect of the law by the judges.[75] The *recurso de casación* is not a new hearing. This means that it is not possible, at this stage, to introduce new facts or to discuss factual problems already raised. The Supreme Court and the *Tribunales Superiores de Justicia* examine only the regularity in the application of the law and certain basic principles of procedure.

The only resolutions susceptible to *casación* are: definitive judgments of *Audiencias provinciales* in proceedings of *mayor cuantía* and in the following judgments of *menor cuantía*, proceedings relating to capacity, civil status of natural persons, filiation, paternity or maternity; proceedings in which the amount of the claim was superior to six million pesetas, and proceedings in which the amount of the claim could not be estimated according to the rules set forth in article 489 *LEC*; resolution by appeal—*autos*—in proceedings for the execution of the judgments referred to above, when these decisions resolve points not decided in the judgment.

The grounds for *casación* are strictly fixed and the *recurso* must be based on one or more of the following: abuse, excess or defect in the exercise of jurisdiction, lack of competence or inadequacy of the proceedings, lack of essential formalities in the proceedings when these amount to leaving one of the parties defenceless, infraction of the law or the *jurisprudencia* applicable to the resolution of the dispute.

Recurso de revisión

The *recurso de revisión* is regulated in article 1796–1810 *LEC*, although some writers disagree as to calling it a *recurso*[76] since this special type of procedure is an appeal against decisions with *fuerza de cosa juzgada*, not because the decision is unfair but because some irregularities were present in the formulation of the judgment. The grounds for the opening of a *recurso de revisión* are fixed in article 1796 *LEC* and include the discovery of decisive documents, the existence of which was known at the time of the proceedings but which were unavailable due to *force majeure*, the

---

[75] The remote origins of the *recurso de casación* can be found in the *querela nulitatis* of Roman Law. Closer origins are found in French Law, in the *Conseil des Parties* of the *Ancien Regime* and the *Tribunal de Cassation* created by the French revolution.

[76] See Ramos Méndez, *op. cit.*, p. 759.

declaration of forgery of documents[77] on which the decision was based, the declaration of falsity of witnesses' evidence[78] or fraud in the proceedings.

The Supreme Court is the court with jurisdiction to hear the *recurso de revisión* but if the decision which is being challenged was given by a court based in an Autonomous Community whose *Estatuto de Autonomía* has a special provision in this respect, the case shall be decided by the Civil Chamber of the *Tribunal Superior de Justicia* of the Community (article 1801 LEC).

The *locus standi* for this *recurso* rests not only with the party to the proceedings who has suffered as a consequence of the fraud, but also with any third parties who have suffered prejudice as a result of the decision made as a consequence of the fraud. The public prosecutor intervenes in the proceedings (article 1802 LEC).

The *recurso de revisión* must be started within three months following the discovery of the documents or the fraud (article 1796 and 1798 LEC) but in any case it is not possible to initiate this *recurso* after five years from the date of publication of the decision (article 1800 LEC). There are no *recursos* against the resolution deciding the *recurso de revisión*.

7. ENFORCEMENT OF JUDGMENTS

GENERAL

In order to enforce a judgment it must be definitive (article 919 LEC). A judgment is definitive when it is not possible to start any *recurso* against it.[79] In some special cases the law will execute decisions which are still not definitive.[80] Foreign decisions which have obtained *exequatur*[81] or have been otherwise recognised can be enforced in the same way as domestic judgments.

---

[77] This declaration must be made in the relevant criminal proceedings according to STS of February 8, 1964.
[78] Again in the criminal proceedings STS of April 28, 1975.
[79] Either because there are no grounds to start the *recurso*, or because the time for doing so has elapsed.
[80] That is, when there is still the possibility of an appeal, if the eventual damage which can be occasioned by the enforcement is less than the damage which could be derived from delaying enforcement.
[81] See below.

ENFORCEMENT OF DOMESTIC JUDGMENTS

The execution or enforcement of judgments corresponds to the ordinary courts. Article 55 LEC states that the court with jurisdiction to decide upon a case also has jurisdiction to enforce the judgment. Proceedings for enforcement of civil decisions are always started by the parties—*principio dispositivo* (article 919 LEC).

Depending on the nature of the decision it is possible to distinguish several types of enforcement of judicial decisions: enforcement of judgments to pay a certain amount of money, judgments to do or not to do something, judgments for the delivery of a specified property, judgments of divorce, separation and matrimonial nullity, judgments to pay an unliquidated sum.

Judgments ordering the debtor to pay a certain amount of money are the simplest to enforce. The court will attach the goods of the debtor and proceed to a judicial sale until the amount of money is obtained (articles 921–7 LEC). Orders for specific performance are enforced by the court by fixing a period for the performance (article 924 LEC). If this period is not met the court will award damages to the plaintiff calculated by the court which previously heard both parties (articles 928–31 LEC). Resolutions on matrimonial proceedings are entered in the Civil Register and the judge will adopt whatever measure are necessary in order to guarantee the enforcement of the conditions agreed during the proceedings (articles 90 and 91 CC). The judge also determines the economic obligations of both parties in respect of maintenance (article 93 CC).[82]

Together with the enforcement of the execution of judgments and arbitration awards—which are equivalent to judicial decisions in terms of execution—there are other documents which can be enforced because they have special characteristics. This means that the right recognised in the document has a high degree of certainty and so it is not necessary to pursue a declarative procedure in order to ascertain it. These documents are basically the documents of article 1429 LEC which can be enforced by the so-called *juicio ejecutivo*. The main documents are public deeds,[83] bills of exchange, cheques and promissory notes and private documents previously recognised as authentic before a judge.[84] The *juicio ejecutivo* presents certain similarities to summary judgments under order 14 RSC because there are limited defences available to the defendant who still has the right to a plenary ordinary procedure where his rights can be decided at a later stage.

---

[82] By the *Ley Orgánica* 3/1989 of June 21, the person who is default in payment of maintenance orders for more than three months commits criminal offence.
[83] *Escritura pública* made in front of a notary. See Chap. 4, pp. 119–121.
[84] This procedure is regulated in articles 1429 to 1531 LEC.

Enforcement of foreign judgements

Before starting proceedings for the enforcement of a foreign judgment in any country, and therefore in Spain, there are some practical considerations which need to be taken into account. The first of these is to ensure that the defendant, against whom judgment is going to be enforced, has assets in Spain. There is little point otherwise in going through the whole procedure of enforcement. Ascertaining the existence of the defendant's assets is however, a difficult matter. The plaintiff can search in the Land Registry of the place where he believes the defendant's property is situated or otherwise seek enforcement at the place of business of the defendant if this is known.

Being a foreign party to the proceedings, as will be the case if, for instance, an English plaintiff wishes to enforce an English judgment against a defendant in Spain, is also expensive and time-consuming and the overall cost implications must be weighed in relation to the value of the judgment and the possibilities of enforcement.

The main costs and difficulties are in relation to preventing the disposal of the defendant's assets before enforcement is granted,[85] obtaining of a power of attorney to conduct litigation in Spain and employing a local lawyer and *procurador* who will, almost undoubtedly, ask for advance payment of their fees and other expenses.

It might be worth considering before the beginning of an action whether it is more convenient to sue directly in Spain and then seek enforcement of the Spanish judgment or to start the action in England and seek enforcement of the later judgment at a later date. Although the enforcement of English judgments in Spain has been considerably simplified since the implementation of the Brussels Convention,[86] the experienced international lawyer will always weigh both possibilities.

Methods of enforcement of foreign judgments in Spain

Before a foreign judgment can be enforced in Spain it needs to be authorised. Once this is done enforcement will proceed in the ordinary ways common to local and foreign judgments. The regulation of the enforcement of foreign judgments can be found in articles 951 to 958 of the *LEC* which differentiate between three different systems.

---

[85] Which can be done by an *embargo preventivo*. See above.
[86] See below.

Conventional system

The first of these systems is the conventional system which applies when there is a international convention with the country of origin of the judgment.[87] In the past most of these treaties were bilateral and established the requirements for the execution of judgments from each signatory country to the other. Today the most important conventions on enforcement of foreign judgments are the Brussels and Lugano Conventions, which articulate a simplified system of enforcement which relies heavily on jurisdictional criteria concerning which country has jurisdiction in the first place to decide the case. If these criteria of international jurisdiction are respected, the enforcement of judgments in other states which are members of the convention is almost automatic.

The Brussels and Lugano Conventions apply only to civil and commercial matters and specifically exclude questions of status or legal capacity of natural persons, rights in property arising out of a matrimonial relationship, wills and succession, bankruptcy, social security and arbitration.[88]

The actual procedure for the enforcement of judgments as implemented in Spain by Instrument 2362 (*BOE* January 28, 1991), states that the court with jurisdiction for the enforcement of foreign judgments in Spain is the *tribunal de primera instancia* of the place where the defendant is domiciled (article 32 BC and article 10 of Instrument 2362). If the defendant is not domiciled in the member state where enforcement is sought, jurisdiction of the relevant court shall be determined by reference to the court of the place where judgment is to be enforced (for instance where the defendant has assets or real property).

The plaintiff must make an application to the court accompanied by the following documentation (article 46 and 47 of Instrument 2362): an authentic copy of the foreign judgment—if judgment was given in default he must also present a copy of the documentation evidencing proof of service of the writ on the defendant—and proof that the judgment is enforceable in the country of origin and that notice of the judgment has been served; if the applicant for enforcement qualifies for legal aid in his country of origin he must present documentation to this effect and he will be automatically entitled to legal aid in Spain (article 44 of Instrument 2362). The plaintiff must also provide the court with an address for service and, when possible, with an address for service on the defendant. As a general requirement for any foreign party to proceedings in

---

[87] Such treaties exist with Colombia, *Convenio* of December 26, 1908; Czechoslovakia, November 21, 1927; Switzerland, November 19, 1896; France, May 28, 1969; Italy, May 22, 1973; Austria, February 17, 1984; Germany, November 14, 1983.

[88] See art. 1 BC. Also see Cheshire and North, *op. cit.*, pp. 288–9.

Spain the applicant must have executed a power of attorney in favour of a Spanish lawyer and *procurador* empowering these persons to act for him. All these documents must be translated into Spanish by a legal translator or a similar authorised person in the country of origin, if requested by the court (article 48 of Instrument 2362).

Once these documents have been presented, the judge cannot examine substantive issues, nor are the parties allowed to intervene or make any representations. A decision must be given by the judge in "a short period of time" (article 34 of Instrument 2362). Recognition, according to the Conventions, can only be refused on the grounds of articles 27 and 28 of the BC and LC, when such enforcement is contrary to the rules of *ordre public*, when judgment has been given in default and service has not been properly effected on the defendant, or when the judgment conflicts with another judgment previously given by the Spanish Courts in an action between the same parties. Recognition can also be refused in cases concerning the status of natural persons, rights in property arising out of matrimonial relationships, wills or succession, in cases in which the court of the state of origin has decided a preliminary question which conflicts with a rule of the private international law of the state in which recognition is sought, unless, however, the same result would have been reached by the application of the rules of private international rules of that state (article 27(4)).[89]

Article 28 provides defences for enforcement in two situations, both when the judgment was given without observing the jurisdictional provisions of section 3 of the Convention (insurance matters, consumer contract or exclusive jurisdiction) because jurisdiction in these matters is to a large extent mandatory,[90] and when the case is provided for under article 59. Article 59 refers to the situation in which a contracting state has entered into an agreement with a non-contracting state as to the non-recognition of foreign judgments given in other contracting states against defendants of that non-contracting state.[91]

The judge is under a duty to examine whether any of these defences applies in so far as this appears from the judgment or is known to the court.[92]

---

[89] Even if the question of status of natural persons is outside the scope of the conventions, a judgment will not be excluded if such matters arise as an incidental issue; for instance, in cases of maintenance orders it would be necessary to determine whether the parties were married. Maintenance judgments are enforceable under the Convention but the state in whose courts the order has to be enforced will not do so if, according to its own private international law rules, the parties were never married in the first case.

[90] See P. North, *op. cit.*, pp. 306–13 and p. 433.

[91] It will refer to cases provided for in the conventions with non-contracting states mentioned in n. 87

[92] Cheshire and North, *op. cit.*, p. 421.

154 CIVIL PROCEDURE

If enforcement of the foreign judgment is authorised, the defendant can appeal to the *Audiencia Provincial* on the following grounds: first, that the rules of Title III of the Convention do not apply; secondly, that the judgment was not enforceable in the country in which it was given; and thirdly, that one of the defences of article 27 or 28 apply. This must be done within the period of one month from when the notification of enforcement was given. The only appeal against the decision of the *Audiencia Provincial* is the *recurso de casación* to the Supreme Court.[93]

System of reciprocity

If there is no treaty between Spain and the country of origin of the judgment, the foreign judgment will have the same effect that Spanish judgments have in that country (article 952 LEC). The person seeking enforcement must prove this.

Suppletory regime—*exequatur*

If there is no treaty or a system of reciprocity has not been established by the plaintiff the foreign decision needs to be recognised[94] before enforcement is possible. This control or authorisation is known as *exequatur* and the Supreme Court has jurisdiction for this procedure. The following requirements need to be complied with (article 954 LEC). First, the foreign judgment must have been given in a personal action; secondly, the foreign judgment must not have been given in default;[95] thirdly, the underlying obligation in the foreign proceedings must be lawful in Spain; and fourthly the foreign judgment must meet all the requirements for validity in the country where it was given, as well as being duly certified according to the requirements for foreign documents in Spain.

The procedure for *exequatur* is complex, expensive and time-consuming. The party initiating the proceedings must submit a translation of the foreign judgment and file all the necessary documents together with a *demanda* to the Supreme Court. The court will then examine the requirements. If it thinks these are met it will start the proceedings according to the procedure for *juicios de menor cuantía*.[96] The burden of proving any alleged fact lies on the plaintiff. The defendant can appear and contest the proceedings. If the Court thinks that all the conditions of article 954 are satisfied, the foreign judgment will be recognised and

---

[93] See p. 148 for the grounds of *casación*.
[94] *Homologada*.
[95] STS of April 15, 1986, relaxes this requirement by demanding proper service on the defendant. If proper service has been effected the judgment can be recognised.
[96] See above.

ENFORCEMENT OF JUDGMENTS   155

then it is possible to enforce it in Spain. Enforcement rests with the Courts of First Instance.

Since *exequatur proceedings* can take one and a half years to complete, the plaintiff would, in most cases, seek an *embargo preventivo* according to the provisions of article 1400 LEC—similar to a Mareva injunction—with the purpose of preventing the defendant from disposing of his assets outside the jurisdiction before the judgment is enforced.

8. JUDICIAL COSTS

Litigating is expensive. It causes expense to the parties who must pay for all those involved on their side and to the State which must organise the administration of justice. It is not surprising that many disputes do not reach the courts because the cost of starting and pursuing the proceedings would be higher than the eventual compensation if the case were to be won.

The costs of litigating are varied. Some of them, including costs for legal advice, certifications and documents, occur before the actual proceedings start. Other expenses arise once the proceedings have started and because of the proceedings. These are known as judicial costs in *stricto sensu*. Although the Ley 25/1986 of December 24, abolished the fee payable to the court—*tasas judiciales*—the costs included in the concept of judicial costs are the fee payable to the *procurador* (regulated by the RD 1030/1985 of June 19), the fees of the *abogado*, experts and other personnel (article 423 LEC) and expenses payable to witnesses (according to articles 644 and 645 LEC).

The general rule is that the party whose claim is rejected is assessed for all costs,[97] with certain limits, unless the judge makes a finding of bad faith, in which case all costs shall be borne by the party litigating in bad faith.

9. LEGAL AID

The burden of judicial proceedings could amount to an effective denial of justice if there were no provision for those with limited economic means to have the possibility of being exempt from judicial costs. Article 119 CE has elevated this principle to a constitutional level providing

---
[97] art. 523 LEC *Criterio de vencimiento objetivo*.

that "justice shall be free in the terms so provided by the law".[98] The *LEC* establishes criteria for granting what is known as *beneficio de justicia gratuita*[99] in article 13. Persons entitled to legal aid will be exempt from any payment to the court[1] or any costs occasioned by the inclusion of public notices or any deposit required to start an appeal, when these are necessary, and they will be appointed a *procurador* and *abogado* without having to pay any fees (article 30 *LEC*).

In order to be entitled to free legal aid the applicant must establish insufficient economic means according to article 14 *LEC*, and therefore his income must be less than twice the minimum salary. This can be adjusted for people whose income exceeds this minimum but is still four times under the minimum salary (article 15 *LEC*) taking into account the number of dependants, and other personal circumstances. In this case the applicant will be exempt from all costs excluding the free appointment of *procurador* and *abogado*.

The benefit of free legal aid must be requested from the judge who is competent to hear the main trial (article 20 *LEC*). The petition will be examined in an oral hearing with the parties and the *abogado del estado*.

If the party who has been granted the benefit of legal aid wins the case he must pay the costs of his defence if these do not exceed a third of the amount obtained in the judgment (article 45 *LEC*). If he is condemned to pay costs he must do so if his economic circumstances change in the three years subsequent to the judgment (article 47 *LEC*).

---

[98] art. 119 CE: "*la justicia sera gratuita cuando asi lo disponga la ley y, en todo caso, respecto a quienes acrediten insuficiencia de recursos para litigar*".
[99] Strictly translated as "benefit of free justice".
[1] Abolished anyway by the *Ley* 30/1986.

Chapter Six
Criminal procedure

1. CRIMINAL LAW AND CRIMINAL PROCEDURE

There are two main types of offences according to the Spanish Criminal Code—*delitos* and *faltas*.[1] *Delitos* are serious offences, and are subdivided into major offences or crimes—*delitos graves*, and less serious offences—*delitos menos graves*. *Faltas* are minor offences. This distinction is important because it will determine the type of procedure to be followed, in the same way as the amount of the claim determines the type of civil proceedings.

There is an important connection between substantive criminal law and criminal procedure. Only the facts described and established in the Criminal Code as constituting a criminal offence[2] can initiate the commencement of criminal proceedings. Substantive criminal law, also, can be applied only by the courts which have the relevant jurisdiction.[3] The importance of the rights involved, and the seriousness of the consequences of infringing those rights, means that only the State, through its courts, decides if a criminal offence has been committed and the punishment that this deserves. Criminal procedure is that branch of procedure which regulates the proceedings by which the courts can punish criminal offences.[4]

2. PRINCIPLES OF CRIMINAL PROCEDURE

The important consequences of the commission of a crime both for the victim and for the perpetrator, and the seriousness of the punishment attached to that commission, means that criminal procedure is subject

---

[1] art. 1 of the *Código Penal* of 1973. *Delitos* (and *faltas*), are the acts or omissions committed with *dolo* or negligence, punishable by the law (art. 1 CP).
[2] Only the law can establish which facts constitute a criminal offence. These facts need to have been previously established by a *ley* according to the principle of legality, as must the punishment attached to the commission of an offence.
[3] art. 117 CE.
[4] J. L. Gómez Colomer, *El Proceso Penal Español para no juristas*. (1993) p. 43.

to a variety of principles which guarantee the rights of both the victim and the accused. Some of these principles are established by the Constitution and therefore can be protected by the *recurso de amparo* before the Constitutional Court.

Criminal proceedings are organised according to different principles from those governing civil proceedings. In civil proceedings the parties control the action and the judge is a qualified spectator of the activities of both parties who could, at any stage, end the proceedings by settling their dispute. In criminal proceedings the judge plays an active role while the parties do not control the commencement or end of the proceedings.[5] This is because in civil matters the parties can determine their relationships and agree a solution if a dispute arises. Criminal law, on the other hand, is a branch of public law which protects the right to freedom in all its possible manifestations. The State has the duty to protect all public and private interests which are infringed as a consequence of the commission of a criminal offence. In order to fulfil this duty, the State has the monopoly of the *ius puniendi*—the right to punish those who attack and endanger freedom. The right of the State to punish is organised according to strict principles in order to avoid the misuse of power. These principles are the principles of criminal procedure, since the only channel by which the State can punish individuals is through a process in which there are a number of guarantees.

Criminal proceedings are the only way by which the State can protect the right of freedom. In this respect criminal proceedings are "necessary".[6] The "principle of necessity" of criminal proceedings encompasses other subsidiary principles. The first of these is the principle of officiality. According to this principle the existence and commencement of criminal proceedings does not depend on the will of the individual.[7] Criminal proceedings are started by the court once it has knowledge of the commission of a crime. Also, even if the parties can bring any evidence they wish, the direction of the proceedings rests on the judge who can refer to and search for any evidence he considers appropriate and necessary without any intervention of the parties;[8] he is unrestricted in the evaluation of this evidence and will give judgment according to his own conscience. The judge, also, directs the proceedings until the end and

---

[5] With the exceptions mentioned below.
[6] Civil proceedings are not "necessary" because the parties can organise their civil relationships and dispose of their rights privately; the State only intervenes when one of the parties so demands.
[7] The only exceptions are the so called "private" and "semi-private" criminal offences. See below.
[8] Especially during the instruction, which is governed by the inquisitorial principle giving wide powers to the judge (arts. 299, 483, 701(vi), 708 and 729–2 *LECrim*).

the parties cannot agree or decide on the termination of the proceedings.[9]

In order to protect individual rights from the great powers of the judge in criminal proceedings, the exercise of these is governed by strict formalities which must be respected or will otherwise constitute a ground for *casación*. Criminal proceedings are oral (article 120(2) CE) and public (articles 24(2), 120(1) CE and 232 *LOPJ*).[10]

Although the parties in criminal proceedings do not stand in an equivalent position to the parties in civil proceedings, it is possible to say that there is a duality of positions, namely one party which accuses and the other party who is accused and who must defend. Both parties are in a position of contradiction, and the party who is being accused has the right to be heard—principle of audience—before she or he can be condemned. The principle of contradiction or audience has constitutional status. Article 24 of the CE prohibits lack of defence and ensures a procedure which has guarantees. Accordingly, both parties have the right to know all the facts and evidence presented in order to organise their defence or accusation. Also, in criminal proceedings, it is not possible to give a judgment in default. If the defendant is not present the proceedings can not take place. Finally, the principle of equality, which also informs civil proceedings, is of paramount importance in criminal proceedings where the parties have the same opportunities to establish their positions and the same rights of audience.[11]

3. SOURCES OF CRIMINAL PROCEDURE

The sources of law vary from one branch of the law to another,[12] depending on the nature of the rights involved and the purpose of the regulation. Criminal law, and therefore, criminal procedure are subject to the "principle of legality", which means that the only type of rule of law which can determine which actions constitute a criminal offence is a rule with the force of *ley*. There is no scope for administrative Regulations or custom in this area.

The main sources of criminal procedure are the Constitution, which establishes the main principles informing the regulation of this type of proceedings (articles 24, 120 CE) and the *Ley de Enjuiciamiento Criminal*

---

[9] Principle of *impulso procesal de oficio* (arts. 237 *LOPJ* and 215 *LECrim*).
[10] Even if there is a preliminary or first stage—*Fase de Instrucción o Sumario*—which is written and secret.
[11] Despite the major role played by the prosecution in the instruction of criminal proceedings.
[12] See Chap. 2.

(Criminal Procedure Act) of 1882.[13] Only the State—the Central State—can regulate criminal proceedings (article 149(1)(6) CE). The Autonomous Communities have no power to legislate on procedural or substantive criminal law matters.

The decisions of the Constitutional Court on matters affecting any rights of individuals which are closely connected with procedural matters, have a binding effect on judges as to the interpretation of constitutional rules (article 40(2) LOTC) and therefore can be included within the sources of criminal law.[14]

4. PARTIES

In criminal proceedings there is a duality of positions: accusation and accused. This is not equivalent to the plaintiff and defendant of civil procedure because the accusation in criminal proceedings is, or can be brought by a variety of persons. This is due to the fact that not only the person suffering the consequences of the crime is a victim, but the whole society may be affected. Therefore, the right to start criminal proceedings is vested in several persons.

The accusation, in Spanish criminal proceedings is drawn up in the first place by the public prosecutor—*el Ministerio Fiscal*.[15] The public prosecutor represents the public interest, not only the interests of the victim. In the exercise of functions all the circumstances of the case will be considered and a request may be made that the proceedings stop or that changes or amendments are made to the original charges, if it is considered that there is not enough evidence against the presumptive culprit. This office is also under an obligation to ensure that all the procedural guarantees are respected (articles 2 and 781 *LECrim*; articles 2–6 EMF).

The main function of the public prosecutor is the prosecution of the "public criminal action" in all criminal proceedings, except in those cases in which the intervention and consent of the victim are necessary for the initiation of the proceedings.[16] For this purpose, criminal offences can be classed as public, semi-public or private, according to who can or must start the proceedings. "Public" criminal offences—which are the majority—are those which should be prosecuted *ex officio*. This means

---

[13] Modifications on criminal procedure have been subsequently introduced by *ley orgánica*. See below.
[14] *ibid.*
[15] See above, Chap. 3, pp. 94–95.
[16] art. 105 *LECrim*.

that the public prosecution can and must initiate the prosecution once it has notice of the commission of the crime, independently of the response of the victim, who can remain passive or even "forgive" the offender. This eventual "forgiveness" does not affect the prosecution of the crime by the State through the public prosecutor. "Semi-public" criminal offences are those in which it is necessary that there has been a previous report of the offence by the victim (or a close relative of the victim, or by the public prosecutor in the case of minors or persons without full legal capacity) in order to commence the prosecution. Once this report has been made the public prosecutor has the obligation to proceed with the accusation. Traditionally these offences were offences against sexual freedom, or domestic offences for which the legislator preferred to give the persons involved the choice as to whether to start proceedings or not.[17] "Private" offences are those in which the public prosecutor does not intervene at any stage.[18]

Together with the "criminal action" the public prosecutor will undertake the "civil action" (article 108 LECrim) if the victim has not reserved the right to start the action for civil damages in civil proceedings.[19]

Not only the public prosecutor can start criminal proceedings. Any citizen can do so subject to a few restrictions. This is a major departure from other legal systems in which the prosecution belongs exclusively to the state—for instance in countries like France or Italy.[20] There is, however, a difference depending on whether the person who starts criminal proceedings is also the victim of the criminal action or not. If he is the victim he is referred to as the "private prosecutor"—*acusador particular*.[21] If he is not the victim, he is referred to as the "popular prosecutor"—*acusador popular*.[22]

The private prosecutor will be the only party in the accusation of "private crimes" in which the public prosecution does not take part. In this case he can discontinue the proceedings, withdraw the charges against the accused or forgive him, in which case there will be no punishment.

---

[17] Today this list has been extended to include rape and sexual abuses (art. 443 CP), slander and libel (arts. 463 and 467 CP and art. 4 of L 62/1978), family desertion (art. 487 CP), public scandal (art. 431 CP), damages for reckless driving when the amount of these is over the compulsory insurance limit (art. 563 CP). For a complete list see. J. Gómez Colomer, *op. cit.*, p. 116.
[18] arts. 104 and 105 LECrim and arts. 463, 467 and 586 CP.
[19] See below.
[20] In England see, The Prosecution of Offences Act 1985 which preserves the right of individuals and certain statutory bodies to institute and conduct criminal proceedings together with the Crown Prosecution Service.
[21] art. 270(II) LECrim. the victim can be a Spanish national or a foreigner.
[22] In this case it is necessary to be a Spanish citizen (art. 101 LECrim).

The victim of the crime can decide whether he or she wishes to request civil damages in the criminal proceedings or prefers to start separate civil proceedings. He has the right to waive the claim for civil damages. This waiver must be express and conclusive (article 110 LECrim) and will not have any consequences on the criminal action which will proceed with the few exceptions of the "totally private crimes".

The "popular" prosecutor can be any Spanish citizen, over 18, enjoying full civil rights. In this capacity it is not possible to prosecute a spouse, except for crimes against close relatives of the prosecuting spouse. The "popular" prosecutor needs to be represented by an *abogado* and a *procurador* and deposit a security with the court (article 280 LECrim). Once he has done so and presented a *querella*[23] he becomes party to the proceedings with full rights and duties.

The defendant in criminal proceedings receives a variety of denominations depending on which stage of the trial he is at: suspect, arrested, presumptive culprit, accused, or simply, defendant. The minimum age for criminal liability is 16 years (article 8(2) CP), and only physical persons can be defendants in criminal proceedings (article 15 (bis) CP.[24] Because of the severe consequences of an eventual judicial decision determining his culpability, the defendant's position is protected by the law. The guarantees or rights of the defendant have the character of fundamental rights and are established by the Constitution in articles 17 and 24. The infringement of any of these is a ground for the *recurso de amparo*. The defendant has, first, the right to an ordinary, pre-determined judge. This means a total prohibition on "exceptional courts" appointed for the sole purpose of judging a particular case, and gives the defendant the guarantee that his case will be decided impartially by a professional judge who will be subject only to the law in arriving at his decision. Secondly, the defendant has the right of defence and the right to be assisted by a professional lawyer (article 24 CE). If the defendant does not designate a lawyer of his choice to conduct the defence of his case, the court will designate one *ex officio* from among the lawyers registered at the local bar. This lawyer is called *abogado de oficio*[25] and his services are free of charge.[26] Thirdly, the defendant has the right to be informed

---

[23] See below.
[24] This raises important and difficult questions as to the responsibility of companies and juristic persons. The general solution is to charge the director of the company. See also articles 238 and 499 (bis) CP.
[25] Similar to the "duty solicitor" in England.
[26] Although Richard Vogler in his book *Spain: A Guide to the Criminal Justice System, Prisoners Abroad* (1989) points out that most of these *abogados de oficio* are inexperienced, the fact is that all lawyers registered with a Bar Association have the obligation to give their services and they will act to the best of their ability to preserve the rights of the

of the charges against him and of the state of the proceedings. Fourthly, the defendant has the right to use all evidence in his defence including the right of not making any declarations which can be prejudicial to his position.[27] Fifthly, every person has the right to the "presumption of innocence", which means that until all charges have been duly and sufficiently proved and the judge has given a verdict of culpability, the defendant is innocent. Consequently, it is the prosecution which must prove and establish the culpability of the defendant, not the defendant who must prove his innocence. Sixthly and lastly, nobody can be arrested except in the cases and circumstances determined by the law.

According to article 19 CP, every person who is criminally liable, is also responsible for the civil damages caused by the commission of the offence. This civil liability, according to article 101 CP and article 100 LECrim, extends to restitution of the object of the crime, if this was against property and/or compensation for physical and moral damages.[27a] The compensation for moral damages extends to the family of the victim.

Criminal liability is personal, and therefore, only the author of the offence can be held responsible for it. However, civil liability arising out of the commission of a criminal offence can extend to persons other than those who committed the offence. If the author of the offence is a minor or does not enjoy full capacity, his parents or guardian are responsible for the civil damages arising from the criminal action. Also persons with a duty of care are held responsible for the civil consequences of actions of the persons under their care.[28]

The instructing judge determines who is the person with civil liability, at the instance of the civil claimant,[29] and will demand that this person provides bail to cover the eventual damages imposed. From this moment the person charged with a civil claim becomes a party to the proceedings with full rights and duties.

---

defendant. Furthermore, for cases involving six or more years imprisonment only lawyers with at least five years professional experience will be appointed. See art. 17(3) CE, art. 520 LECrim, arts. 436–442 LOPJ, arts 57–60 RD 2090/1982 of July 24, (*Estatuto General de la Abogacía*) and RD 118/1986, of January 24, regulating the contributions of the State to the scheme.

[27] This right commences from the moment when the presumptive culprit is conducted to the police station where he can insist on keeping silent and insist on answering only to the judge (art. 520.2(a) LECrim).

[27a] Pain and suffering.

[28] See arts. 21 and 22 CP, also art. 8 in cases of circumstances reducing or eliminating criminal liability.

[29] This can be the private prosecutor or the public prosecutor.

5. THE COURT

The court with jurisdiction to hear criminal cases is determined by taking into account the importance and severity of the punishment attached to the actual offence. This criteria also determines the type of offence—*delitos graves* (crimes), *delitos menos graves* (serious offences) and *faltas* (minor offences). Together with this, some offences are heard by specific courts taking into consideration the capacity of the person committing the offence; in this context offences perpetrated by Members of Parliament are judged by the Criminal Chamber of the Supreme Court, irrespective of the classification of the offence.

Minor offences (*faltas*) are decided by the *Juzgado de Instrucción*[30] of the place where the offence was committed (article 14(1) *LECrim*) with the exception of very minor cases in which a decision can be made by the *Juez de Paz*.[31] For the decision of serious offences (*delitos menos graves*)[32] either the *Juez de lo Penal* of the place where the offence was committed or the *Juez Central de lo Penal* has jurisdiction. Cases involving crimes (*delitos graves*) are decided by the *Audiencia Provincial* of the province where the crime was committed.[33]

In criminal proceedings, at least for serious offences and crimes, there are two clear and differentiated stages—the *instrucción*,[34] and the public hearing. These are carried out by different courts in most cases and always by different judges. The court with jurisdiction for the "instruction" of criminal cases is the *Juez de Instrucción* or the *Juez Central de Instrucción*. For cases decided by the *Tribunal Supremo* or *Tribunal Superior de Justicia*, a special judge is designated from the Criminal Chamber of these courts to carry out the *instrucción* of the case. This judge will not participate in the public hearing or in the final decision since the Constitutional Court has declared unconstitutional the decision of a criminal case by the instructing judge.[35] Appeals against criminal decisions, when these are possible,[36] are decided by the superior courts. The enforcement is always made by the judge or court which gave judgment.

---

[30] See above, Chap. 3 under section on *Juzgados de Primera Instancia e Instrucción*.

[31] arts. 385, 590, 594, 596 and minor offences of Tit. I and II of the Criminal Code.

[32] *Delitos menos graves* are those offences which are punishable by imprisonment of less than six years, a fine of whatever amount, deprivation of a driving licence or any other punishment of less than six years.

[33] For information on which cases are decided by the *Audiencia Nacional*, *Tribunales Superiores de Justicia* or *Tribunal Supremo* see Chap. 3, pp. 80–94.

[34] See below for the meaning of the *instrucción*.

[35] STC of July 12, 1988. This decision of the Constitutional Court has been reflected by the LO 7/88 which specifies the obligation to nominate a separate judge for the instruction of the cases decided in the *Tribunal Supremo* and the *Tribunal Superior de Justicia*.

[36] See below.

CHART OF CRIMINAL COURTS

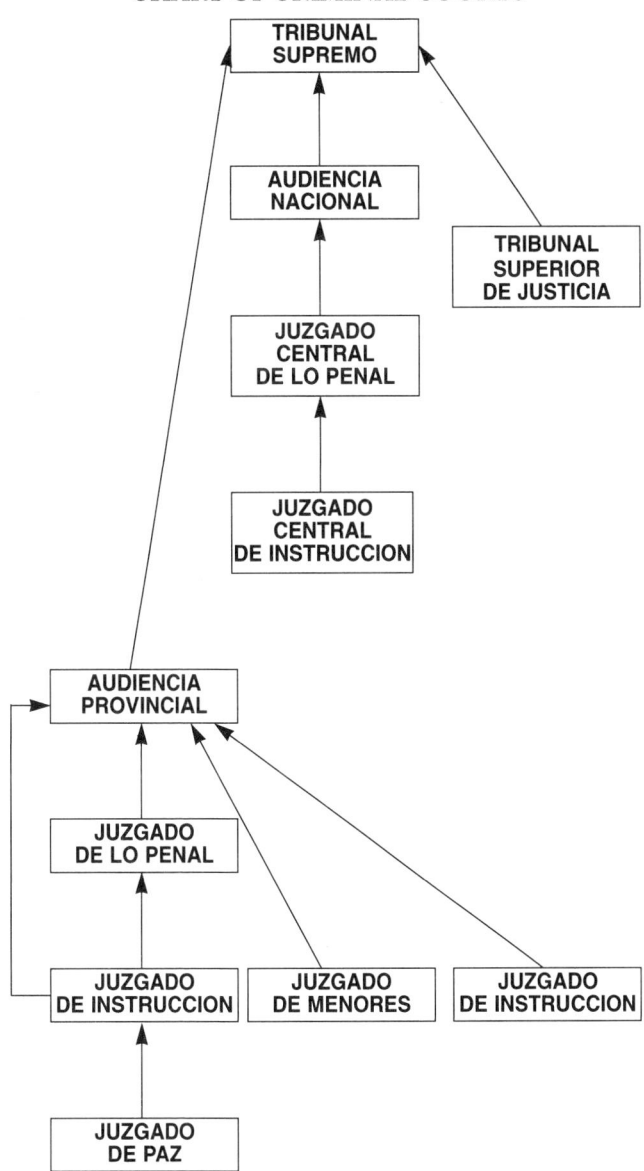

Note: The arrows indicate the system of appeal to higher courts.

6. MAIN CRIMINAL PROCEEDINGS

There are four different types of ordinary criminal proceedings in Spain.[37] First, there is the ordinary criminal procedure for serious crimes (*Procedimiento penal ordinario por delitos graves*)[38] secondly, the abbreviated procedure (*Proceso penal abreviado*), introduced by the LO 7/88 of December 28, (article 770–97 LECrim) and thirdly, the abbreviated procedure with an immediate oral hearing (*Proceso penal abreviado con juicio oral inmediato*), introduced by the Ley 10/1992 of April 30, article 790–2 LECrim) and fourthly, the procedure for minor offences (*procedimiento de faltas*) originally introduced by the LECrim but modified by the Ley 10/1992.

Together with the ordinary proceedings there are what are called special proceedings which depend not on the seriousness of the offence or of the punishment, but on the character of the person charged, or on the subject matter of the offence, or on both. These consist of the procedure against *Diputados* and *Senadores*,[39] the procedure against members of the Autonomous Parliaments,[40] the procedure for extradition,[41] the procedure for defamation,[42] the procedure for terrorist activities,[43] the procedure for crimes against fundamental rights,[44] and the procedure for monetary crimes.[45]

Other proceedings are special because they deal with facts and activities which are not offences typified by the Criminal Code but by other laws. These are the *proceso por peligrosidad social* by which "special measures" are imposed on those who are "socially dangerous". This procedure is an anachronism of the Franco era and includes several unconstitutional provisions. It is currently under review and has been subject to constant criticism by the majority or writers. There is also the *proceso*

---

[37] To these can be added the new procedure for those cases in which there is a jury according to the LO 5/95. See below.
[38] This was the original procedure regulated in the LECrim for all crimes. All references will be to this procedure unless otherwise stated.
[39] arts. 71 CE, arts. 750–756 LECrim, arts. 10–14 *Reglamento del Congreso* and arts. 21 and 22 *Reglamento del Senado*.
[40] Regulated in the *Estatuto de Autonomía* of each Community.
[41] Ley 4/1985 of March 21.
[42] arts. 804–823 LECrim, arts. 3 and 4 Ley 62/1978 of December 26.
[43] Due to the gravity of these activities the LO 3/1988 and 4/1988 of May 25, have introduced rules which modify issues of jurisdiction, precautionary measures and the right of defence. See arts. 384 (bis) 504 (bis) 520 (bis) 533 and 779 LECrim.
[44] Ley 62/1978 of December 26, which establishes fast and expeditious mechanism for the protection of fundamental rights.
[45] Regulated by the Ley 40/1979 of December 10, and art. 9.2 of the LO 10/1983 of August 16.

MAIN CRIMINAL PROCEEDINGS   167

militar penal[46] for crimes specified by the Military Criminal Code, and the *proceso tutelar de menores*,[46a] by which the *Tribunal Tutelar de Menores* decides on the appropriate measures to be imposed on those who have not attained the age for criminal responsibility (16 years).

The main ordinary proceedings and in particular the *procedimiento ordinario por delitos graves*, will be examined with references to the others where appropriate.

In criminal proceedings there are several clearly differentiated stages. Some of these take place before the actual court commencement of the proceedings and their function is to establish whether or not there is enough evidence to initiate criminal proceedings against the defendant.

PRELIMINARY STAGE

Before criminal proceedings can be started it is necessary to determine various issues, the first being whether an offence has actually been committed and the circumstances in which this happened. In order to do this, several investigations need to take place. These investigations are usually carried out by the judicial police. Secondly, and once it has been established that a criminal offence has been committed, it is necessary to determine who is the person responsible for it. Further investigations are then required in order to find and identify the author (unless he presents himself to the judge or the police and confesses to the commission of the crime).[47] These investigations are also carried out by the judicial police.[48] Only after these two points have been established can the prosecution start the criminal procedure.

(i)   The judicial police

The body of the judicial police[49] is an auxiliary of the judicial power,[50] the public prosecution and—since it performs a public service—to some extent of the citizens.[51] Article 126 CE states that the function of the judicial police is to assist the judge and the public prosecutor in the

---

[46] LO 4/1987 of July 15, on military jurisdiction; LO 2/1989 of April 13, on military procedure.
[46a] *Ley* 4/92 of June 5 *Ley Reguladora de la Competencia y el procedimiento de los Juzgados de menores*.
[47] This is not conclusive because in any event a procedure is necessary before anybody can be convicted of a criminal offence.
[48] See below.
[49] Although according to J. L. Gómez Colomer, *op. cit.*, pp. 154 and 155, the denomination "judicial police" is inaccurate.
[50] See above, Chap. 4, p. 118.
[51] J. L. Gómez Colomer, *op. cit.*, p. 152.

investigations of crimes and the identification of the person responsible for these. The judicial police are subject to the orders received by the judge and the public prosecutor (article 283 LECrim).

The judicial police will start investigations once it has been instructed to do so and will communicate any knowledge of facts which might constitute a criminal offence to the judge. If the criminal offence is a *delito público*, then the judicial police has the duty to investigate all the events which took place in the territorial district under their jurisdiction. If the offence is a *delito privado*, which can only be prosecuted if the victim so desires, the judicial police will have the same obligation to investigate the facts and to identify the criminal once it has been requested to do so.[52]

The judicial police body is dependent on the Ministry of Internal Affairs (*Ministerio del Interior*) (article 31 LO 2/1986) even if its members are subject to the orders of the judge or public prosecutor. They will perform any acts in which public coercion, entry into and search of private dwellings are necessary.

(ii) **Starting criminal proceedings**

The initiation of criminal proceedings requires an act—just as civil proceeding are started by the issue of complaint—which can be carried out by citizens or by the State. Citizens can start the proceedings by a *denuncia*[53] or by a *querella*.[54] The State can initiate the proceedings *ex officio* or by special requirement of the Executive.

La denuncia

A *denuncia* is a declaration of knowledge by a private person who has notice of the commission of a criminal offence and thereby communicates this knowledge to the court. This can be done orally or in writing. The *denuncia* is made to the judge, usually the duty judge—*Juez de guardia* (article 259, 262 and 264 LECrim)—the public prosecutor or the police. As a result of its general duty to investigate and report every fact which might constitute an offence, the reports of the police (*astestados policiales*)—according to article 297 LECrim—are also a

---

[52] Their obligations are specifically regulated in the RD 769/1987 of June 19, which develops the LO 2/1986 of May 13.
[53] This term could be translated by "complaint" or "information". The original Spanish terminology will be used because there is another type of complaint, *querella*, with special characteristics.
[54] There is no direct and accurate translation of this term into English. This is a special type of complaint in those criminal offences which can only be prosecuted with the consent of the victim.

denuncia. The person who makes this declaration of knowledge does not necessarily become a party to the proceedings although he will at least be called as a witness.

Although every citizen has a general ethical duty to report any knowledge of the commission of a criminal offence, certain persons, due to their personal characteristics or their relationship with the offender, are excepted from this duty. These are minors and mentally disabled people (article 260 *LECrim*), the spouse, close relatives and descendants of the perpetrator (article 261 *LECrim*), the lawyers of the offender (article 263 *LECrim*) and Catholic priests in respect of facts, knowledge of which was acquired under confession, according to canon law (article 263 *LECrim*). On the other hand some people have a special duty or obligation to report their knowledge of the commission of a criminal offence because of their profession, for example the police and the public prosecution service.

Once a *denuncia* has been made, the court has the obligation to start investigations. If the report was made to the police, it will be passed on to the judge who will determine whether the facts reported constitute a criminal offence. If so, the judge will pass the information to the public prosecutor and to the persons who are accused of the commission of the offence (article 118 *LECrim*). If the facts reported do not constitute a criminal offence the *denuncia* will be dismissed.

The person making the *denuncia* has no further obligations, unless he wishes to become a party in a private or popular accusation, depending on the circumstances. He will also be protected if his security is endangered by the fact of reporting the criminal offence. However, if he acted maliciously when making the *denuncia* he could be criminally liable (article 325 CP—*denuncia falsa*—and article 338 CP—*simulación de delito*).

La querella

The second type of declaration which starts criminal proceedings is called *querrella*. This is a complaint made with the intention of becoming a party to the proceedings. This complaint is made formally, in writing, to the judge with jurisdiction to hear the case.[55]

The distinction between public, semi-public and private criminal offences becomes relevant again in order to analyse who can make a *querella*. In the case of public criminal offences—*delitos perseguibles de oficio*—this report or complaint can be made by the victim,[56] any Spanish

---

[55] This is different from the case of a *denuncia* which could be presented to the duty judge, the police or the public prosecutor.
[56] Which will become the "private" accusation.

citizen,[57] or the public prosecutor. The latter, is under an obligation to do so.[58] In cases of "semi-public" offences, once the victim has presented the *denuncia*, the public prosecutor has the duty to prepare and present a *querella*. The victim can also do so if he wishes.[59] No other person is entitled to make a *querella* in this case. In "private" criminal offences only the victim can formulate a *querella*.[60]

This complaint is a formal declaration which must be signed by an *abogado* and a *procurador* and addressed to the court with jurisdiction. It must identify the person against whom it is made, give a detailed account of the facts believed to constitute a criminal offence and the relevant law, with a request to carry out whatever investigations are necessary in order to determine the actual commission of the offence by the suspect. It also has to state any precautionary measures to be taken and include a petition as to the civil liability or otherwise state the reservation of the right to start civil proceedings later. With the *querella* it is necessary to enclose the power of attorney of the *abogado* and *procurador* and any other documents relevant to the case.

If the *querella* is accepted by the court there are important effects. The person signing it becomes a party to the proceedings, the judge will order the carrying out of the investigations requested, unless these are against the law or unnecessary (articles 311 and 312 *LECrim*) and will serve it on the defendant who now becomes the accused and as such has the rights of defence stated in article 118 *LECrim* and should be represented by a lawyer.

Initiation ex officio

The judge who has knowledge of the commission of a criminal offence must communicate this knowledge to the public prosecutor in order to allow him to make a *querella*. The court which has decided a case can also initiate criminal proceedings against the person who started these if there is a case of *denuncia falsa*.[61]

A special form of criminal proceedings applies in the case of defamation against foreign Heads of State or diplomatic personnel because of the political connotations. These cases can only be started when the Executive so requests.[62]

---

[57] The "popular" accusation.
[58] See art. 271 *LECrim*, art 19(1) *LOPJ*, and arts. 3, 4 and 5 *EMF*.
[59] arts. 104, 105 and 270 *LECrim*.
[60] art. 104 *LECrim*, art 467 *CP* and art 4(1) Ley 62/1978.
[61] art. 325 (II) and (III) *CP*. False Indictment.
[62] art. 467 (V) and (VI) *CP*.

(iii) Precautionary measures

If in civil proceedings it is sometimes necessary to impose certain precautionary measures in order to ensure that the judicial decision can be enforced in the future, this is even more necessary in criminal proceedings. The investigations can take a long time and the period between the completion of these and the date of the public hearing can vary considerably. If one considers that the author of the offence could face a punishment amounting to imprisonment of up to thirty years, it is not surprising that he may try to hide, to leave the country or to change identity. Also, in the same way as the civil defendant might try to dispose of his assets and alienate these from his estate in order to frustrate the claims of the plaintiff, the person who is liable for civil damages arising out of a criminal offence may also try to alienate his estate or change the ownership of it in order to frustrate a monetary punishment or liability for civil damages.

Precautionary measures in criminal law try to avoid the above situations. These measures can apply to persons or over property. Measures imposed on persons are the *citación cautelar* (cautionary summons), *detención* (arrest), *prisión provisional* (pre-trial custody), *libertad provisional* (freedom on bail). Measures applied to property are basically two, *la fianza* (bail) and *embargo* (attachment).

La citación cautelar

This is a summons to the person whose participation in the criminal acts appears likely from the investigations of the judge to appear and make a statement to the instructing judge or to the public prosecutor (articles 486 to 488 *LECrim*). If the person summoned to appear and make a statement does not do so he will be arrested (article 487 *LECrim*).

La detencion[63]

Since freedom of movement is a constitutional and fundamental right (article 17(1) CE) a person can only be arrested according to the rules established in the Constitution and the *LECrim* (article 17 CE and 489 *LECrim*). It is also necessary to distinguish between arrest as a precautionary measure before the trial and arrest as an executory measure.

As a precautionary measure it is only possible to arrest a person who is about to commit a crime (article 490 *LECrim*), or who is caught in flagrant commission of a crime. The courts are very strict on the need to

---

[63] See the useful and clear explanation of this measure in Richard Vogler, *op. cit.*, pp. 28–39.

establish these circumstances and the police must justify and prove that they exist.

Preventive detention or arrest can only last for a maximum of 72 hours. After this time the person arrested must either be conducted to the judge to declare or he must be allowed to go (article 17(2) CE). Only in cases of terrorist activities can this detention be extended to a maximum period of five days (article 520 (bis)(1) *LECrim*). This detention can be carried out by the police in the circumstances mentioned above or ordered by the judge.

The person arrested has the right to be told of the reasons for his detention; his rights also include the right to remain silent (article 520 *LECrim*), the right to request the assistance of a lawyer to help with the enquiries at the police station or by the judge, the right to communicate the detention to a member of the family or any other person, the right to be examined only by a doctor, the right to a translator if the person arrested does not speak or understand Spanish, and, in the case of minors or people with disabilities, the right to notify parents or guardians at once.[64] If any of these rights are denied, or the person arrested has suffered ill-treatment or been held at the police station for longer than the maximum allowed[65] he is entitled to ask for *Habeas Corpus*. *Habeas Corpus* is a fundamental right that each person has to request judicial protection against illegal detention or other violation of rights deriving from it. It is recognised in article 17(4) CE and developed by the LO 6/1984 of May 24.

The *Ley de Seguridad Ciudadana* (LSC) of 1992 has introduced a special type of "arrest"[66] the features of which are constitutionality more than dubious. Effectively article 20 of the *LSC* allows the police, while exercising their functions of protecting citizens' security,[67] to request any person to identify himself. If the person so requested fails to produce proof of identity,[68] or refuses to do so he can be taken to the police station and arrested. In order to make the detention legal the conditions of article 490 *LECrim* must be present,[69] if not the detention is illegal and article 20 of the *LSC* cannot derogate from article 490 *LECrim* and even less article 25(3) or 17(2) CE.[70] The police should, therefore, be cautious in

---

[64] In the case of a foreigner the consular authority must also be notified of the detention.
[65] 72 hours, or five days in cases of terrorism.
[66] Called *retención*.
[67] Which of course, is not a clear concept.
[68] In Spain every citizen has an identity card, *Documento Nacional de Identidad* (DNI), which he is obliged to carry or to produce for the Police and other authorities on request. Foreigners must produce their passports.
[69] Flagrant commission of a crime.
[70] arts. 25(3) and 17 CE—rights of freedom and security. Nobody can be deprived of

the exercise of the powers given to them by the LSC and ensure that the person who is being arrested falls under one of the categories of article 490 LECrim.

La prisión provisional

This pre-trial custody, which must be sanctioned by a warrant from a judge, consists of a limitation of the personal freedom of a person suspected of having committed a criminal offence when there is enough evidence that the person might escape and thus frustrate the enforcement of the eventual punishment. The judge will take into account the circumstances of the suspect, his criminal record, the danger to society that the freedom of the suspect might create and the social reaction provoked by the commission of the crime.[71] Custody will also be ordered if the suspect has not appeared to give a statement to the instructing judge.

Pre-trial custody can have different degrees: communicated—the prisoner can communicate with his lawyer, the judge, his family or friends (article 523 LECrim); uncommunicated—when there is a danger of frustrating the investigations of the judge and the police (articles 506 to 508 LECrim); and mitigated—when the illness of the suspect makes it necessary to allow him to remain in his home or in a public hospital (article 505 LECrim).[72]

Pre-trial custody can only be imposed for a maximum period which depends on the duration of the possible prison sentence that the commission of the crime attracts (article 504 LECrim).

Libertad provisional[73]

Freedom on bail, is allowed to those suspects for whom an order of pre-trial custody is not justified. It consists of the imposition of certain obligations on the suspect which limit his freedom and the performance of which is guaranteed by the bail given to the court (article 529–42 LECrim). It usually consists of obliging the suspect to appear before the court periodically[74] and to remain at the disposition of the court (article 530 LECrim), not being allowed to leave the country or to change residence without previous notification and the consent of the court.

---

freedom and provisional detention cannot last longer than strictly necessary and never more than 72 hours.

[71] For example pre-trial custody was ordered in 1994 for famous bankers due to the social concern that arose as consequence of the monetary crimes committed.

[72] See arts. 501–525 LECrim and J. L. Gómez Colomer, op. cit., pp. 337–339 for more detail on the different regimes of pre-trial custody.

[73] Freedom on bail.

[74] Customarily on the 1st and 15th of each month.

Other measures

Other measures imposed by the court can be directed against the property of the suspect in order to satisfy any eventual fine, the civil liability and the legal costs of the proceedings. These can be imposed at the same time as a personal measure limiting freedom, or independently. Basically there are two such measures: *embargo* (attachment)—which has the same characteristics as the attachment ordered in civil proceedings—and *fianza* (bail).[75]

The final type of measures that the judge can impose before the trial are connected with the punishment attached to certain offences. These include suspension of office for judges, public prosecutors, *secretarios judiciales*, and any other personnel auxiliary to the judge, in criminal cases brought against any of these persons in connection with the exercise of their functions; and the provisional forfeiture and suspension of driving licence (article 529 bis CP).

LA INSTRUCCIÓN

Once criminal proceedings have been formally started, the first stage of the proceedings, *la instrucción*, begins. *La instrucción* has the object of ascertaining the facts and the perpetrator of the crime in order to formalise the request for punishment. In this respect this is a preparatory stage for the oral public hearing—*juicio oral*—during which the judge will definitively establish the innocence or culpability of the accused.

The *instrucción* is conducted by a judge—*el Juez Instructor*—who must be different from the judge conducting the public hearing. The instructing judge has wide powers in order to clarify all the circumstances and facts which might or might not constitute a criminal offence. These powers can imply the restriction of some fundamental rights in order to guarantee the success of the investigations and are therefore carefully regulated by the *LECrim*.

The *instrucción*, also called summary—*sumario*—is clearly inquisitorial and usually secret, with a judge who controls the proceedings, orders investigations and has wide powers concerning the imposition of any urgent measures considered necessary for the clarification of the facts or the identification of the presumptive culprit.

Whilst the judge has the power to conduct any investigations he thinks appropriate, the parties—both the prosecutor and the defendant—can request the judge to undertake further investigations. These will be carried out by the judge himself or with the assistance of the

---

[75] See arts. 589–614 *LECrim*.

judicial police or experts—for example, forensic doctors, graphologists or ballistic experts.

Investigations by the judge

The first act of investigation that the judge will undertake[76] is a visual inspection (*inspección ocular*) by personally going to the place where the events took place. He will then make a report describing what he has seen and will take any fingerprints or any other evidence available, take photographs or interrogate witnesses if they are available. This is regulated in article 326–33 LEC.

The judge will then, examine the object of the crime (*cuerpo del delito*). This can be a person or an object. If it is a person it might be necessary to identify the corpse, or to carry out an autopsy in order to determine the time and causes of death.[77] It might also be necessary to conduct other medical examinations in cases of physical injuries not amounting to death. If it is an object, the judge will describe it if this is possible, and make enquiries about its previous state. He will also try to determine the value of the object, which is important in order to determine the punishment[78] and the civil liability.

The next investigation by the judge is directed at the suspect and its purpose is the identification of the author of the offence. Once the judge has done this, he will have to determine if the presumptive author has the necessary capacity to be held criminally liable, *i.e.* the presumptive author will not be criminally liable if he is under 16, or mentally disabled. The judge can also request information about the suspect[79] from any public authorities. After this, he will take a statement from the suspect. At this point it is important to remember that the right not to incriminate oneself and the presumption of innocence are recognised by article 24 of the Constitution. The defendant in criminal proceedings might have already been arrested by the police. If this is so, he must be brought before the instructing judge to make a statement within 24 hours. In his statement, besides the right to remain silent and not to declare anything which may be prejudicial to his position, the suspect cannot be compelled to take an oath. He can demand the presence of his lawyer and, if he is a foreigner, of a translator. Any kind of coercion or torture is strictly forbidden and will give rise to criminal liability of the persons involved

---

[76] He is obliged to do so by art. 336 *LECrim*.
[77] This is necessary in all cases of violent death or when there is suspicion of foul play concerning the cause of death (art. 343 *LECrim*).
[78] See arts. 505 and 515 CP.
[79] The circumstances of the accused can be taken into account for the punishment. For example, if he has already been convicted of the same crime previously the punishment will be increased (art. 10(15), 61(2) and 61(6) *LECrim*).

in these acts.[80] The aim of this interrogation is to confirm or determine the identity of the suspect and his participation in the commission of the criminal offence. To this effect the judge can, for example, request the suspect to write some words in order to check if he is the author of documents which were allegedly written by him. The judge will enquire about previous conduct or morals and the general life-style of the defendant but these questions may not be trick questions intended to entrap the suspect. The clerk (*secretario judicial*) will keep a record of everything which is done. The statement given by the suspect is written down and everybody who is present—suspect, judge, suspect's lawyer, court clerk and translator—will sign it. The suspect cannot be obliged to sign it unless he totally agrees that what has been written is exactly his declaration. If the suspect admits the facts, this does not amount to a confession with the same effects that a confession has in civil proceedings,[81] because it is only possible to convict somebody at the public hearing. If the suspect was previously arrested by the police and made a statement in the police station, he might not be required to do so again, but simply to ratify the previous one before a judge. The suspect has the right to make as many statements as he wishes to the judge (article 400 LECrim).

Once the judge has taken a statement from the suspect, he will do the same with any witnesses.[82] If there are any discrepancies between the statements of the witnesses and the defendant, or between the different defendants if there are more than one, the judge will arrange a confrontation (*careo*).[83] This confrontation takes place in front of the judge and the *secretario judicial*. The latter will read to all the parties present at the confrontation, the statements already made and remind the witnesses that these have been made under oath and the consequences of false declarations. He will then ask each of the witnesses if they confirm their statements. If there are contradictions at this stage the judge will request the parties to agree in their statements. The *secretario* will keep a record of the whole procedure and this record will be given to all the parties to sign.

Some of the investigations conducted by the judge during the *instrucción* could, as indicated previously, limit the fundamental rights recognised by the Constitution or international conventions ratified by Spain.[84] Most of these investigations will, in practice, be carried out by

---

[80] Spain is a party to the European Convention on the Prevention of Torture, November 26, 1987.
[81] See Chap. 5, pp. 140–142.
[82] Witnesses make depositions under oath (arts. 410–450 *LECrim*).
[83] arts. 451–455 *LECrim*.
[84] For instance the Rome Convention of Human Rights and Individual Freedoms of 1950 (ratified by Spain in 1979).

the police who must in any case possess a warrant from the judge authorising their activities. The types of activities include entry to public or private places,[85] and the interception of personal communications which can be postal, telephonic or telegraphic and presumably nowadays, informatic. This interception of personal communications can only be made in respect of the person accused of the commission of a crime, and in no case can it affect the lawyer in charge of the case since he is under a duty of confidence to his client.[86]

Since the establishment of a democracy in Spain, these activities have been performed with sufficient guarantees, always with a judicial warrant and any proof obtained outside the judge's authorization is considered illegal and inadmissible. However the approval of the *LO de Seguridad Ciudadana* by Parliament has created controversy among lawyers, politicians and citizens. This law allows the police to enter and search a private dwelling when the police know that a drug-related offence is being committed. While fully appreciating the importance and magnitude of the problem of drug-related crime in Spain in recent times, this regulation seems most unfortunate in that it does not require any judicial intervention before the police can enter a private residence. This will, no doubt, give rise to complaints that will have to be decided by the Constitutional Court, since the *LSC* clearly infringes constitutional and internationally recognised fundamental rights.

The final investigation which can be authorised by a judge and which can conflict with a fundamental right is a physical inspection in the form of blood, semen, saliva, urine or other body fluids' tests. Vaginal or anal inspections, X-rays, psychiatric or psychological tests, alcohol and drugs tests must only be carried out when it is strictly necessary since article 15 of the Constitution guarantees the right to physical integrity. In order to carry out any of these investigations it is necessary to obtain a judicial warrant. They can never be ordered or carried out at the request of the public prosecutor or the police unless the person subject to them expressly consents and they will only be undertaken by an expert, *i.e.* a doctor. The only exception to this is in the case of alcohol tests taken by the police during routine checks in order to determine whether the offence of driving under the influence of alcohol (article 340 (bis)(a)1 CP) is being committed. This test can be used as evidence at the trial and it is carried out by the police in accordance with the *LECrim* and various administrative regulations on the matter.[88] The Constitutional

---

[85] This is contrary to art. 18 CE which guarantees the inviolability of private dwellings.
[86] See J. Tome, *op. cit.*, p. 238.
[87-88] Base 4, *Ley* 18/1989, July 25; art. 12.2 of the *texto ariculado* approved by RDL 339/1990 of March 2; and arts. 20–25 of the *Reglamento General de la Circulación* approved by RD 13/1992 of January 17.

Court has declared that this investigation does not infringe any constitutional rights and has established special guarantees[89] in order to ensure that the rights of defence and the principle of contradiction are respected. The public prosecutor has the right to be kept informed of the progress of the procedure by the instructing judge (article 306 LECrim) and in certain cases (article 785 (bis) and 789(3) LECrim) carries out some of the preparatory enquiries.[90]

Charges: *el procesamiento*

Charging somebody means formally accusing that person of the commission of a certain crime.[91] This is necessary in order to open the oral hearing and it is done by the instructing judge (article 384 LECrim). In order to charge the suspect it is necessary to establish the existence of "rational evidence of the commission of a crime by a specific person".[92] This decision of the judge—*auto*—can be appealed.[93] The charge is not necessary in the abbreviated proceedings nor in proceedings for minor offences.[94]

Once the judge considers that all the investigations are complete he will end the *sumario* (article 622 LECrim). The prosecutor can then request that the dosier is sent to the *Audiencia Provincial*. If the judge who carried out the *instrucción* considers that the facts constitute a minor offence (*faltas*), he will send the dossier to the *Juez de lo Penal*. If he considers that it is a major offence or a crime (*delitos*), the judge will send the dossier with all the documentation to the court which has jurisdiction to decide the case—the *Audiencia Provincial* or the *Tribunal Superior de Justicia*. This decision will be communicated to the private prosecution, if there is one, even if he is only acting as civil actor, requesting him to appear at the *Audiencia Provincial* within 10 days or at the *Tribunal Superior de Justica* within the period of 15 days. A copy of all these documents will be sent to the public prosecutor (article 623 LECrim). The *Audiencia Provincial* or the *Tribunal Superior de Justicia*, will examine the dossier sent by the judge and will confirm whether the *instrucción* is complete or not. If the court thinks that further inves-

---

[89] STS 5/1989 and STC 3/1990, of January 15. See J. Tomé, *op. cit.*, pp. 226–227.
[90] The role of the public prosecutor is greater under the Abbreviated Procedure. See below.
[91] Mozley & Whiteley's Law Dictionary *op. cit.*, p. 234.
[92] art. 384.I LECrim.
[93] art. 384 LECrim.
[94] In proceedings for minor offences the person is charged by being notified to appear at an oral hearing (art. 962(I) LECrim). In the "abbreviated proceedings" (art. 790 LECrim) the person is charged when any precautionary measures are taken against him by an *escrito de acusacion*.

tigations need to be carried out it will send the documents back to the "instructing" judge with instructions as to any new investigations which need to be undertaken (article 631 *LECrim*). If the *Audiencia* or the *Tribunal Superior de Justice* considers that the *instrucción* is complete it will dictate a resolution declaring that this is so and decide whether the public hearing should take place or whether the proceeding should be stayed because of lack of evidence (article 632 *LECrim*).

THE PUBLIC HEARING

Submissions by the parties

Once the case has been admitted for public hearing, the parties to the proceedings need to elaborate certain documents in order to make their petitions and positions clear and definitive in the light of the evidence provided by the *instrucción*.

In proceedings for *delitos graves*, this consists of the presentation to the court of the *escrito de calificación provisional* by the prosecutors, in which they request the presentation of the evidence they deem necessary. The same document must be presented by the accused indicting the evidence he intends to rely on for his defence. The court will decide whether to accept the evidence proposed and indicate a date for the start of the public hearing. This will be notified to both parties. Once this is done some preparatory activities must be undertaken in order to present the proposed evidence, for example notifications to the witnesses and experts and requests for documents.

The trial

The court for the trial will be composed of three judges,[95] one of whom will be the President who will control the proceedings. Until the *LO* 5/95 of May 22, there was no jury in Spain although the Constitution had a provision for this in article 125. This article has now been developed and although at the time of writing trial by jury has still not been implemented, the new regulation will be considered below.

The trial is public unless it necessary to protect the victim or his family (article 680 *LECrim*) and the Press is admitted. The defendant is present and he is represented by his *abogado* and *procurador* and a translator if he does not speak Spanish (article 688–740 *LECrim*).

The trial will start with the clerk reading aloud the background to the

---
[95] In cases for *delitos* heard by the *Audiencia Provincial* or *Tribunal Superior de Justicia*.

case and all the details of the file, including the commencement of the *sumario*, the investigations undertaken and any precautionary measures taken, for instance whether the defendant is in custody or at liberty on bail. He will also read the submissions of the parties (*calificaciones*), the evidence proposed to be presented by them and whether it has or has not been accepted by the court (article 701 *LECrim*).

Then, depending on whether the offence with which the defendant is charged carries a punishment involving imprisonment of more than six years or not, the judge will ask the defendant whether he accepts the facts or not, including civil damages. If the offence committed is punishable with imprisonment of more than six years the case automatically proceeds to trial and the court will not ask the defendant whether or not he pleads guilty. If the offence carries a punishment of less than six years imprisonment or other type of penalty, the president of the court will ask the defendant in clear and concise terms whether he pleads guilty or not. The defendant is under no obligation to answer at this stage, and he or his lawyer can demand that the case proceeds to trial. Even if the defendant pleads guilty, the court has to demand the consent of his lawyer. If the lawyer refuses to accept the plea of guilty the case has to proceed to trial despite what the defendant has said. Also, the court must be satisfied from the file that the defendant is guilty before sentencing. If the court is not satisfied, the case will proceed to trial, even if the defendant and his lawyer have accepted the plea of guilty (article 688–99 *LECrim*).

The trial by jury

On May 22, 1995 the *LO 5/95 Ley Orgánica del Tribunal Jurado* introduced the institution of the jury to Spanish criminal procedure according to the general provision of article 125 CE. This provided that the participation of citizens in the administration of justice was to be effected by two main mechanisms, the "popular action"[96] and the jury.

The *LO 5/95* of May 22, is due to enter into force six months after its publication[97] and there have already been some "test-runs" for trials with a jury. The institution of the jury in criminal proceedings has had a controversial history in Spain. Traditionally favoured by liberals and condemned by conservative governments,[98] the institution of the jury appears today to be related to the fundamental right of citizens to

---

[96] See above.
[97] *Disposición final quinta LO 5/95* with the exceptions made in this disposition concerning chapter II of the law (Selection of Juries) and the *disposición transitoria tercera*, which will become enforceable two months from the date of publication. The *LO 5/95* of May 22, was published on May 23, 1995.
[98] There were provisions for a jury in the Constitutions of 1812, 1837, 1869 and 1931.

participate in public matters (article 23.1 CE) and, in particular, in the administration of justice (article 125 CE).

Being a juror is at the same time, and according to the LO 5/95, a right and a duty of citizens. Chapter II of the LO 5/95 specifies who can and should be a juror, how jurors are to be appointed and duties of jurors, as well as the roles which are incompatible with that of being a juror.

Trials by jury are limited to certain types of crime. These are crimes against human life (articles 405–10 CP), crimes committed by civil servants in the exercise of their duties (articles 362–6, 385–96 and 400–404 (bis)(c) CP), the crime of omission of duty of help (article 489 CP), trespass[99] (articles 490–2 bis CP), crimes against freedom (article 493 CP) and crimes against the environment (articles 553 (bis)(a)–(c) CP). Jurisdiction for these trials traditionally belonged to the *Audiencia Provincial* and the intervention of the jury is limited to trials in the *Audiencia Provincial* or another court with jurisdiction according to the status of the person accused.[1] There is no intervention of a jury in trials in the *Audiencia Nacional*.[2]

The *Tribunal del Jurado* is composed of nine jurors and a judge who acts as the President. The function of the jury is to give a verdict declaring whether the facts indicated by the presiding judge are proved or not. The jury also declares whether the accused is guilty or not guilty of the criminal actions accepted as forming the charge by the judge (article 3 LO 5/95). The judge in turn issues a sentence according to the jury's verdict, imposes a punishment and decides, if it is applicable, the civil liability of the accused.

The introduction of trial by jury made necessary the modification of certain procedural rules which did not provide an adequate framework for this new development. In this respect, the *Exposición de Motivos* of the LO 5/95, makes some important remarks and explains the reforms which are to be introduced in Spanish criminal proceedings for trials by jury. Contrary to the theory that it is only necessary to modify that part of the procedure in which the jury intervenes, that is, the *juicio oral*, the legislator has opted for some changes in both stages of the Spanish system.[3] Article 24 of the LO 5/95, effectively creates a new type of criminal proceedings, the Trial by Jury, which is regulated in article 24–

---

[99] Note than in Spain trespassing is a criminal offence.

[1] *i.e.* Special jurisdiction in cases concerning Members of Parliament and members of the Government. See above.

[2] Which in any case has special jurisdiction because of the subject matter of the crime. See above, Chap. 3, p. 87.

[3] Since the *LECrim* has to be modified according to this *disposición* and actual trial by jury has still not been implemented it is necessary to wait until further developments take place in order to be able to make a detailed assessment of the system.

70 of the *LO 5/59*, while the *LECrim* provides subsidiary guidelines for matters not specifically provided for in the new regulations. The aim of these reforms is to adapt the most difficult technicalities of Spanish criminal proceedings, which were initially designed for professional judges, to the needs and limitations of non-professional jurors on one hand, and on the other, to reinforce the value of evidence stated in the *juicio oral*, since most judges in fact decide on the basis of the evidence available from the *sumario* or *instrucción*. In order to achieve these two main aims, the main changes introduced are: the need for a well-founded claim for the start of oral proceedings—in which the facts that are going to be subject to evidence are clearly stated; reinforcement of the neutrality of the investigating judge by establishing that a party— different from the judge —needs to start the accusation while the judge decides whether it is convenient to proceed with the investigations or not; and, the introduction of several dispositions relating to the oral trial itself addressed to provide an adequate framework for the decision of the jury (article 42–65 *LO 5/95*).

Evidence

At the public hearing, the witnesses will make their statements under oath.[4] First, the witnesses for the prosecution are called and then the defence witnesses. Witnesses must wait outside the courtroom and are called by the president in the order proposed by the parties in their submissions. All persons called to be witnesses in criminal proceedings must attend, otherwise they face a severe penalty (article 410, 420 and 702 *LECrim*). They can also be criminally charged for false statements (article 433 *LECrim* and articles 326–8 *CP*). If a witness, because of illness or disability, cannot appear at the court hearing the judge will take a statement at his home and read this at the hearing. The witnesses are questioned first by the lawyer of the party who called them and then by the other party. The defendant can be called to give evidence either by the prosecution or by the defence. He is the only person who does not need to take an oath as he can not be forced to declare against himself. The president of the court can intervene at any time to clarify matters. He must also prevent, either on his own initiative or at the request of the prosecutor or the defence lawyer, questions which are captious, suggestive or impertinent (article 708 *LECrim*). The witness can refer to documentary or other evidence if this has already been accepted by the court (article 712 *LECrim*). If the witnesses contradict each other or the defendant's and the witnesses' statements are con-

---

[4] arts. 701–722 *LECrim*.

tradictory, the judge can call a confrontation (*careo*) ensuring that no insults or threats happen during this confrontation. The defendant can remain silent, although this might be seen as indicative of guilt.

After the witnesses have made their statements any other evidence is produced. There are no fixed rules concerning the weighing up of the evidence by the court. The court is free to attach whatever weight it thinks appropriate to all statements and evidence presented, although it cannot act unreasonably. No evidence which has been obtained illegally, for instance illegal telephonic interceptions, or the opening of correspondence without a court warrant, will be accepted. Nor will evidence obtained as a result of a violation of basic human rights, for instance by torture, be accepted (article 11 *LOPJ*).[5]

Definitive submissions

The original submissions of the parties (*escritos de calificaciones*) were based on the investigations and evidence available during the instruction. At this stage the parties have heard all the evidence of the oral hearing and might wish to alter their original submissions.

After the presentation of evidence the parties have two choices; either they can confirm their original submissions, in which case, they may do so orally and the court clerk will make a note which will be added to the dossier or, the parties, or one of them, can decide to alter the original submissions. This must be done in writing. At this stage, the prosecutor can charge the defendant with a different offence which may be more or less serious.

The definitive submissions or the ratified ones—*calificaciones definitivas*—form the basis for the accusation.[6] These submissions are the ones by which the court is bound in its decision, since the sentence dictated by the court must resolve all the points raised in these submissions, and only those.[7] According to the *principio acusatorio*[8] a person needs to be charged before he can be convicted. It is, therefore, not possible for the court to charge somebody with a crime of which he has not been accused by the prosecution and consequently against which he has not had the possibility of defending.

However, different problems can arise at this stage. For example, the court might believe that once all evidence has been heard a crime has taken place and that it has been committed by the defendant. The

---

[5] The persons involved in obtaining such evidence can be charged in criminal proceedings.
[6] See J. Tomé *op. cit.*, p. 313.
[7] *Principio de congruencia*.
[8] Which govern criminal proceedings during the second stage, or public hearing.

prosecution might, on the other hand, have withdrawn the charges. If the court were to condemn the defendant without accusation it would amount to an infringement of the accusatory principle. It also could amount to denial of the right of defence if the crime the court believes the defendant has committed is different from the crime with which he was originally charged, because, in this case, the defendant would not have been given the opportunity to be heard and to conduct his defence. Conversely a similar problem may arise when the court believes that mitigating circumstances exist and these have not been pleaded by the accusation or the defence.

The solution to these problems can be found in article 733 of the LECrim which provides that "if on the basis of the evidence presented, the court understands that the specification of charges has been made on the basis of *clear mistake*, the president of the court can ask the prosecution and/or the defence whether they believe the facts constitute the offence that has been described in the specification of charges or a different one as suggested by the court, or whether the prosecution or the defence think that any mitigating circumstances have taken place".[9]

This exceptional power of the court should be applied with moderation. There is considerable *jurisprudencia* of the Supreme Court on the application of this provision of the LECrim by the courts.[10] In general it is possible to charge the defendant with a different offence if this is of the same nature,[11] provided that a circumstance exempting or reducing liability has not been raised by the prosecution or the defence.[12] It is not possible, however for the court to suggest that a circumstance increasing liability has taken place because it would amount to a denial of the right of defence.[13]

The definitive submissions are made orally to the court. First, the president of the court permits the public prosecutor to speak, followed by the lawyer of the private or popular prosecution and then the lawyer of the civil plaintiff, if any. The last person to make definitive submissions is the defence. These submissions must state the facts which the party

---

[9] art. 733 LECrim "*si juzgando por el resultado de las pruebas entendiera el tribunal que el hecho justiciable ha sido calificado con manifiesto error, podra el Presidente emplear la siguiente formula: Sin que sea visto prejuzgar el fallo definitivo sobre las conclusiones de la acusacion y la defensa el Tribunal desea que el Fiscal y los defensores del procesado le ilustren acerca de si el hecho justiciable constituye el delito de . . . o si existe la circumstancia eximente de responsabilidad a que se refiere el num . . . del art 8 del CP*".

[10] See J. Tomé, *op. cit.*, pp. 314–316 for a detailed explanation of this point.

[11] STS of November 4, 1986, and June 16, 1988 and STC of April 18, 1981, October 10, 1986 and December 29, 1989.

[12] STS of September 30, 1988.

[13] STC of December 29, 1989; STS of November 4, 1986, June 17, 1989 and February 25, 1991.

making the submission considers proved according to the evidence put forward during the trial, the legal clarification of those facts, i.e. which offence is charged, any extenuating, aggravating or mitigating circumstances and the evidence supporting these.

After all parties have submitted their conclusions and before the president declares the trial to be *listo para sentencia*,[14] he will ask the defendant if he wishes to make any final statement. After this, the President announces that the trial is closed (articles 739 and 740) and will ask the public to leave the courtroom. All the parties will be asked to sign the record.

The court will then retire to consider its verdict.

The *Sentencia*

Once the trial has been closed the court has five days in which to give a verdict. However, because of the overload that Spanish courts have, this period can be longer. The court will conduct its discussions privately on the same day or the next business day. One of the judges of the court—*el Magistrado Ponente*—is in charge of summarising the case and gives his opinion on the case. After this all the judges vote. Decisions are made by a simple majority of votes and all issues must be considered separately (articles 741–2). The court must decide on the innocence or guilt of the defendant and the issues of civil liability raised. It must be remembered that up until now the presumption of innocence applies[15] and any doubts or deadlocks must be decided in favour of the defendant— *in dubio pro reo*.

The *Sentencia* must acquit or condemn the defendant (articles 141 and 742 *LECrim*). The document containing the *sentencia* has three parts. The first part is called *encabezamiento*, and states: the place and date of the decision, the court dictating it, the facts leading to the opening of the proceedings, the names, addresses and occupations of the parties, and the name of the *Magistrado Ponente* and the other judges. It also has a number as required by the *LOPJ* in order to keep a special record of all decisions, and an indication as to whether the public prosecution has been a party to the proceedings or not.

The second part is a summary of the facts—*antecentes de hecho*[16]—in which all the facts connected with the final verdict must be stated. It is also necessary to make a clear declaration as to the facts considered to

---

[14] Literally "ready for sentence".
[15] Except in serious drug related offences.
[16] The *LOPJ* has substituted the traditional denomination *resultandos* by the term *antecedentes de hecho*.

be proved[17] and of the conclusions of the parties, including whether the court has used the power included in article 733 LECrim.[18]

The third part of the decision is called *fundamentos de derecho*, in which the court, according to article 142 LECrim, expresses the application of the law to the facts proved. It must contain the legal and doctrinal justification as to the classification of the facts considered to be proved as a criminal offence.[19] It must also explain, in legal terms, the participation of the defendant in the commission of the offence and the existence of any aggravating, or mitigating circumstances. In a separate paragraph it must state the legal implications as to civil liability and the imposition of the *costas*.[20] All legal rules applicable to the case must be stated and properly cited.

The last part of the decision is the verdict—*el fallo*—which will declare whether the defendant is guilty or innocent and decide the *costas* and any civil liability (article 142 LECrim).

The judgment—*sentencia*—must be written and signed by the judge or judges. It must be made public by being read aloud by the *Magistrado Ponente* in court. After this the original is filed in the record of judgments (article 159 LECrim and article 266 LOPJ) where all judgments have a number and are kept in chronological order. A true copy is made by the clerk who will include it in the record of the case. The judgment will be notified to the parties and their *procuradores*.[21].

7. RECURSOS[22]

Depending on which court dictated the judgment the parties have different possibilities of challenging the decision.

For judgments given in abbreviated proceedings,[23] it is possible to appeal the decision of the *Juez de Paz*, *Juez de lo Penal*, or the *Juez Central de lo Penal* (article 795 LECrim). The *recurso de apelación* must be made within ten days from the date of judgment. In order to be admissible the

---

[17] It is not possible to declare somebody guilty of an offence which has not been proved, STS of November 14, 1981.
[18] See above, p. 184.
[19] For instance the court will say: "the facts declared to be proved constitute a criminal offence, typified in art ... of the Criminal Code with the punishment of..."
[20] The expenses caused by the proceedings. See below.
[21] Remember that the role of the *procurador* is to liaise between the court and his client. See Chap. 4.
[22] The Spanish terminology is retained because, as explained earlier, this word has a wider meaning than the term "appeal".
[23] And in *juicios de faltas*, where an appeal is possible to the *Juez de Primera Instancia*.

party appealing must have suffered prejudice as a result of the judicial decision. The appeal must be made in writing, stating all relevant submissions and include a petition to the court (article 795(2)). This appeal must be lodged with the trial court. The grounds of appeal depend on a mistake of the facts by the trial judge, or a mistake in law or in procedure.

The judge, if he considers that there are grounds for appeal, will pass the submissions to the other party who has the right to make his own declarations, and will then refer the whole dossier to the higher court for decision. This higher court[24] will then re-try the case. It is possible to introduce new evidence in the circumstances stated in article 795(3),[25] although the appellate court must abide by the evidence already accepted in the original trial. The procedure at this stage is mainly written and there is no need for a public hearing (article 795(8)) although this is possible. The court will then give its judgment (article 796 LECrim).

Further appeal is only possible either by the *recurso de casación* or the *recurso extraordinario de queja* and only on the specific grounds fixed for each of these.

The judgments of the *Audiencia Provincial* and the *Audiencia Nacional* in proceedings for serious crimes (*Procedimientos por delitos graves*) are final. the only appeal against them which is possible is the *recurso de casación* and the *recurso de queja*.

The *recurso de casación* is only available on points of law or procedure, never on the appreciation of the facts by the court. This *recurso* is not possible against the decisions of the Supreme Court (article 847(II) LECrim) or decisions of the *Juez de lo Penal* and the *Juez de Paz* in proceedings for minor offences.[26]

The grounds for *casación* depend on a mistake in law—*infracción de ley* (article 849(1) and (2) LECrim) and the breach of formalities in the proceedings—*quebrantamiento de forma*, (articles 850 and 851 LECrim).

Mistakes in law can be of two types: infringement of a substantive rule of law, *i.e.* a rule of the Criminal Code; or mistakes in the appreciation of documentary evidence. Although the Supreme Court does not analyse questions of fact or evidence, an exception is made when the judge clearly made a mistake as to the evidence presented by documents which was not contradicted by other evidence.

Infringement of procedure or lack of formalities can occur either during the proceedings or during the elaboration of the judgment by the court.

---

[24] The *Audiencia Provincial* in appeals against decisions of the *Juzgados de lo Penal* and the *Audiencia Nacional* for appeals against decisions of the *Juzgado Central de lo Penal*.
[25] Evidence which could have been presented before, or the presentation of which was wrongly rejected by the trial judge.
[26] Against the latter two the *recurso de apelación* is available.

If the Supreme Court considers that there has been a mistake in law, it will pass its own judgment to resolve the case. In accordance with the principle of *reformatio in peius* (article 902) this new judgment cannot impose a punishment higher than the punishment imposed in the first and now annulled judgment.[27]

If there has been lack of formalities, the case will return to the original trial court which must re-try it from the point in the proceedings where the infringement happened (article 901 (bis)(a) and dictate a new decision.

The last available *recurso* is the *recurso extraorinario de revisión*. This is an extraordinary procedure against definitive judgments which can only be initiated when new facts prove that the person has been punished on erroneous grounds because new facts or documents are discovered after the end of the proceedings. The court with jurisdiction to hear of this *recurso* is the Supreme Court. *Locus standi* for the commencement of this *recurso* lies with the prosecutor of the Supreme Court—*Fiscal del Tribunal Supremo*—(article 957), but the person who was wrongly punished, or his relatives, can request the Minister of Justice to open investigations in order to ascertain the existence of the grounds for *revisión* (article 955 *LECrim*). If these grounds exist, the Minister will request the Prosecutor of the Supreme Court to initiate the *recurso*. The grounds for the *recurso de revisión*—which are stated in article 954 *LECrim*—are, first, when more than one person has been condemned and contradictory sentences have been passed for the commission of an offence which only one of them could have committed; secondly, when a person was condemned on the basis of evidence provided by documents or witnesses' statements which were later declared false in a criminal procedure; thirdly, when a person was condemned for the manslaughter of a person who is proved to be alive after the sentence; and fourthly, when, after the sentence, new facts establish the innocence of the person condemned.[28]

The procedure for the *recurso de revisión* is written; the prosecutor and the person condemned make their submissions to the court. The Supreme Court will decide whether the decision needs to be annulled and, depending on the circumstances of the case, whether a new trial is necessary. If the person condemned is later found to have been innocent, he or his next of kin will be entitled to compensation for damages by the State and to the rehabilitation of his name. Even if the person wrongly declared guilty is already dead his widow or descendants can

---

[27] STC of 84/1985 of July 8.
[28] The Constitution guarantees compensation by the State for judicial error (art. 121; also the *LOPJ* arts. 292–297).

request the procedure of *revisión* in order to rehabilitate his memory and prosecute the real author of the offence.[29]

8. COSTS AND LEGAL AID

Since the abolition of the courts' fee in 1989,[30] the costs incurred in criminal proceedings include the fees of the *abogado* and *procurador*[31] (articles 241(2) and (3) *LECrim*), the fees payable to experts, the expenses of witnesses and any other expenses, such as public notices in official journals (article 241(4) *LECrim*).

The judge in the final judgment must make a decision as to liability for costs. The principle, in criminal procedure, is that the winner does not pay any costs, but that these are borne by the person who loses. This principle is complemented by the rule of bad faith, by which any party who started the proceedings in bad faith will have to pay the costs.[32] In respect of the defendant, there are two possible situations. The first is that he is declared guilty, in which case he will have to pay all costs (article 240 *LECrim* and article 109 *CP*). The second is that he is declared innocent in which case he will not have to pay costs (article 240 *LECrim*) in respect of expenses incurred by the proceedings, but he will still have to pay his lawyers, witnesses and experts (article 242 *LECrim*), unless the person bringing the private accusation acted in bad faith. The costs are calculated according to the criteria of article 242 *LECrim*.

There is provision for legal aid or *beneficio de justicia gratuita*, for those persons who do not have sufficient economic means to litigate. The *beneficio* will be awarded according to the criteria of article 123–5 *LECrim*, taking into account the economic circumstances of the claimant and his family (articles 126 and 127 *LECrim*). If legal aid is awarded, the beneficiary will be exempted from payment of any fees and will be represented by an *abogado* and *procurador de oficio* paid by the State (article 440(2) *LOPJ*).

The judge who has jurisdiction over the case will decide on the award

---

[29] arts. 960 and 961 *LECrim*.
[30] Ley 25/1986 of December 24. See above under the section on Judicial Costs.
[31] The latter charges an *arancel* or fixed fee.
[32] The application of this principle in criminal procedure is however, reduced because if the judge or the public prosecution do not think that the facts amount to a criminal offence or that the evidence available indicates that the defendant might have committed the offence, they will order a stay of the proceedings. The private prosecutor will then have to pay the costs incurred up to that stage.

of free legal aid. Both Spanish citizens and foreigners can enjoy this benefit.

9. ENFORCEMENT

Judgments in criminal proceedings, unless these end in acquittal, need to be enforced by the State. Article 117 CE establishes that the execution or enforcement of judgments in all cases must be carried out by the judicial power. The different types of sentences that can be imposed will require a different machinery of enforcement. Punishments in Spain can be divided into the following groups: imprisonment, punishments restrictive of rights other than freedom, punishments restricting freedom of residence, others.

The first type of punishment, imprisonment, is the most important because of the consequences it has for the person condemned. Prison sentences are arranged in steps and degrees.[33] Their duration can vary from one month—*arresto mayor*—to 30 years—*reclusión mayor*. There is no death penalty in Spain except for military crimes in times of war.[34] If the person condemned has not got a criminal record and the punishment imposed is imprisonment for less than a year, the judge can suspend the sentence (article 92 CP) on condition that the person condemned does not commit any offence in the next five years. This measure was introduced in order to solve two problems—overcrowding in Spanish prisons, and the constitutional mandate that punishments should be directed at the re-education and rehabilitation of the delinquent and that consequently the effects of imprisonment for less than a year could theoretically be worse than leaving him at liberty.

In all cases of prison sentences there are two types of judges who intervene in the enforcement of the sentence, the judge who dictated it and the *Juez de Vigilancia Penitenciaria*.[35] This latter type of judge was created by the LO 1/1979 *General Penitenciaria* (LGP) with the specific function of supervising the enforcement of prison sentences, safe-guarding respect for the fundamental rights of inmates and any other matters connected with the above, for instance: granting parole, authorising sanctions against inmates in prison, concessions of benefits to inmates, changes of regime or remission.[36]

There are three types of prisons in Spain: *Establecimientos preventivos*—

---

[33] See Richard Vogler for a chart on prison sentences, *op. cit.*, p. 71.
[34] art. 15 CE.
[35] Prison Judge.
[36] See J. L. Gómez Colomer, *op. cit.*, pp. 309–311 and R. Vogler, *op. cit.*, pp. 89 and 90.

remand prisons—(articles 7(a) and 81(1) LGP), *Establecimientos de cumplimiento de penas*—ordinary prisons—which can be of two types, ordinary or open (articles 7(b) and 9 LGP) and *Establecimientos especiales*— special prisons— *i.e.* psychiatric hospitals, general hospital or "rehabilitation" centres (articles 7(c) and 11 LGP).

Each prisoner is subject to an examination by a team composed of a criminologist, a psychologist, a social worker and a teacher, in order to determine the "criminological type", and the possibilities of rehabilitation and social reintegration. They will decide to which type of prison the prisoner must be sent to and will give him a "grade" (article 74(2) LGP and article 242(2) RLGP). There are four grades: first grade or closed prison regime (article 46 RGP), in which case the convicted prisoner is sent to an ordinary prison; second grade or ordinary regime (article 44 RGP), whereby the prisoner is also sent to an ordinary prison, but the regime is more open than in the first degree; third grade or open regime (article 45 RGP), for prisoners sent to an "open prison", where the prison regime is based on two elements, namely the trust given to the prisoner and the absence of obstacles preventing escape;[37] and fourth degree or parole (article 58 RGP and article 98 CP), for prisoners who have already served three-quarters of their prison sentence and who provide guarantees that they will live a "normal life".[38]

Fines are enforced by the court, which will request payment from the convicted. If he refuses to pay the court will execute the fine in the same way in which civil monetary decisions are enforced,[39] or, if this is unsuccessful the court will arrest the convicted person for a maximum period of six months if the offence was a serious offence or a crime, or up to 145 days if it was a minor offence (article 91 CP).

Other type of punishments can consist of the restriction of certain rights other than freedom of movement, for example, deprivation of driving licence (article 789(2) *LECrim*) suspension from public office or restriction on the exercise of private professions (articles 35 and 36 CP) deprivation of Spanish nationality;[40] or a public admonition by court (article 89 CP).

---

[37] The advantages, according to J. L. Gómez Colomer, are that this system is more in accordance with the aims of social rehabilitation, improves physical and mental health, stimulates "normal" family relationships, is less expensive, encourages and facilitates the finding of employment and solves the sexual problems of prisoners. The only inconvenience is the possibility of escape, which, according to the same author, is statistically very low. *op. cit.*, p. 318.

[38] A good account of the prison regime in Spain is provided in Richard Vogler, *op. cit.*, pp. 84–123.

[39] See Chap. 5, p. 150.

[40] Only for foreigners who have obtained Spanish nationality (art. 34 CP); persons with Spanish nationality "of origin" cannot be deprived of it (art. 11(2) CE).

Glossary

abogado	A practising lawyer in charge of providing advice for, and the defence of, clients.
abogado de oficio	A duty solicitor.
abogados en ejercicio	practising lawyers
actor/demandante	plaintiff
acusador particular	A private prosecutor.
acusador popular	A "popular" prosecutor.
Administración del Estado	Central State Administration
Administraciones Autónomicas	Autonomous Communities' Public Administrations
Administraciones locales	local public administrations
allanamineto	The acceptance of plaintiff's claim by the defendant.
arancel	The fixed fee charged by *procuradores*.
aseguramiento de bienes litigiosos	Attachment of the property in litigation.
atestados policiales	Police reports about crimes.
Audiencia Nacional	Court with jurisdiction over the national territory in certain criminal, administrative and employment matters.
Audiencia Provincial	A Higher Court with seat on the capital of the province.
auto	A decision of the judge ending the proceedings without deciding about the subject matter.
beneficio de justicia gratuita	legal aid
bufetes, despachos	law firms
calificaciones	submissions

194 Glossary

calificaciones definitivas	definitive submissions
careo	confrontation, means of evidence in criminal proceedings
carga de la prueba	burden of proof
Cartas pueblas	The laws granted by the king to Christian settlers on territories bordering with the Muslims.
Catedrático	university professor
citación cautelar	cautionary summons
Código de Comercio	Commercial Code.
Código Penal	Criminal Code.
Colegio de Abogados	Bar Association.
Colegio de Notarios	Notaries Professional Association.
Colegios profesionales	Professional associations.
Comisión de Codificación	A special commission created for the drafting of the different codes.
Comisiones	The commissions (in Congress).
competencia funcional	The jurisdiction to hear appeals and enforce judgments of a given court.
conflicto de atribuciones	conflict or dispute between constitutional organs of the state as to the extent of their powers.
conflicto de competencia	conflict of powers between the State and the Autonomous Communities.
congruencia	When the judgment must meet the petitions of the parties.
Consejeros	advisers
Consejo de Ministros	The Council of Ministers.
Consejo general de la Abogacia	The General Council of Lawyers
Consejo General del Poder Judicial	The General Council of the Judiciary; the government body of the judiciary.

constitución	A special type of law passed by the king (historic law).
contestación a la demanda	answer (to a complaint)
Corporaciones públicas	public corporations
Cort General	Parliament in Catalonia consisting of nobles, churchmen and the representatives of the cities.
costas	costs originated by the proceedings.
costumbre	custom
cuantía del litigio	The amount of the claim in civil proceedings.
cuerpo del delito	The object of the crime.
decisión	A judicial decision (see *sentencia*).
declinatoria	A dilatory exception in civil proceedings for denouncing lack of territorial or international jurisdiction.
decretos	by-laws
decretos legislativos	A statute made by the executive by delegation from Parliament.
decretos-leyes	A type of statute made by the executive in special circumstances.
Defensor del pueblo	The Ombudsman.
delitos	crimes
delitos graves	serious crimes
delitos menos graves	less serious offences
demanda	A complaint; document opening civil proceedings.
demanda de reconvención	counterclaim
demandado	defendant
denuncia	information or complaint.
denuncia falsa	false information or complaint
Derecho	Law

derecho	right
Derecho administrativo	administrative law
Derecho civil	civil law (private law)
Derecho común o general	common law (as opposed to regional—*foral* law)
Derecho penal	criminal law
Derecho procesal civil	civil procedure law
derechos forales	The regional customary laws.
derogación expresa	The express derogation of laws.
derogación implícita	The implied derogation of laws.
desamortización	The compulsory sale of Church-owned property in Spain in the eighteenth century.
despacho colectivo	Partnerships of a maximum of twenty lawyers.
detención	arrest
Dictamen	The draft legislation presented by the commissions.
Diputación	The organ of government of the provinces.
Diputados	Deputies; members of the lower chamber of parliament.
disposiciones transitorias	transitional law
doctrina legal	doctrinal writings
Documento Nacional de Identidad	identity card
Dret Comú	The *ius commune* in Catalan.
dúplica	rejoinder
El Congreso de los Diputados	Congress (Lower Chamber of Parliament)
El Pleno	The plennary session (in Congress).
El Senado	Senate (Upper Chamber of Parliament)

embargo preventivo	attachment
emplazamiento	A summons to appear at the proceedings on a certain date.
Equidad	equity
escrito de calificación provisional	The submission of a report to the judge by the prosecution, requesting the presentation of evidence and provisional conclusions.
escritura pública	public deed
Escuela Diplomática	The Diplomatic School.
establecimiento especiales	special prisons
establecimientos de cumplimiento de penas	ordinary prisons
establecimientos preventivos	remand prisons
Estado de sitio, alarma o excepción	state of siege, alarm or exception
Estatuto de Áutonomía	The supreme law of the Autonomous Communities.
Estatuto de los Parlamentarios	The status of Members of Parliament.
excepciones dilatorias	dilatory exceptions
falta de jurisdicción	The lack of jurisdiction of a court.
falta de personalidad del demandado	The defendant's lack of capacity to stand in court.
falta de personalidad del demandante	The lack of capacity of the plaintiff to stand in court.
faltas	minor offences
fase de alegaciones	allegations
fase de conclusiones	The conclusive stage of the proceedings.
fase de enmiendas	The period of amendments (for legislation).
fase de instrucción	The first stage of criminal proceedings in which the judge directs investigations.

fase de plenario	An oral trial in criminal proceedings.
fase de prueba	The evidentiary stage.
fianza	bail
Fiscales	public prosecutors
Fiscal General del Estado	The Attorney-General.
Fiscalía ante el Tribunal Constitucional	The public prosecution office at the Constitutional Court.
foral	regional
formalización de objecto litigioso	Statement of the grounds for litigation.
Fueros municipales	The municipal laws of medieval Spain.
Fuerza de ley	The position of certain laws in the hierarchy of sources.
fundamentos de derecho	Legal principles applicable to the facts specified in the *demanda*.
Furs	The *fuero* in Catalan.
hechos	facts
hechos extintivos	mitigating circumstances
hechos impeditivos	mitigating circumstances
Hermandades	Associations of neighbours in the cities of the Basque country with certain legislative capacity.
Inciativa popular	popular initiative (for the elaboration of laws)
infracción de ley	A mistake in law (one of the grounds for *casación*).
inspección ocular	visual investigation by the judge.
Instituciones públicas	public institutions
interdicto de adquirir	An injunction granting possession.
interdicto de obra nueva	An injunction against new buildings.
interdicto de obra ruinosa	An order for the demolition of an old, dangerous building.

interdicto de retener o recobrar	An injunction restoring possession.
interdictos	injunctions
interpretación auténtica	The interpretation of a law by Parliament.
interpretación usual	The interpretation of a law by the judge.
investidura parlamentaria	The declaration by which Parliament invests its confidence in the President.
jueces	judges
jueces temporales	temporary judges
Juez	judge
juez de guardia	duty judge
Juez de lo Penal	A judge in the Criminal Court.
Juez de Paz	Justice of the Peace.
Juez de Vigilancia Penitenciaria	prison judge
Juez Instructor	investigating judge in criminal proceedings.
juicio de cognición	The procedure (civil) for small claims.
juicio de mayor cuantía	The procedure (civil) for large claims.
juicio de menor cuantía	The procedure (civil) for lesser claims.
juicio ejecutivo	A special summary procedure for the enforcement of monetary liquidated claims.
juicio verbal	The oral procedure for minor claims.
Junta de Portavoces	The Assembly of representatives (in Congress).
Juntas	See *hermandades*.
Jurados	jurors
jurídico	legal
Juriprudencia constitucional	constitutional case-law
jurisdicción	jurisdiction

200 Glossary

Jurista	jurist, lawyer
Justicia	justice (n)
Justicia Mayor	A special institution of Aragón with some resemblances to the Ombudsman.
Justo	just, fair
juzgado	A unipersonal court.
Juzgados centrales de instrucción	The courts in charge of the investigation of certain crimes.
Juzgados contencioso-administrativos	The courts for administrative matters.
Juzgados de Familia	Courts of First Instance in charge of family matters (civil).
Juzgados de lo penal	criminal courts.
Juzgados de lo social	courts for employment matters.
Juzgados de menores	juvenile courts
Juzgados de Paz	Peace Courts
Juzgados de Primera Instancia	First Instance Courts
Juzgados de Primera Instancia e Instrucción	Courts of First Instance in civil and criminal cases.
Juzgados de Vigilancia penitenciaria	prison courts
La Jurisprudencia	Case law of the Supreme Court.
Las Cortes Generales	Parliament.
Letrados del Estado	Lawyers who represent the State and the Public Administration.
Ley	law, statute
Ley Cambiara y del Cheque	Bills of Exchange Act.
Ley de Bases	Law drawing the main guidelines to which subsequent legislation should adhere to.
Ley de Enjuiciamiento Civil	Civil Procedure Act
Ley del Mercado de Valores	Stock Market Act.

Glossary

Ley de Matrimonio Civil	Civil Marriage Act
Ley de Sociedades Anónimas	Companies Act.
Leyes	laws, statutes
leyes de presupuestos	General budgetary laws of the State.
Leyes Orgánicas	"Organic" laws—a special type of legislation.
Leyes temporales	provisional laws
Ley ordinaria	An ordinary law or statute approved by Parliament.
libertad provisional	freedom on bail
licenciado en derecho	Bachelor in Law.
Magistrado Ponente	The judge who drafts the main judgment.
magistrados	A higher category of judges.
Magistrados suplentes	temporary judges (see *magistrado*)
materias troncales	core subjects
medidas cautelares	provisional remedies
medidas cautelares	precautionary measures
medidas cautelares innominadas	non-specific precautionary measures
Mesa	The Board (in the Congress).
Ministerio Fiscal	The Public Prosecution Service.
ministro	minister
municipios	municipalities
Notarios	notaries
Oficiales	The officials at the service of the courts.
Oficina judicial	The judicial office run by the Court Clerk.
Ordenanzas	Rules dictated by the *Hermandades* or *Juntas*.
Ordenes	by-laws
órdenes jurisdiccionales	jurisdictional orders

Glossary

pacto de quota litis	contingent fee agreement.
pacto palmario	A variety of the contingent fee agreement with a premium in case of victory.
Pactos de hospitalidad o clientela	The agreements between Iberians extending the application of personal laws.
partidos judiciales	judicial districts
pasante	Unofficial category of lawyers similar to trainee solicitors.
Pase foral	The non-application of the laws dictated by the King of Castille by the different territories and kingdoms in medieval Spain.
poder suficiente	power of attorney
policía judicial	The judicial police.
pragmáticas	The laws dictated by the King of Castile without consultation with Parliament.
principio de oficialidad	principle of officiality (procedure).
principio dispositivo	dispositive principle (procedure).
Principios generales del derecho	general principles of law.
prisión provisonal	pre-trial custody
procedimiento abreviado para delitos menos graves	The abbreviated procedure for less serious crimes.
procedimiento por delitos graves	The procedure for serious crimes.
Procedimineto Abreviado	The abbreviated procedure (criminal).
Procurador	lawyer whose function it is to liaise between the court and the parties.
Profesor Titular de Universidad	University lecturer.
proposición de ley	A proposal for legislation presented by the Chambers of Parliament.

GLOSSARY 203

Protocolo notarial	Notaries' registry of acts and transactions.
provincias	provinces
Proyecto de ley	The project for legislation presented by the Executive.
prueba tasada	legally-weighted evidence
quebrantamiento de forma	A breach of formalities during the proceedings (ground for *casación*).
querella	A special type of information or complaint by the victim of a crime.
recurso contencioso-administrativo	The judicial appeal against administrative dispositions.
recurso de amparo	Procedure of appeal to the Constitutional Court for the protection of fundamental rights.
recurso de apelación	ordinary appeal.
recurso de casación	An appeal to quash a decision of inferior courts.
recurso de inconstitucionalidad	appeal challenging the constitutionality of a law.
recurso de injusticia notoria	appeal "for notorios unfairness".
recurso de nulidad	nullity appeal.
recurso de queja	petition in error.
recurso de reposición	motion to set aside.
recurso de súplica	petition for reconsideration.
recurso extraordinario de revisión	extraordinary appeal for review.
recusación de magistrados	The removal of judges from particular cases.
Reglamento del Congreso	A statute governing the functioning of Congress.
Reglamento del Senado	A statute governing the functioning of the Senate.
reglamentos	regulations

reglamentos administrativos	The regulations about the organisation of the Administration.
Reglamentos de las Cámaras	A law for the regulation of the functioning of each Chamber of Parliament.
reglamentos jurídicos	The regulations affecting rights and duties of citizens.
réplica	reply
Salas	Chambers (of the Courts)
sanción y promulgación	The formal procedure for the passing of legislation consisting of the King's signature and "approval".
Secretario judicial	court clerk
Senadores	Senators; Members of the Upper Chamber of Parliament.
sentencia	A judicial decision ending the proceedings and resolving the subject matter of the dispute.
sumario	See *fase de instrucción*
tasas judiciales	The fee payable to the court.
titulos ejecutivos	Documents upon which it is possible to start enforcement of a debt without previous declarative proceedings.
Tribunal	A court with more than one judge.
Tribunal Central de Trabajo	Central Labour Court (seat in Madrid).
Tribunal Constitucional	Constitutional Court.
Tribunal del Jurado	Jury.
Tribunal Militar Central	The Central Military Court.
Tribunal Superior de Justicia	The Superior Court of Justice with seat in each Autonomous Community.
Tribunal Supremo	The Supreme Court of Spain.
turno de oficio	The duty to give free legal advice to those entitled to legal aid.

vacatio legis	Period between the publication of a statute in the B.O.E. and its application.
vecindad civil	Civil domicile; connecting factor for the application of *foral* or regional laws.
via normal	The normal route for achieving autonomy.
via rápida	The quick route for achieving autonomy.
Villas	The cities in medieval Northern Spain.
vista pública	public hearing.

Index

Abogados
  duties of, 110
  fees of, 110, 155, 189
  training of, 109–110, *see also* Legal Professions
Absolutism, 13–15
Appeals (*recursos*), 147–149, *see also* Civil Proceedings, Criminal Proceedings
Attorney-General (*Fiscal General del Estado*), 80, 102
Audiencia Nacional (National Court), 86–88, 130
  administrative matters, 87
  appeals as to foreign judgments, 154
  appeals to the, 147, 187
  criminal matters, 87, 181
  labour matters, 87
Audiencias Provinciales
  appeals to, 148, 154, 187
  civil matters, 91
  criminal matters, 91, 178–179, 181
  jurisdiction of the, 91
Autonomous Communities, 37, 38
  appeal of unconstitutionality and the, 99
  approval of the, *leyes orgánicas*, by, 48–49
  basic institutional rule of the, 48–50
  creation of the, 48
  distribution of matters defence, 50
  fixing of municipal limits, 50
  Estatuto de Autonomía, 48–50
    approval of the, 48
    drafting of the, 49
    meaning of, 48
  jurisdiction of the, 48, 50

Autonomous Communities—*cont.*
  law of the, 47
  relationship between State law and, 47–51, 103
  legal advice to the, 113
  legislation by the, 49
  legislative initiative of the, 64
  ley of the, 49
  powers of the, 47, 48, 49, 103
  unity of jurisdiction and the, 78
Autonomy
  concept of, 49–50
  definition of, 47

Bronzes of Vispasa, 3
Brussels Convention, 126–127, 151, 153–154

Citizen's initiative, 65, 66
Civil Code, 21–22
  criteria for interpretation of laws, 51–53
  establishment of customs as a source of law, 41–42
  non-retrospective effect of the law and, 55
  regulation of sources of law, 29–30, 43, 46, 54–56
Civil Domicile, 54
Civil law countries, 28
Civil procedure, 123–156
  Code of, 131
  courts of first instance, 129–132
  forum for, 131
  generally, 123–124
  jurisdiction of Spanish courts, 125–129, 129–132
    international, 125–129
    submission to the, 137–138
      dilatory exception, 137–139
  oral, 124–125

Civil procedure—*cont.*
  public, 125
  sources of, 125
  written, 124–125
Civil proceedings, 132–156
  appeals, 147–149
    cassation, 141, 148, 154
    extraordinary, 148–149
      review, for, 148–149
    motion to set aside, 147
    ordinary, 141, 147
    petition in error, 147
    petition for reconsideration, 147
  declarative, 134–135
    allegations, 135–140
      counterclaim, 139
      writ, 135–140
        filing of the, 136
        rejoinder, 140
        reply, 140
        response to the, 137–139
        service of the, 136–137
    evidence, 140–142
      admission of, 141
      burden of proof, 141–142
      concluding, 143
      form of, 141
      generally, 140
      means of, 141
      pre-trial discovery, 141–142
      presentation of, 141
      presumptions, 141–142
      weighing up of, 141
    judgment, 144
  enforcement of judgments, 149–154
    domestic, 150
    foreign, 151–155
      conventional system, 121
      exequatur, 149, 154–155
        jurisdiction for, 154
        procedure for, 154–155
      generally, 151
      reciprocity, system of, 154
      suppletory regime, 154–155
    generally, 149

Civil proceedings—*cont.*
  judicial costs of, 155
  juicio de cognición, 130, 146
  juicio verbal, 130, 146
  legal aid for, 155–156
  lesser claims, 130, 144–145
  provisional remedies, for, 132–134
    injunctions, 133
    precautionary measures, 133–134
      attachment, 133–134
      miscellaneous, 134
      non-specific, 134
Code of Criminal Procedure, 1872, 18
Codex, 3, 7
Codification, 15
  civil law, of, 20–22
  commercial law, of, 23–24
  criminal law, of, 22–23
Common law, 76
  countries, 28
Congreso (Congress), 59–60, 62
  expedited procedure of, 38
  law-making procudure of, 66
  legislative initiative of, 64–65
Consejo General del Poder Judicial, 79–80, 83, 84, 97, 109, 113, 114, 115
  composition of the, 79
Constitution, 16–20
  attribution of powers by the, 47
  Church and State, relationship between, 24–25
  criminal principles established by the, 158
  drafting of the, 24–26
  education, as to, 25
  form of government, as to, 24, 48
  fundamental rights and freedoms
    limits on, 170–173, 176–178
    movement, of, 171
    not to incriminate oneself, 175
    presumption of innocence, 175
    protection of, 24–26, 98
      guarantees for the, 26

Constitution—*cont.*
 guaranteed by the Monarchy, 58
 international treaties identified in the, 33–34
 leyes orgánicas subject to the, 31–32
 non-retrospectivity of the law and the, 55
 purpose of a, 16
 reform of the, 59
 source of law, as a, 30, 77
 supremacy of the, 96
 territorial organisation by the, 25
Constitutional Court, 30, 31, 32, 35, 38, 95–104
 appeals against unconstitutionality, 98–99
 composition of the, 97–98
 creation of the, 77
 decisions of the, 46, 100, 164
 derivative law of the EC, incompetence to control the, 99
 functions of the, 97, 8
 judicial power distinguished, 95–96
 nomination of members of the, 59
 organisation of the, 98
 origins of the, 96–97
 powers of the, 59, 95
 procedures of the, *recurso de amparo*, 101–103 *and see* Recurso de Amparo
 procedures of the, 98–104
  conflictos de atribuciones, 104
  control of international treaties, 101
  el recurso de inconstitucionalidad, 98–100, 101
  la cuestión de inconstitucionalidad, 100–101
 proceedings before the, 95, 158, 177
 resolutions of the, 49, 50
Constitutional history, 16–20

Constitutional State, 24–26
 defence of the, 113
 institutions of the Constitutional Court, 95–104, *see also* Constitutional Court
 Public Administration, 71–75, *see also* Public Administration
 Public Prosecution Service, 94–95 *see also* Ministerio Fiscal
 Crown, the, 57–59
 Government, 67–71, *see also* Government
 judiciary, 76–94, *see also* Judiciary
 Parliament, 59–66, *see also* Parliament
Contingent fees, 110
Convention on Special Missions, 1969, 127
Corporaciones Publicas, 73
Corpus Iuris Civilis, 3, 6–8
Council of Ministers, 40
 deliberations of the, 70
 Government, identified with, 68
Courts, classification of the, 80–104
Criminal Code, 1870, 18
Criminal Code, 1973, types of offences, 157
Criminal procedure
 Codes, 18, 19
 costs of, 189–190
 Court, as to the, 164–165
  different stage of proceedings, dependent on the, 164
  type of offence, dependent on the, 164
 Criminal Code, 157, 187
 criminal law and, 157
 legal aid, 189–190
 offences
  private, 161
  public, 160–161
  semi-public, 161

Criminal procedure—*cont.*
  parties, 160–163
    defendant, 162–163
      denominations of the, 162
      rights of the, 162–163
        infringement of the, 162
      liability for civil damages, 163
      minors, of, 163
      person under a duty of care, of, 163
      person without full capacity, of, 163
    popular prosecutor, 161, 162
    representation of the, 162
    spouse of the, 162
    private prosecutor, 162
    public prosecutor, 160–161
  principles of, 157–159
    legality, 159
    necessity, 158
  sources of, 159–160
    Constitution, the, 159
    Criminal Procedure Act, 1882, the, 159–160
    decisions of the Constitutional Court, 160
  victim, as to the, 162
Criminal proceedings, 166–191
  appeals, 186–189
    cassation, 187–188
    extraordinary, 188
      review, for, 188–189
    ordinary, 186–187
    petition in error, 187
  enforcement of the judgment, 190–191
  stages of, 166–167
    judgment, 185–186
    preliminary, 167–186
      initiation, 168–170
        denuncia, by a, 168–169
          false, 169
        ex officio, 170
        querella, 169–170
      investigations by the judicial police, 167–168

Criminal proceedings—*cont.*
  stages of—*cont.*
    preliminary—*cont.*
      precautionary measures, 171
        arrest, 171–173
        attachment, 174
        bail, 174
        cautionary summons, 171
        freedom on bail, 173
        pre-trial custody, 173
        suspension of office, 174
      public hearing, 179–185
        definitive submissions, 183–185
        evidence, 182–183
        submission by the parties, 179
        trial, 179–185
          jury, by, 180–182
      summary, 174–179
        charges, 178–179
        investigations by the judge, 175–178
          object of the crime, 175
          physical inspection, 177–178
          suspect, 175–176
          visual, 175
          witnesses, 176
  types of, 166–167
Custom, types of, 42
Customary laws, 1, 4
  Basque, 13
  characteristics of, 41
  definition of, 41
  evidence of, 1, 4
  features of, 1
    independent source of law, 42
    personal laws, 1
    subsidiary source of law, 42
  requirements to be satisfied as rules of law, 41–42
  types of, 42

Decreto Legislativo, 38–40, 49
  decreto-ley compared, 39

Decreto-Ley, 37–38, 49
  conditional on ratification of Congress, 38
Defensor del Pueblo, 59, 74–75, 99, 102
Delegated commissions, 40
Derogacion Expresa, 55
Derogacion Implicita, 55
Digest, 3, 7

Equity, role of, 53
Estatutos de Autonomía, 48–50
  reform of the, 59
  see also Autonomous Communities
European Community Law, 37–37
  supremacy of, 34
Executive
  control of the, 97
  law-making procedure of the, 66
  laws of the, 64
  legislative initiative of the, 64–65
  powers of the, 37, 39, 58, 64
  proceedings against the, 102

Fiscal General del Estado (Attorney-General), 80, 102
  appointment of the, 95
Fueros Municipales, 5–13, 21–22
Fundamental rights and civil liberties, protection of, 24–26, 74, 102

Government
  British compared, 67
  composition of the, 67–68
  functions of the, 70–71
  legislative initiative of the, 64–65
  Ministers of the, 69–70
    duties of, 70
    immunity of, 70
  monarchy distinguished, 67
  powers of the, 68
  President of the, 68–69, 99
  Vice-President of the, 69

Habeas Corpus, 92, 172

Hospitality Agreements, 1

Injunctions, 133
Instituciones Publicas, 73
International jurisdiction of the courts, 125–129
International treaties, 33–37, 127
  Constitution, subject to the, 35
  hierarchical position of, 35
  incorporation into the legal system of, 33–34
  ordinary laws and, 35
  types of, 33–34
Ius Puniendi, State monopoly of the, 158

Judiciary
  anonymity of the, 115
  appointment of the, 114
  control of the, 97
  costs of the, 155, 189
  freedom of the, 44
  government of the, 79
  powers of the, 76–78
  role of the, 76
  status of the, 114–115
Juicio de Mayor Cuantía, 130, 135–144
Juicio de Menor Cuantía, 130, 144–145, 154
Jury
  composition of a, 181
  function of a, 181
  intervention of a, 181–182
  trial, by
    introduction of, 180–182
    jurisdiction for, 181
    limited, 181
Justice, dual nature of imparting, 77
Juzgados
  centrales de instrucción, 93, 164
  de lo contencioso-administrativo, 93
  de lo penal, 92–93, 186, 187
  de lo social, 93–94
  de menores, 92, 94
  de paz, 92, 94, 186, 187

Juzgados—cont.
  de primera instancia e instrucción, 91–92, 130, 164
  de vigilancia penitenciaria, 92, 94, 190

King *see* Monarchy

Latini, 2
Law
  concept of, 27, 27–28, 44
  non-retrospective effect of, 55–56
  private, 28, 54
  public, 28
  qualifications required to practice, 105–107
  retrospective effect of, 55–56
  sources of, 29–55, *see also* Sources of Law
Law-making process, 63–66
Legal aid, 110, 155–156, 189–190
Legal certainty, principle of, 55–56
Legal education, generally, 105–107
Legal history, 1–16
  absolutism, 13–15
  canon law, 7–8, 12, 22
    influence of, 12
  codification of law, 15, 20–24, *see also* Codification
  constitutional law, 15–16, *see also* Constitution
  early influences of, 1–6
  ius civile, 1, 7, 54
  ius commune
    formation of, 6–8
    integration of
      Aragon, into, 10
      Basque country, into, 12
      Castile, into, 11–12
      Catalonia, into, 10–11
      Mallorca, into, 11
      Navarra, into, 9–10
      Valencia, into, 11
    reception of, 8–9
  ius gentium, 2, 54
  ius pereginum, 2
  lex provinciae, 2

Legal history—*cont.*
  local laws 5–13, *see also Fueros Municipales*
  natural law, 15
  role of the judiciary, 76
Legal Professions, 105–122
  classification of, 107–122
    abogados, 107–111
      advocacy of, 109
      Code of Ethics and Conduct for, 109
      de officio, 162
      del estada, 113, 156
      duties of, 110, 170
      E.C. regulations, application of, 113
      remuneration of, 110, 155, 189
      requirements to become, 108
    auxiliary personnel, 118–119
    civil servants, 118, 119
    European Community lawyers, 111–112
    judges, 113–116
      appointment of, 114
      responsibilities of, 115
      status of, 114–115
      temporary, 114, 115
      training of, 114, *see also* Judiciary
    judicial police, 118
    magistrates, appointment of, 114
    notaries, 119–121
      dual role of, 119–120
      functions of, 119
      regulation of, 119
    procuradores, 111–113, 155, 189
      E.C. regulations, application of, 113
      requirement to act, 112, 170
    public prosecutors (*fiscales*), 116–117
    secretarios judiciales, 116, 176
      E.C. regulations, application of, 113

Legal Professions—cont.
  educational requirements for the, 105–107
  qualification required to practice the, 105–107
Ley, 30–33
  definition of, 30–31
  ordinaria, 32, 37
    ley orgánica compared, 32
    Parliament, approved by, 37
  orgánica
    Constitution, subject to the, 31–32
    regulation by, 31–33
    subject matter of a, 32
    retrospective effect of a, 38
    types of, 31–33
Ley de Divorcio, 56
Ley de Matrimonio Civil, 56
Liber Iudiciourum, 4
  application of the, 5–6
  influence of the, 12
Licenciado en Derecho
  attainment of, 105–107
  meaning of, 105
Lugano Convention, 127, 153–154

Military Criminal Code, 78
Ministerio Fiscal (Public Prosecution Service), 94–95, 101, 117, 118, 160
Monarchy, functions of, 58–59
Monist System, 33
Muslim
  law, 5
  presence, 4–6

National Court, 86–88, see also Audiencia Nacional
NATO, participation of Spain in, 34
Novella, 3

Official Journal of the Autonomous Communities, 49
Ombudsman (defensor del pueblo), 59, 74–75, 99, 102
Opinio Iuris, 40

Organic Law of the Judiciary, 1870, 18

Pandectas, 3
Parliament
  Chambers of, 60–61
    Comisiones of the, 61
    Dictamen of the, 61
    Juntas of the, 60–61
    Mesas of the, 60–61, 65
    regulation of the, 62
  composition of, 59–61
  control of, 96
  delegation by, 39
  freedom of, 59
  functions of, 59
    law-making process, 63–66
  members of
    Estatuto de los Parlamentarios as to, 62–63
    immunity of, 63
    remuneration, 63
    status of, 62–63
  supervision of, 59
  supremacy of, 96
Parliament Monarchy, principle of, 57
Patent law, 131
Personality, principle of, 54
Pleno (plennary session), 60–61
Popular initiative see Citizen's initiative
Presumption of innocence, right to the, 163, 175
Provincial courts, 91–92, see also Audiencias Provinciales
Public Administration, 71–75
  categories of the, 72–73
  composition of the, 71
  concept of, 72
  control of the, 74–75
  functions of the, 72, 74
  principles of the, 73–74
  proceedings against the, 102
Public prosecution service (El Ministerio Fiscal), 94–95, 101, 117, 118, 160
Punishment, 190–191

Index

Rationae Materiae, 34
Reconquista, 5, 9
Recurso de Amparo, 74, 97, 98, 158, 162
Reglamentos
  Autonomous Communities, of the, 49
  classification of, 40
  Congreso, of the, 62, 66
  Executive, of the, 40–41, 64
  formalities of, 40
  Public Administration, of the, 40
  Senado, of the, 62, 66
  types of, 40
    circulares, 40
    decretos, 40
    instrucciones, 40
    ordenes, 40
Res Iudicata, 100, 144
Reunification, 13
Road Traffic Code, 40
Rome
  fall of, 3
  first invasion of, 1–2
  influence of, 1–13
  law of
    absolutist, 3
    influence of, 22
    vulgar, 3
Rome Convention of Human Rights and Individual Freedoms, 1950, 176

Senado (Senate), 59–60, 62
  law-making procedure of, 66
  legislative initiative of, 64–65
Sentencing, 190–191
  death penalty, 190
  deprivation of driving licence, 191
  deprivation of Spanish nationality, 191
  fines, 191
  imprisonment, 190–191
    types of, 191
  public admonition by the court, 191
  suspension from office, 191

Sources of law
  application of, 51, 53–56
  Civil Code, 29–30
  complementary, 44–46
    case law, 44–46
    decisions of the Constitutional Court, 46
  Constitution, 30
  custom, 41–42
  efficacy of, 53–56
  European Community Law, 36
  explanatory, 47
  generally, 29–30
  interpretation of, 51–53
    private and public distinguished, 52–53
  legislation, temporary, 55–56
  ley, life-span of the, 54–56
  Parliament, 29, 30
  primary, 30–43
    administrative dispositions, 40–41
    custom, 41–42
    European Community Law, 36–37
    general principles of law, 43
    international treaties, 33–37
    legislation, 30–33, 54–56
    ley, 30–33
      decretos legislativos, 38–40
      decretos leyes, 37–38
      leyes ordinarias, 37
      leyes temporales, 55
    natural legal principles, 43
  role of equity and, 53
Stare Decisis, concept of, 44
State of Autonomies
  consequence, of, 72
  definition of, 47
  federal state distinguished, 47–48
  unity of jurisdiction and the, 78
Supreme Court 45–46, 81–86, *see also Tribunal Supremo*

Territorial laws, examples of, 54

Territoriality
  application off, 53–56
  principle of, 54
Trade Marks Law, 131
Treaty of Accession to the European Communities, 33–34
Treaty of Rome, 111
Treaty of the European Union, 101
Tribunal Constitucional, 95–104 *see also* Constitutional court
Tribunal de Casación, 44–45
Tribunal de Cuentas, 74, 104
Tribunal Supremo (Supreme Court), 45–46, 81–86
  Administrative Chamber of the, 84–85
  Chamber of Conflicts of the, 129–130
  Civil Chamber of the, 83
  composition of the, 82
  Criminal Chamber of the, 84, 98, 164
  jurisdiction of the, 82, 130, 147, 188
  Military Chamber of the, 86
  Social Chamber of the, 85

Tribunales Superiores de Justicia, 88–90, 130
  administrative matters, 89
  Audiencias Territoriales, replacing, 88
  civil matters, 89, 130
  criminal matters, 89, 164, 178–179
  jurisdiction of the, 89–90, 130, 147, 148
  social matters, 90

Ultra Vires, 39, 104
Unitary State, definition of, 47
Urbanisation of society, 2
Usage, 40

Vecindad Civil, 54
Vienna Convention on Consular Conventions, 1963, 127
Vienna Convention on Diplomatic Relations, 1961, 127
Visigoths
  kings, fall of the, 4
  legal works of the, 4
  monarchy of the, 4
  presence of the, 3–4
  resistance of the, 5–6